My First Aquarium Collectors Edition

"The Joy of Tropical Fish Keeping in Classic Retro Style"

By Alastair R Agutter

My First Aquarium Collectors Edition

BOOK COVER DESIGN:

By Alastair R Agutter

ORIGINAL ARTWORK AND IMAGES

By Alastair R Agutter

PHOTOGRAPHS

By Alastair R Agutter, Ian Russell, Wikipedia (CC)

AUTHOR WEB SITE

www.alastairagutter.com

COPYRIGHT

Copyright © Classic Retro Mono First Edition 2016

PUBLISHED BY

Create Space Independent Publishing

An Amazon Group Company

First Edition Published: 26th November 2016

Released Internationally 26th November 2016

ISBN-10: 154065771X

ISBN-13: 978-1540657718

ALL RIGHTS RESERVED

ABOUT THE AUTHOR

Alastair Agutter is one of a select few world-wide to successfully breed the Discus (symphysodon) species King of the Aquarium in captivity and an authority on these tropical fish species and others, as an accomplished Best Selling Author of Specialist Books Internationally.

Alastair began keeping and breeding tropical fish as a hobbyist from the age of just 9 years back in 1967 (nearly 50 years ago) and has successfully bred many species.

Alastair began keeping and breeding tropical fish as a hobbyist from the age of just 9 years back in 1967 (nearly 50 years ago) and has successfully bred many species. He was one of the very first Aquarists in the United Kingdom breeding cichlids from the Great Lakes (Malawi and Tanganyika) in the early and mid-nineteen-seventies.

His enthusiasm as a dedicated Aquarist continues today with a number of projects underway; including the development of new biological filtration systems (Polyatomic-ion Biological Reactors), to help improve the success survival rate for keeping thriving plants with tropical fish species. Other projects include breeding a number of endangered species including original strains of the symphysodon family and other smaller indigenous species native to South America mainly inhabiting the Great River Amazon.

Alastair also continues today designing and making his very own aquariums and equipment for his projects, and also endeavours to write more tropical fish hobbyist reference books as a freelance full-time author, in the interests of further serving the local and wider Community Internationally.

My First Aquarium Collectors Edition

CONTENTS OF BOOK

Introduction – To Classic Collectors Edition   *page 06*

Chapter 1 - A Little History of the Pastime   *page 11*

Chapter 2 – New Aquarist Getting Started   *page 16*

Chapter 3 - Tropical Fish Aquarium Theme   *page 28*

Chapter 4 - The Aquarium Size, Stand and Positioning   *page 46*

Chapter 5 - Aquarium Substrates and Furnishings   *page 77*

Chapter 6 – Growing and Keeping Aquarium Plants   *page 109*

Chapter 7 - The Aquarium Filtration System   *page 154*

Chapter 8 - Aquarium Water Conditions   *page 182*

Chapter 9 - Heating and Thermostats   *page 222*

Chapter 10 - The Aquarium Lighting Methods   *page 229*

Chapter 11 – Fish Species Behaviour   *page 236*

Chapter 12 - Aquarium Fish Species   *page 256*

Chapter 13 - Feeding Fish Species   *page 293*

Chapter 14 - Aquarium Early Days Care   *page 315*

Chapter 15 - Aquarium Maintenance   *page 319*

Chapter 16 - Fish Species Safety and Health Care   *page 321*

Continued over…

My First Aquarium Collectors Edition

CONTENTS OF BOOK - *Continued*

Chapter 17 – Fish Diseases and Cures   *page 323*

Chapter 18 – Aquarists Reference Tables   *page 331*

Chapter 19 - Aquarists Products and Accessories   *page 343*

Chapter 20 - Breeding Tropical Fish Tips   *page 371*

Chapter 21 – Additional Notes   *page 379*

INTRODUCTION

Welcome to **"My First Aquarium Collectors Edition"** of the book, a publication I have wanted to write for many years, so I can share my experiences with tropical fish hobbyists and dedicated aquarist around the world who share such a passion.

One of the Author's Naturally Planted Community Aquariums – Photo by Alastair R Agutter

I decided to have published this *"classic edition"* of the book for a good number of reasons in these modern and uncertain times. One of the reasons being I am sure like many, I like to think I am a romantic and very often look back on the past with very fond memories mostly, whist we exist today in this high tech world of ours and with many challenges ahead.

For our very young millennials who I know are good caring and loving folk, I wanted to write and share this book documenting often times of old, so you all know that whilst the lines of time become forever marked upon my face, deep within is a very caring spirit and heart that is always alight holding a beacon of hope for your generation and all majestic wonders of creation we have come to love and know on this very small Earth we know as home.

Tropical Fish Keeping, is without doubt a time honoured and noble pastime. And has served as a place of learning and discovery, now for more than ah 100 years in the modern era of industrialization. And now today such a pastime and knowledge contributes to serving as part of an academic ark, as we begin to confront reality in these times. Such knowledge in this book and others may well in fact hold the key to knowing how we can preserve our marine life as many dwindle each day from climate change. And so such knowledge should be shared by one humanitarian to another and reachable for all.

I genuinely believe through my faith that we all have a path and destiny to follow if we search deep enough within ourselves to find such answers. Skills found so often, varied and hidden, are talents to be unleashed through God's will, so we all work together and learn how to become good shepherds, as our fellow species of the world tell us through their eyes how they seek our help.

So if as a young millennial or senior in our world seeking to explore this interest for the very first time, the "Collectors Edition" will help you navigate into the future on the right path, whilst gathering a sense of the historical past that has been shared by countless millions of dedicated aquarists and for a small affordable investment price for all.

In our fast changing world of technology today, the digital world has provided an opportunity for all who seek knowledge. And the tablet, pc and smart phone devices of modern times, enables us to unlock knowledge and this has been their greatest achievement. Before such a world, our path to seek knowledge came from the written words found in books, and from such knowledge, fuelled ones imagination. I like to think even in our world of digital media, can be found a place for the printed book, for through such sharing of knowledge between the reader and the book, can also be found the keeper of wisdom.

Before writing this introduction I looked through a book that I am privileged to hold at this time in my life written by William T. Innes titled *"Exotic Aquarium Fishes"* that was first published if I recall back in 1936. A period in time of the Golden Age of American Baseball and written only a year after the legend *"Babe Ruth"* called time on his career as a professional player. The writing of this book by William T. Innes of our tropical fish keeping pastime, tells us far more than just information about our hobby. The way the book was written and the style of pictures inside, allows us to return to such days in history. It demonstrates to me therefore, a book can hold many wonders and where it is evident, even a book, as a valued companion, can possibly have a soul or shares our very own, where such experiences and memories are held very deep and dear in our heart.

Today as we all know the printed book is to some degree in decline and this is unfortunate as production costs on smaller printed book runs and volume of work is affected and becomes costly. But I believe it is still imperative that the written word reaches every corner of our world to bring hope and light, especially for young folk born into ignorance and who need help to be lifted out of ignorance through knowledge. So to continue my path and journey as a humanitarian, I have endeavoured to make it possible that this book can be reached and enjoyed by all in various printed and digital editions and styles for all folk in all corners and parts of the world.

For me writing this book has been a tried and tested pleasure and also a very humbling experience, as I try to recall all, by opening up those old grey cells of the past, and back to when I acquired my first aquarium at the age of just 9 years. I became captivated with the magic of tropical fish keeping by visiting a close School friend's house one Winters evening in early November back in 1967. As we both entered the hallway from the cold dark early night, I was greeted with this breath-taking scene of an illuminated underwater world before my very own eyes.

The Aquarium and stand was all gold in colour made from angle iron with ornate corners, and the tank itself was bow fronted, standing proudly in the hallway. To me then the size of the aquarium appeared massive, but now over the years and upon reflection, I know the aquarium measured around 3 foot in length and about 18 inches in height and 12 to 15 inches in depth. The scene within the aquarium was of a fine algae aged gravel floor, with part of a sunken galleon and a shell that opened occasionally, as the bubbles built up from the air stone disguised in the ornament. There was a small corner filter, powered by an air pump, filled with just activated charcoal and cotton wool, or filter floss described by the commercial world of aquatics. Other furnishings included some live and plastic plants that had aged with the presence of algae on the leaves, but this aged looked only added further beauty to the majestic scene before me. The aquarium inhabitants consisted of some swordtails, platies, danios, guppies and various barbs and tetras. One particular barb that took my fancy had a beautiful claret sheen and ruby colouration on the body and fins. The specie in question was a rosy barb (*Pethia conchonius)*, a member of the spotted barb genus Cyprinidae family, and the species today a native to many parts of Central, Eastern and Southern Asia including Afghanistan, Sri Lanka, Bangladesh and has since been found in parts of

Mexico and also in Columbia and other Central and Southern parts of America over the years.

I cannot recall the conversation with my Father upon returning home that particular evening, but I know the talk mainly consisted of Tropical Fish Keeping over the dinner table. Knowing today how my Daughter negotiates with me, I am sure he was quickly becoming press ganged into my wishes, as my birthday was only a matter of days away, November the 28th in fact. On a following Saturday morning before my Birthday, I was taken by my Father to a home that had been advertising a second hand tropical fish tank with a stand. The Aquarium (24" x 12" x 18") was again the old fashioned angle ironed type and again painted, sprayed or galvanized in gold. There was a little rust coming, but the aquarium putty between the angle iron and the glass panes was maintaining a seal and did not leak, as the aquarium was still housing in the seller's dining room hundreds of guppies and platies swimming up and down. The fish in question in the aquarium consisted of all shapes, types, sizes and colours. You can imagine my joy as my Father agreed to buy the aquarium for me. Now that was the easy bit, the second part got a little harder, as we had to drain the aquarium and then bag up all the guppies and platies. Eventually we made our way home and then the project began for me in earnest, as I was left to my own devices regarding the positioning of the aquarium in my bedroom. I then had to begin the process of washing the gravel again and the family bath seemed a good idea. When I started washing the gravel, this was quickly followed by screams by my Mother, insisting I make sure I clean the bath thoroughly. After washing the gravel, I began to return the substrate to the aquarium, along with the external thermostat, internal heater, external small box filter that clipped onto the side of the fish tank, and the lights (light bulbs), that were housed in the fish hood (lid) of the aquarium. Then finally, I began to fill the aquarium very gradually and slowly with water again, before floating the fish in bags, once a suitable temperature had been reached of around 76 degrees, before returning the fishes to the aquarium again. Of course as you can imagine, I did have some casualties from my new exploits and it was now well past midnight filling up the aquarium.

In those days I read many books once I was hooked on tropical fish keeping, even taking them to School to read and particularly enjoyed looking at the pictures of the very many colourful species of fish and exotic plants for the aquarium.

For me in the 1960's and 1970's where existed many Aquarist Clubs across the Country for help and advice, I can now reflect and think how fortunate we all were in the hobby and like so many I joined the local Aquarist Club (Southend

Leigh and District Aquarists Society, founded in 1935). I managed to obtain a regular lift to the Club by my friend's Father (Mr Victor), who owned the bow fronted aquarium. The club was an invaluable venue for picking up aquarium bargains and advice from local members. Soon I found myself attending shows, visiting other aquarist's homes and learning more each day about my new found pastime and love of tropical fish keeping. Now, nearly some 50 years on today, I fondly recall those very magical early days of tropical fish keeping. To me they were very special and innocent days for a small boy, where folk took the time to teach and help each other.

Today, I find myself being just as passionate about this fabulous pastime, as I build and add more aquariums to my fish house, so I can write more books to share my findings with folk. I hope when looking back on my Childhood, that many more younger folk and members of our society today also become engaged and take up the pastime of tropical fish keeping, a very meaningful hobby, teaching us all the importance and values of caring, creating and preserving life. I truly hope therefore, the information and advice found in this book and others based on nearly five decades of experience, including the successful breeding of some of the most difficult species on Earth, will be of great value and serve you well with proven methods practiced over many years, as you begin this new enjoyable journey of tropical fish keeping that could well be the grounding in a career as a Marine Biologist (the world needs you).

Finally, it heartens me that my very youngest sibling and Daughter Ellenna has taken up tropical fish keeping with a passion, and where this leads me on to the inspiration I found behind writing this book and the many others I have planned and wish to complete if allowed through God's good graces. This is in the hope as mentioned earlier, the young folk especially, will find inspiration and also take up this traditional time honoured and noble pastime of tropical fish keeping. Then alas, delivering from participating in the hobby, many years of joy and the most priceless gifts of all these being memories, coupled with greater enlightenment of the World around us that is currently under threat from Climate Change.

It just leaves me to wish you all the very best in your new found hobby and where I sincerely hope you find many years of great joy and happiness.

My sincere best wishes for now and always,

Alastair R Agutter

Aquarist, Humanitarian and Author

CHAPTER ONE

History of the Pastime

Aquariums and Tropical Fish Keeping in Western Society in truth was born from the old European Empires of the past and in Asia, with fish keeping dating back many centuries, regarding the keeping of ornamental fish in bowls and containers, mainly Goldfish.

Author's Breeding Pair of Turquoise Discus – History In the Making over 25 years ago

One thing I have learnt from studying Natural Law for over 50 years, regarding the realms of Quantum Mechanics and Natural Branching. Is that there does exist a sense of order to "evolve and refine" when we reference Quantum Mechanics, to a seeming "chaos and uncertainty" when we reference Natural Branching. Yet both phenomena event cycles go hand in hand, and are dependent upon each other, regarding further advancement here on Earth and beyond throughout the Cosmos.

Western European Empires when reaching many far out posts around the World in Victorian times, saw in conjunction with military personnel and equipment, an army of enthusiast collectors for plants, many we enjoy today in our Gardens that we often believe to be native to our Countries and Regions. As a result of such interest for ornamental plants, the gardening revolution began in earnest in those grand Victorian times and was very quickly followed by the building of ornamental ponds and water features for many Family homes. The great green houses of the past also saw more unusual and exotic plant species appearing from the tropics and saw the beginning of tropical fish keeping as we knew it then, with the creation of terrariums and vivarium's as a prelude to our pastime today.

The Goldfish bowl was introduced to Europe in the 17th century from China. The first recorded aquarium however, was in the 19th century around 1850 in England, and shortly afterwards, aquariums began to populate and adorn many a room in middle to upper class resident homes throughout Britain, especially affluent areas of the South and Southeast of England. Climate conditions and temperatures in these regions were more favourable for such a new and challenging pastime we know today as tropical fish keeping.

Around the same time in Germany, a teacher began to keep tropical fish, although the pastime was not yet known to have such a name and where rectangular containers began to be used, and was the prelude to today's most popular aquarium shape.

There was little known in those days about filtration and the purification of water. However, as ardent gardening experts both in Germany and England, water plants with the use of soils, peat and fine substrates, produced some fine tropical plant specimens and with the introduction of iron into the substrate from old nails, this served the inhabitant plants very well. Water quality surprisingly enough in those days, was of a considerable condition and in fact better than many parts of the world today. However, regular water changes had to be made almost on a daily basis, to avoid stagnation and a further high death count to fish species.

The movement of fish species in those early days can only be described as tragic, as the fish species had to endure and survive many weeks in transportation from these far out regions of the world. In those days all specimens of tropical fish were wild species, as breeding in any form did not happen or exist until more was learnt and known some years later and especially regarding filtration.

However, in the Victorian industrial age of rapid change and exploration, many middle to upper class homes in these societies of the Victorian age and period had some form of interest, or passion, to pursue. From such dedication and interest of pastimes in those days, the process of learning from trial and error began in earnest and began to evolve most rapidly in the form of hobbies and pastimes we have come to love and know today.

As years past, many species began to be bred successfully in captivity. Aquariums began to be powered by conventional light bulbs from electricity and the heating of aquariums was initially provided by the use of gas flamed heating to slate bottom aquariums. As the years past paraffin became a regular fixture in many a fish house or gardeners greenhouse as a form of heating. However, some species alluded even the most dedicated of aquarists until the late 1970's and early 1980's, when finally Jack Wattley, Dr Eduard Schmidt-Focke, myself, and a handful of others around the World, began to breed successfully Wild symphysodon, the Discus, the King of the Tropical Fish Aquarium in captivity. In the mid 1980's when writing my first book to share with the community my experiences and findings, it seemed a period of closure on the last great unknown surrounding tropical fish keeping and breeding. At the time, it seemed as if there was far greater effort being made by many great aquarists to breed these majestic species and I am sure subconsciously it was for fear of extinction. For as industrial man reached the deepest regions of South America, deforestation begun in earnest, wiping out many wild species of plant and animal life to these regions for commercial gain. I personally felt time was short and running out, as I recall writing in the introduction of "The Discus Book" my concerns surrounding climate change even over 25 years ago and with dire warnings even then.

Three original copies of the Tropical Fish Hobbyist Magazine published back in the 1960's and early 1970's (Nov 1967, Aug 1972, Mar 1968). Photograph taken by Author Alastair

I think the historical heyday of tropical fish keeping was in many respects the late 1960's through to the early 1980's, as many an aquarist club existed and folk were always friendly and keen to share their ideas. Aquarist hobbyists would also very often invite you to their homes, to see their collection of tropical fish. Such times were inspiring and invaluable for gaining greater knowledge first hand, especially if a young aquarist.

Tropical fish keeping has also played its significant role through history surrounding invention and cures for illness. Not just from the commercial world, but many dedicated aquarists.

I recall on one visit to Holland collecting fish and visiting fellow aquarists and breeders, I had the great honour to meet Dr Theo Sternberg, where Theo had a substantial breeding program underway of White Cloud Mountain Minnows and Killie Fish, as he continued his research to advance the Sciences in finding cures for Cancer, Alzheimer's and Parkinson's disease.

I even recall from my very own humble endeavours when breeding Discus, where I discovered and found that these majestic species and others, could catch colds. I also found fish species also suffered from airborne viruses as we humans do, and one notable I found and discovered to be particularly challenging, was respiratory distress syndrome. Very often sadly the outcome for the victims of this infection was fatal. I eventually discovered the problem and found a cure for such a condition was as a result of corporate industrialization to the region and therefore alas environmental changes to the water chemistry of the Rivers and Tributaries causing an explosion of **"Nitrite"** (NO_2^-, polyatomic ion) poisoning that triggered the condition.

Water quality advancements in the history of tropical fish keeping had predominately played its part for the eventual successful keeping of tropical fish, since those early times.

Today, the Dutch Masters of Irrigation and Filtration, owes in fact a great deal to the Victorian's and the humble Aquarist over the years developing trickle filter systems and other gadgetry methods for the pumping and purification of water. Also the eventual recorded works available in the form of information found in reference books, where many hours can pass, often spent on research by Aquarists and Biologists, has greatly helped to advance this field.

The studying over history of the natural environment regarding water movement and purification flows over substrates for more than a century now, has also greatly helped to find many perplexing answers for countless species surrounding ichthyology (Greek, fish) when kept today in aquariums by tropical fish hobbyists, where we can in most cases see healthy thriving tropical fish.

Collection of Tropical Fish Hobbyist Magazines back covers of the past showing products of the day and how things have changed since the 1960's). Photograph taken by Author Alastair

Therefore today the joy of tropical fish keeping as being far more informative and resourceful in the way of products and solutions is greatly owed to our Victorian Ancestors, who journeyed into the unknown and from their endeavours and dedication as Aquarists, laid the foundations for our pastime to grow and become so successful, a hobby that now spans the globe today, reaching every corner and part of the World.

CHAPTER TWO

New Aquarist Getting Started

One of my aims with this book is to make every part of taking up your new pastime of tropical fish keeping exciting and enjoyable, with help at every step along the way!

A Perfectly Healthy Happy Female Swordtail (Xiphophorus) Looking for Food in one of the Author's Planted Aquariums – Photograph by Alastair R Agutter

When I began Tropical Fish Keeping back in the 1960's, I had in my local community a good number of small retail outlets to acquire equipment and fish. Looking on Google now, at the same region there are far fewer shops today and many have been replaced with the emergence of what I describe as Pet Superstores. These new stores today are more commercially driven and with many staff, in comparison to the old tropical fish stores of a bygone era and past, where so very often you were purchasing long established reliable proven product brands and able to seek advice on an item directly from the retail shop owner, who was always a passionate tropical fish hobbyist and very often a member of the local Aquarist Club.

More Products for today's Aquarist – Photo by Alastair R Agutter at Maidenhead Aquatics

As a regular patron to such retail establishments of the past, relationships were built up on trust between customer and shopkeeper. The retailer also got to know you as a customer and would always go that extra mile and inform you of a new product, if he or she believed it would be of benefit or of interest to you. Shopkeepers in days gone by would also make it their business to spend considerable time with customers, to ensure their patrons received the correct advice and the right equipment.

If today you become fortunate to find such a tropical fish shop establishment in your local community, such as the boys and girls at Maidenhead Aquatics, stick with them. For at times their help and advice will be invaluable and this is some of the very best advice I can give!

Today in our commercially driven world, we are presented with many varying brands and products. This can be at times both confusing and daunting, especially if you are taking up the hobby for the very first time. Even I, nearly after 50 years of tropical fish keeping, sometimes find myself standing in one of these large retail outlets looking perplexed and confused, as I seek out a particular product, plant or fish species.

Tropical Fish Hobbyist Magazines First Issue Published in September 1952 spanning over 5 decades – Photograph Compilation Created by Alastair R Agutter

With reference to reading material on the subject, today we are very fortunate to have more tropical fish books and information in the way of guides, specialist tropical fish books and magazines, plus the World Wide Web to some degree? This is very much a contrast from the past, where in my early days embarking on the hobby, Dr Herbert Axelrod and the Tropical Fish Hobbyist Organization (T.F.H. Inc.), were the primary source and providers of reading material, producing a monthly magazine for the Aquarist of the day for greater knowledge and new ideas.

If I recall, my library of tropical fish books in the 1960's consisted of around 6 books and two of those being Tropical Fish Keeping Encyclopaedias with hundreds of various fish species and plants produced by TFH Inc. (Tropical Fish Hobbyist) and by William T. Innes.

My First Aquarium Collectors Edition

Early Specialist Books 1/. Schmidt-Focke's Discus Book published 1989 2/. Handbook of Discus published 1985 3/. The Discus Book published 1989 – Photograph by Alastair R Agutter

Now today, I find myself in the way of books just on one species a lone, running into the 10's, 20's and 30's. So seeking the right advice to ensure you are on the right track when taking up this hobby of tropical fish keeping, can sometimes be confusing regarding some publications with contrasting and contradictory views. This I wanted to avoid when writing "My First Aquarium", for I want all folk to enjoy this new noble pastime from the very outset, even when it comes to acquiring the correct equipment.

They say it takes all sorts to make a world, this ideology can also be found across many hobbies and pastimes in the way of Aquarists techniques and advice, to the actual hobbyist itself. Aquarists can have many varying ideas and opinions regarding what they want from the hobby. Across such diversity in society, it is physically impossible to please all, but I will try in this book to the very best of my ability, by providing detailed information and techniques I have used that are proven and work successfully over many decades. Some of my methods may be far different from others who write on the subject of tropical fish keeping and this can very often be the case. For when Jack Wattley, Dr Eduard Schmidt-Focke and I bred Discus successfully in captivity, each one of us had our very own different techniques and methods, yet most importantly they all worked. Beyond the products, species, chemistry and other, I have found successful tropical fish keeping comes first and foremost from the simplest of ingredients, this being love and care. Some may say I am old school in my methods, but alas over the years the older and wiser I have become, I know now, one such day will arrive regarding yourself, where from your views and interests, you will also be judged as old School and the word that comes to mind is "evolution", but at the same respecting Natural Law in the form of Quantum Mechanics relating to balance, to "evolve and refine". Regarding tropical fish keeping and all walks of life, I believe in risk aversion and this is well worth considering and remembering. For the more complicated we make something, the greater the risk of something going wrong. I know some folk when taking up the past time seek instant results in our fast changing world today of instant gratification. But this does not happen in tropical fish keeping, as we are all directly governed by the rules of Mother Nature and she has a timeline all of her own. With regards to tropical fish keeping there is no silver bullet, only the golden rule of love and care that will bring successful results and joy, especially when it comes to wanting to breed various fish species. Regarding the latter above, I hope many of you now embarking on this new joyous pastime will decide to go down the road of wanting to breed tropical fish, for many of our beautiful wild species of tropical fish today face extinction in the wild and only in captivity do some species still exist from commercial breeders based in Holland, Germany, Britain, American, Asian and more recently India and Africa.

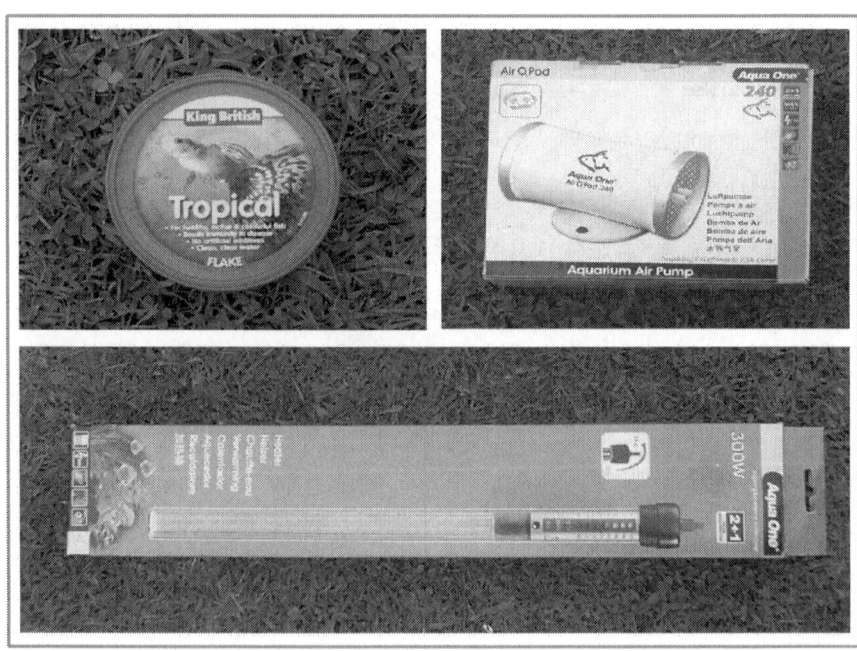

1/. King British Tropical Fish Flake Food 2/. Aqua One Two Valve Aquarium Air Pump 3/. Aqua One Combined 300 Watt Heater Thermostat – Photograph by Alastair R Agutter

As a humble soul and frugal with my hard earned money, I am always mindful when it comes to the need for acquiring the right products and their costs to folk. I particularly take interest here, as I know many of our younger Aquarists pursue their pastime and enjoyment from a limited pocket money budget.

At this point of the book as we discuss products, I feel it is only proper to mention that all the products I recommend, are ones I have purchased and use myself. Therefore I am not commercially influenced in anyway, as I believe this would not be in the spirit of this book or the hobby. In the above picture as an example, are of three products I use today.

The first being King British Tropical Fish Flake Food, a product I have used since the very beginning of my Tropical Fish Keeping back in 1967, when I was introduced to the Flake Food by a fellow member of our local Aquarist Club. The second image above is of an Aqua One two valve aquarium air pump, which is considerably powerful and significantly quieter when running. The pump reminds me of the Aquarium Whisper Pumps used year's gone bye (picture below of old Whisper Aquarium Air Pump), that were very popular in the 1970's and 1980's for their greater silence when running, compared to other pumps on the market.

Picture three above on page 20, is of an Aqua One 300 Watt Aquarium Heater Thermostat, the type I use today and far better made than earlier makes, where you had to use a screw driver to adjust the temperature.

The Aqua One Heater Thermostats pictured above, today have an easy knob control adjustment and indicator, to tell you the temperature setting. All the products above are of great value for money and are affordable to meet every Aquarists budget. The Heater Thermostat for example at the time of publishing this book costs approximately $20.00 in price or around £15.00 in the UK. The King British Fish Food costs around $3.90 at the time of publishing or £2.20 in UK money sterling and finally, the Aqua One two valve aquarium air pump costs around $30.00 US or £20.00 in UK sterling.

Above, are just a few examples of products as we get started, but in the book throughout, I will provide detailed information and a number of easy solutions and options that are available to you as the Aquarist, to meet all budgets when we look at the equipment required, for enjoying and keeping tropical fish for the very first-time. Or further information provided for a fellow inquisitive existing Aquarist, who has chosen to acquire this book for more ideas, to ensure greater success with regards to their endeavours.

Above a picture of an old Whisper Aquarium Air Pump that were very popular in the 1970's and 1980's especially for their quieter running – Photograph by Alastair R Agutter

Before actually getting down to writing this book, I had spent nearly three years in planning it out, for my main aim is to make the book straight forward, easy to follow and informative. I truly hope therefore on this first attempt of writing "My First Aquarium", the book covers the entire topic of tropical fish keeping sufficiently for folk taking up the pastime for the very first time and it to be comprehensive for today's new Aquarists.

My first aquarium as mentioned earlier in the book introduction was a naturally planted one, and I am sure this is the desired type of aquarium for most folk taking up the pastime of tropical fish keeping for the very first time.

So by writing this book on a naturally planted aquarium environment primarily, it enables me to breakdown easily the areas we need to cover. The primary areas of tropical fish keeping to consider are; Location, Aquarium, Substrate, Heating, Lighting, Filtration (Water) and Theme (plants and species).

Now the last point covered above, is the theme and may throw you slightly, but be rest assured, there is logic to my insanity. For certain types of plants and fish species survive in different water conditions and temperatures.

One of the Author's Naturally Planted Community Aquarium's with the introduction of his 'New' Bio Dom Filters (Polyatomic-ion Biological Reactors) for a balanced functioning eco-system Photograph by Alastair R Agutter

A naturally planted aquarium when taking up the hobby of tropical fish keeping is also a very helpful and wise decision, as you will get a great deal of help from Mother Nature, regarding the eco-system balance created in your aquarium.

However, I will also cover other themes in the book such as sterile bare-bottom Aquariums for certain species and breeding, plus rocky and reef-like environments for Rift Lake Cichlids.

In our commercial world, tut, tut, many folk read, hear and see many products and solutions regarding water conditioning, especially when it comes to setting up a new aquarium for the first time.

In this book you will **NOT** hear much about the introduction of commercial **"Chemicals"** or artificial additives at all, for any form of chemical or additive can very often come with serious consequence.

When correctly setting up a naturally planted Aquarium, no chemicals are required if the instructions laid out in the book are followed to the letter as they say.

The Great Amazon under threat from Corporate Industrialization that threatens all Life on Earth from Climate Change – Photograph Compilation Created by Alastair R Agutter

Regarding Naturally Planted Aquariums and our Natural Wild, if we briefly pause and step back for a moment, we can consider the impact today from chemicals in our World surrounding the health of the planet, that is now under serious threat, a topic we describe as climate change and where the common denominator is corporate industrial pollution (chemicals, Co2, No2, So2 etc.) the main menace and cause.

In the book "My First Aquarium" I will cover areas of how we can naturally alter certain water conditions using natural minerals and organic material, in the event that any of my fellow Aquarist readers need to change the water quality, to suit certain fish and plant life species surrounding a desired theme, or to address certain domestic water supply quality issues.

I truly hope as a new Aquarist reading through the book the advice becomes straight forward and makes common sense, thus serving as an enjoyable step by step guide.

Please excuse the pun, but after a few weeks of Tropical Fish Keeping as a new Aquarist "you will be like a fish to water" and take everything in your stride, starting to really enjoy your new found pastime after the initial period.

As like in the realms of Natural Law concerning Quantum Mechanics to "evolve and refine" failure is not an option and will not happen if you follow each of the steps in the book. I have endeavoured to be as thorough as I possibly can, but at the same time making the information hopefully straight forward.

A GOLDEN RULE TO REMEMBER

One point very rarely covered in tropical fish books and worth mentioning as we begin, is to always wash your hands in warm water before and after feeding or maintaining the Aquarium.

Having a Gardening background and interest can be very helpful and advantageous when taking up Tropical Fish Keeping as a Pastime - Photograph by Alastair R Agutter

Ladies like perfume and men like after shave, both of which on hands taint the food and serve as a poison to the fish and can contaminate the water.

GREEN FINGERS ARE USEFUL

If by chance you are a keen gardener already, many parts of the book "My First Aquarium" will make absolute sense when discussing the Naturally Planted Aquarium concerning water chemistry, substrates and plants.

Part of the Author's Fish House showing a Naturally Planted Aquarium on the left and a Bare-Bottom sterile Aquarium on the right Breeding Angel Fish (Pterophylium Scalare) - Photograph by Alastair R Agutter

Many Gardeners can also be very knowledgeable, inventive and resourceful, when it comes to locating certain items and products. This may well help and aid in the hobby of tropical fish keeping, and especially if you really get the "bug" and become so engrossed, as an Aquarist in your new-found pastime. You decide to transform part, or all, of your old garden shed to a fish house.

Fish houses are worth mentioning for back in the 1960's and 1970's especially, tropical fish keeping and breeding in garden sheds was very much a popular in thing. In fact, fish houses made from garden sheds and garages were very often the birth place of many specialist tropical fish breeders and none more so than fellow Aquarist Jack Wattley of Turquoise Discus fame pictured below.

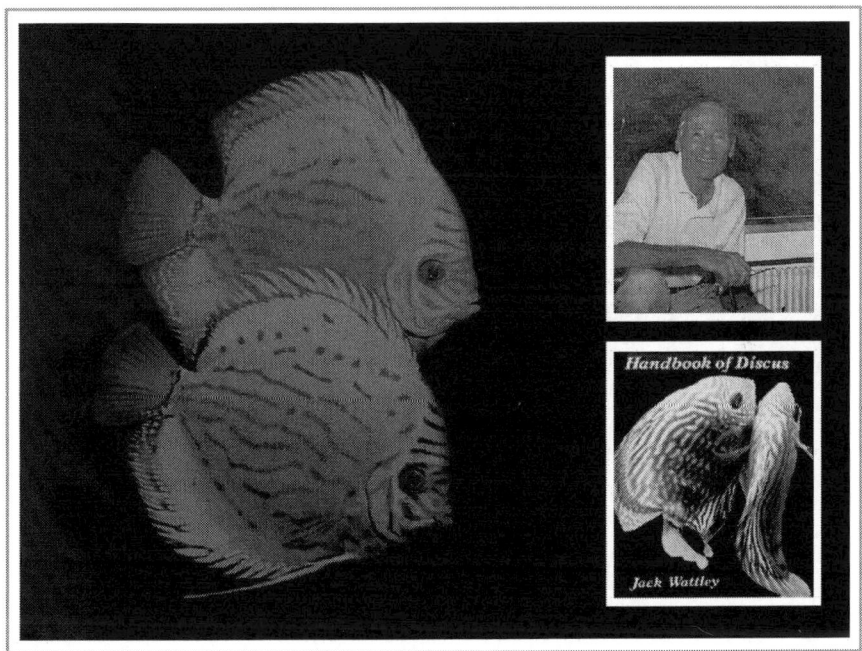

Picture showing the Famous Jack Wattley Turquoise Discus successfully bred from Jack's Garage Fish House in Florida along with Picture of Jack Wattley and his Book – Photograph Compilation Created by Alastair R Agutter

Today Jack Wattley is World renowned and has an International thriving Wholesale Business for the distribution of Discus (symphysodon) and cichlid fish food, but it all began in a garage, or shed, like so many.

I hope in the coming years, we will again see a renaissance period for Fish Houses, as they bring so much joy and satisfaction to folk's lives, especially when successfully breeding fish species today that are no longer found in the Wild.

We as humans today are no longer part of just the human story, but the very custodians as primate species, regarding the story of all life on Earth for today, tomorrow and all future generations.

CHAPTER THREE
Tropical Fish Aquarium Theme

This may well be the very first time you have come across such a chapter dedicated to themes, but in truth every book on community tropical fish keeping should have such a section.

Map Courtesy of NASA and Illustration created and compiled by Alastair R Agutter

As you can quickly see from looking at the map above, we can see how certain different fish species reside in specific locations around the World and also surviving in varying water, temperatures and weather conditions.

Some species even, such as the Swordtail, has now become established in many parts of Asia, many thousands of miles the other side of the World from the species original native location being Central America and Mexico.

With a contrast of temperatures and conditions, it is very easy to quickly see not all can fit successfully in one environment and so choices and decisions will need to be made. But as we move through this chapter, I know I can shed further light on this discussion to make decision making far easier.

CENTRAL AMERICA AND MEXICO

This region in the World of Central America and Mexico offers for fish species inhabitants not the highest of temperatures found in tropical fish keeping. On average temperatures are around 73 to 78 degrees Fahrenheit or in Centigrade terms around 21c to 24c.

Author's Aquarium showing A Male Platy (Xiphophorus Genus but without tail) in the foreground and Female in the background – Photograph by Alastair R Agutter

Popular community aquarium species to Central America and Mexico are Platies, Mollies, Swordtails and Guppies (livebearers).

SOUTH AMERICA AND AMAZONIA

This region in the World of South America and Amazonia offers up a plethora of fish species inhabitants and where temperatures become much higher and noticeably different and with further changes to water conditions across this vast area. On average temperatures are around 78 to 86 degrees Fahrenheit or in Centigrade terms around 24c to 28c.

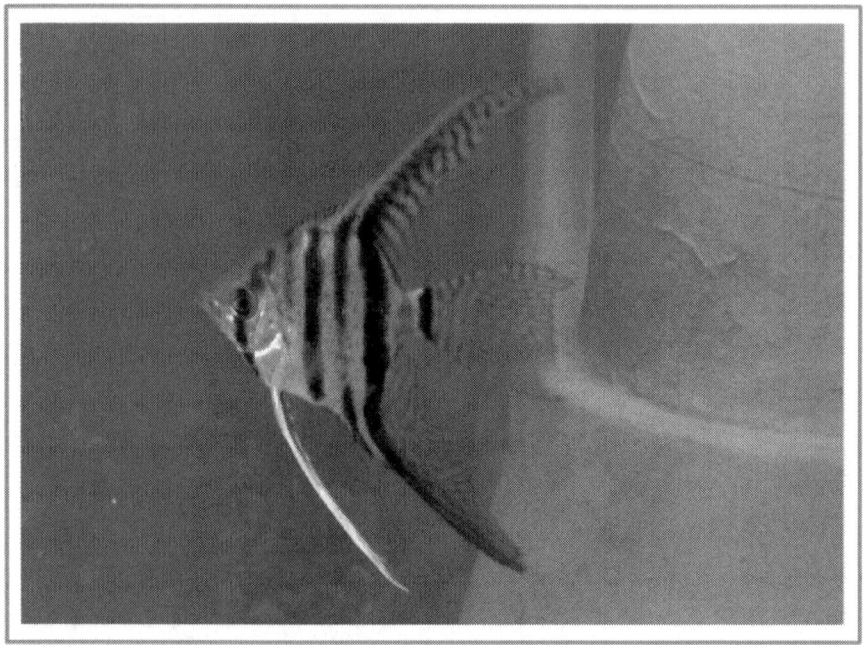

Author's Breeding Aquarium showing a Male Angel Fish (Pterophylium Scalare) a popular Community Aquarium Cichlid Family Member – Photograph by Alastair R Agutter

Popular community aquarium species from South America and Amazonia include Angel Fish, Catfish and many varying species of Tetra's, some cichlids such as Ramirez (Venezuela and Columbia) are suitable for community aquariums. The Amazon and adjoining Rivers such as the River Tefe and others, is the native regions and home to the famous Discus (symphysodon), King of the Aquarium.

CONTINENT OF AFRICA

The Continent of Africa is the home of the Great Lakes, Malawi and Tanganyika for Rift Lake Cichlids that include countless colourful species and many more species becoming into being today, as these cichlids continue to cross breed and morph.

Rift Lake Cichlids can be very aggressive, but are very attractive and colourful. They can very often be mistaken for Marine Fish, especially when in an Aquarium with artificial coral, rocks and white sand as a substrate. These species are always very active, marking out territorial areas with warnings to other approaching fish.

My First Aquarium Collectors Edition

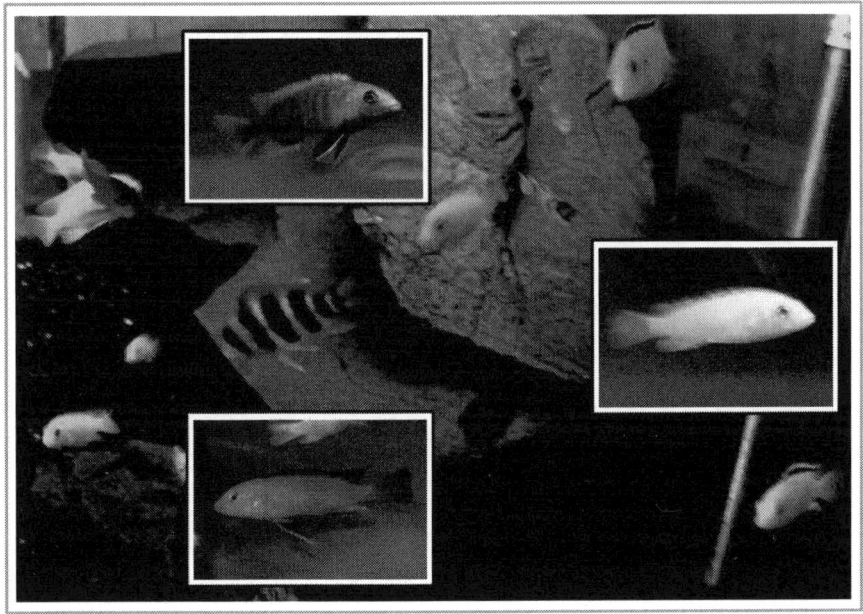

Rock Dwelling Malawi Cichlids from the Great Lakes of Africa, Members of the Pseudotropheus Genus in 1, 2, 3 and background images – Photographs taken and Compiled by Alastair R Agutter at Maidenhead Aquatics, England

Water conditions in these regions are vastly different to the other environments thus far mentioned, with a higher PH (greater hardness) and where temperatures are lower in comparison to the other above regions mentioned earlier. Temperatures normally range between 70 to 78 degrees Fahrenheit, or in Centigrade terms around 20c to 24c.

CONTINENT OF CENTRAL ASIA

The region of Central Asia namely Pakistan and India offers up for fish species again much higher temperatures found in tropical fish keeping and on average a neutral PH but with poorer brackish water quality. On average temperatures are around 78 to 86 degrees Fahrenheit or in Centigrade terms around 24c to 28c.

Popular community aquarium species to Central Asia in these regions of Pakistan and India include a large array of Gourami's (bubble nest builders). Some of the most popular tropical fish Gourami species of this genus are the Dwarf, Pearl, Opaline (Three Spotted or Marbled) and Kissing Gourami (Thailand and Indonesia).

Three Spotted Gourami's (Trichopodus trichopterus) often called Opaline or Marbled Gourami at home with some Clown Loaches (Chromobotia macracanthus) – Photograph by Alastair R Agutter at Maidenhead Aquatics

CONTINENT OF EASTERN ASIA

This region in the World of Eastern Asia offers for fish species inhabitants again not necessarily the highest of temperatures. On average temperatures range between 73 to 78 degrees Fahrenheit or in Centigrade terms around 21c to 24c.

Popular community aquarium species of Eastern Asia including Borneo; are members of the Barb Family and where there are numerous species including Cherry Barbs, Rosy Barbs and Tigers Barbs the latter is one of the most popular species for the community aquarium, however barbs can nip and be very aggressive in community aquariums, upsetting many of the other residents in the Aquarium.

The Cherry Barb is a particularly aggressive species and I would not recommend this fish being in a community aquarium, as they will race around nipping other fish species causing a great deal of stress and anxiety and sometimes resulting in death.

Tiger Barbs (Puntius tetrazona) are a magnificent sight in a large shoal and kept with larger species, but renowned for nipping – Photograph by Alastair R Agutter at Maidenhead Aquatics

In chapter 12 titled "Aquarium Fish Species" covers a series of full colour plates along with the tropical fish species common and Latin names.

PLANT SPECIES CONDITIONS

Another valid point to consider is the plant species tolerance to temperatures and conditions in community aquariums.

Some plant species can thrive in very hot temperatures, where others cannot and will only die.

This can also be the case surrounding water conditions regarding the PH for plants, where there are varying differences between acid and hard water condition.

Two quick examples I can give, is that Amazon Sword Plants will thrive in hot neutral to acid water conditions. Whereas some member species of the Vallisneria family will suffer in very hot temperatures and do far better in cooler temperatures, ranging from 70 to 78 degrees Fahrenheit and in Centigrade terms being 20c to 24c and with a more neutral PH.

An Author's Naturally Planted Aquarium with Twisted Vallisneria Spiralis in the foreground and Amazon Sword (Echinodorus) Plants in the background – Photograph by Alastair R Agutter

The health and condition of plants is also dependent upon the substrate conditions provided and the related filtration used. These factors and issues will be explained in detail in the respective Chapters throughout the book covering Substrates and Filtration in addition to the water chemistry conditions.

So at this point in the book, as we discuss the suitability of fish and plant species, with reference to Tropical Fish Aquarium Themes. This Chapter is essentially gently easing you in to the hobby and familiarizing you with the great diversity implications surrounding Tropical Fish Keeping, giving a summarized insight to help get you thinking about your dream aquarium in your home, or fish house and the inhabitants you wish to keep.

The World of Tropical Fish Keeping is fascinating as a pastime and hobby, where we are spoilt for choice when we consider the countless thousands of fish and plant species. I seem to recall back in the late 1970's and early 1980's when studying Marine Biology even then, there had been discovered over 33,000 species of vertebrate fish and over 550 cartilaginous fish, namely sharks and armoured catfish species.

Once you start to get an idea about the type of theme you desire, the plants if applicable and fish species you wish to keep. We then have to consider the best way of stocking the Aquarium with the chosen species and this relates to the age and size of the fish species in question.

FISH BEHAVIOURAL CONSIDERATIONS

This part of the subject aptly leads on from the above, for another factor we have to consider when establishing and stocking a tropical fish community aquarium, is not only age and size of the new planned inhabitants, but also the fish species themselves, regarding their behavioural characteristics.

One of the Author's Male Angel Fish (Pterophylium Scalare) being very diligent guarding his territory and ready to fend off any visitor threatening the breeding pair, where the eggs are laid on the purposely made polyatomic-ion biological reactor – Photograph by Alastair R Agutter

Cichlids for example are members of the tooth carp family of fish species genera and many are very aggressive predators in their native regions of the wild habitat. I know many species today are tank bred but the DNA structure gene code instincts still exist within these species regarding predatory behavioural patterns.

Some species of cichlids are just fine in community aquariums with the slight exception being at times of breeding taking place and where cichlid parents become very maternal and territorial, chasing out any community fish species that threaten their eggs or young brood.

Some cichlid species suitable for the tropical fish community aquarium are Angel Fish *(Pterophylium Scalare)*, Ramirez *(Mikrogeophagus ramirezi)* Cichlids and Discus *(symphysodon)*.

Even the small iridescent Neon Tetra (Paracheirodon innesi) has a pecking order and can excerpt aggressive behaviour towards each other – Photograph by Alastair R Agutter

Upon reading the above, it may be the assumption that only cichlids are pro-active territorial aggressive species. But the reality is all species of fish evolve through natural selection and within such a grand plan that includes quantum mechanics and natural branching, even the most timid of species will try to establish a hierarchy with territorial areas.

When studying Neon Tetra's for example pictured above, a tropical fish species that is renowned for being a beautiful shoaling fish from South America. But upon studying the species, one can clearly see territorial behavioural patterns and a hierarchy among the other Neon Tetra species in the aquarium. The only time such behaviour decreases is at feeding times, when each member of the shoal has other things on their mind.

Further on in the book we will discuss fish behavioural patterns in far greater detail, but like all subjects, sometimes various topics become relevant, or overlap with others, and I felt it was important to start thinking about these factors, so it helps towards deciding on the most desired tropical fish aquarium theme.

When we look at all the above regions and examples of the contrasting species from around the World, and the tropical fish species available to us, there are similarities across regions in the way of temperatures and water chemistry. However, there is one area where there is a big gulf regarding themes, temperatures and water quality and this relates to the Great Lakes and Rift Lake Cichlids.

GREAT RIFT LAKE AQUARIUM THEME

In the early 1970's, I had the great opportunity to be one of the very first to receive and breed some of the Rift Lake Cichlids in captivity, namely members of the Pseudotropheus genera from Lake Malawi.

As always when first beginning to breed a new fish species collected from the wild, little is known and when it comes to literature, material is always very sparse first of all and in the mid to late 1970's it was really thin on the ground, in fact very few articles at all available.

So very often it was a question of scratching around researching and exploring further, using publications such as the National Geographic to see if one could find the odd article, or column, to try and dissect more information about the regions geology regarding the species, so one could further understand the mysterious underwater world of the Great Lakes in Central Africa.

The environment that Rift Lakes Cichlids exist within is far different to the naturally planted aquarium we are very often accustomed too. The floor to most parts of these Great Lakes is very barren with the occasional rock formation in parts and the occasional signs of plant life.

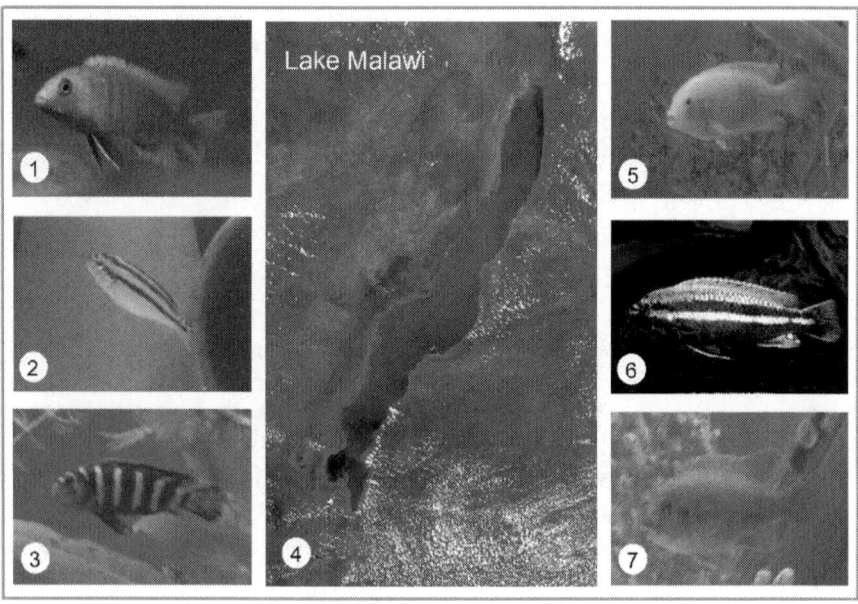

1/. Pseudotropheus (male) 2/. Melanochromis auratus (female) 3/. Pseudotropheus elongatus (male) 4/. Lake Malawi 5/. Pseudotropheus (female) 6/. Melanochromis auratus (male) 7/. Pseudotropheus (female) – Photograph Compilation Created by Alastair R Agutter

When it comes to food for these Cichlids, the main staple diet of these species seems to be what-ever is available from small fish, weed, dead fowl, drowned animal carcasses and also included, the eating of algae from rock surfaces forming part of their diet.

Regarding the reproduction and morphology of the species found in the Great Lakes Malawi and Tanganyika. Cichlid species such as members of the Pseudotropheus family are in fact mouth brooders, when it comes to breeding and reproduction. The eggs are normally laid in a shallow well created in the lakes substrate and after fertilization, the eggs are collected up in the mouths of the Parents, where they begin the process of incubation, so eventually the eggs hatch inside the mouths of the parents and very often by the male.

Even after hatching, the brood will swim around inside the mouths of the Parents. The fry will be occasionally freed from the mouths of the Parents, by gently blowing out the fry into the surrounding water environment, so the fry can have a quick swim about in those very early days for a few seconds and minutes and then again be scooped up into the mouths of the Parents, so the fry are again protected from predators.

The average water temperatures to keep these species are between 72 to 76 degrees Fahrenheit and in centigrade terms, between 21c to 24c. These were the temperatures I found to be the most suitable for the species, when I began to successfully breed these fish back in the early, mid and late 1970's.

I also discovered the water whilst very clear in these Great lakes, the PH is relatively hard and as I recall, had to adjust and create a consistent PH hardness for breeding of around 7.4 to 7.8 PH.

The Rift Cichlids of the Great Lakes in the Wild are ferocious predators and life for these species to survive and reproduce is very harsh. So they are not suitable to keep in a community aquarium with other fish species from many other parts and regions of the World.

Behavior problems with Rift Cichlids is not the only consideration, for as mentioned earlier just briefly, there is a great gulf between temperatures and water chemistry in comparison to many other tropical fish species found throughout the World.

However, if you are seeking hardy and very active colourful fishes and an aquarium for show purposes in your home. A Rift Lake Aquarium can be designed where it can almost look like a Marine Aquarium, by using fine white sand, gravels and rocks to form nooks and crannies created to replicate a reef effect and where after time, can look stunning, as algae becomes established, or where moss forms and grows.

Aquarists today can also acquire these mosses from tropical fish retail outlets, normally available and grown successfully on coconut shells.

Certain forms of lighting can also further enhance the vibrant colours of these Rift Lake Cichlid species, by using namely Grolux tube systems.

Members of the Pseudotropheus genera have always been my favourite, especially when so often species have vibrant iridescent blue males and bright canary yellow females in most cases, but this is not a given as the species continues to morph creating new species.

Picture above showing one of the Author's Pseudotropheus in an aquarium landscape created with white gravel, flower pots and artificial coral. Photograph by Alastair R Agutter

Malawi Cichlid Members of the Auratus (*Melanochromis auratus*) family of Cichlids, also known as the golden mbuna and Malawi golden cichlid offer also stunning colourations from striped gold to orange, yellow and iridescent blues. Males are less colourful and normally black or very dark stripped.

When a collection of 20 to 30 of these Malawi cichlid species are swimming around, the scene in an aquarium can be absolutely stunning.

Later in the book regarding fish behaviour, we will talk about these species as they are very territorial and this can lead to some problems in an aquarium if not managed correctly and how to address and combat these issues will be covered for you.

Rift Lake cichlids in most cases are particularly fast swimming species and so any aquarium housing such fish, will always show a hive of activity for any viewing member of the family, or inquisitive visitor admiring your underwater world creation.

When planning a Rift Lake cichlid aquarium, bear in mind the fish tank needs to be on the larger size, as these species will grow considerably and I would suggest a minimum of an aquarium being 30 gallons plus.

Rift Lake Cichlids can also be very destructive, moving gravel and small rocks when digging. Plants will therefore of course suffer and most likely not survive in such an environment.

As mentioned briefly earlier most Rift Lake Aquariums consist of rocks, bog woods and artificial corals, as just a few examples of what can be housed in these fish tanks for ornamental value purposes.

NATURALLY PLANTED AQUARIUM THEME

Without doubt a Naturally Planted Aquarium in Tropical Fish Keeping can be the jewel in the crown for any home, or fish house, and when set up correctly with the right equipment, will deliver a balanced environment with thriving fish and plants.

An Author's Naturally Planted Community Aquarium alive with activity and healthy thriving plants and fish – Photograph by Alastair R Agutter

There are countless hundreds and thousands of water plant species throughout the World for the natural aquarium and so for the Tropical Fish Hobbyist there is a utopia of choice.

For the ardent Gardener taking up the pastime for the very first time, can open up endless possibility and further interest, with the opportunity especially to propagate aquarium plants for full lush aquatic scenes in the tropical fish aquarium. Whether in the home, or having a fish house that resembles an aquatic greenhouse, one can grow many interesting and curious plant species, especially when set up correctly and where there is an opportunity to bring such plant species into bloom.

Greater details on how to grow plants, the right conditions and techniques for healthy thriving species can be found in the dedicated plant Chapter Six, titled "Growing and Keeping Plants" in the book.

CHOOSING AN AQUARIUM THEME

I hope at this point in the book you have begun to gather some thoughts and ideas on the type of Aquarium you would like to create as your first project.

Short of divorce in a family, one Aquarium project normally leads onto another, and so the idea of a fish house by converting the garage, or a garden shed, may be something to consider in the not too distant future and where such a plan can be devised and designed over those long dark winter nights.

Essentially, when it comes to choosing a theme for your first tropical fish aquarium in general terms, comes down to about five categories. 1/. The Naturally Planted Aquarium, 2/. The Bare Bottom Sterile Aquarium, 3/. The Rift Lake Cichlid Aquarium, 4/. Novelty Aquarium and finally 5/. Chic Modern or Artistic Creative

We can expand further on the themes when it comes to deciding on the type of fish species and plants. For example you may opt for a Naturally Planted Tropical Fish Aquarium, but plum for a South American Amazonian theme with plants and bogwood. Or on the other hand, you may want to have a Naturally Planted Tropical Fish Aquarium, but with an Oriental theme, where parts of the aquarium has a substrate and other areas include ornamental furnishings, even tiers and different levels of substrate in the aquarium.

CHIC MODERN ARTISTIC AND CREATIVE AQUARIUM THEMES

You may even decide to go modern chic and express your creative talents by designing a theme with submerged ornate pots and containers, similar to Bonsai displays, but with aquatic plants in a bare bottom aquarium and where the bottom and background colours of the aquarium are specific to complement a modern and diverse artistic theme, finally complimented with a light system incorporating spots lights for example.

As they say, the world is your oyster when it comes to creating an aquarium theme. So much more can be created, designed and achieved when thinking out of the box. One of my current ideas, is to design a Discus Aquarium with potted tropical lilies in flower, how spectacular is that idea!

This ideally leads us onto the next part of the book by choosing now the correct Aquarium size, the style of the Aquarium, the location and the most suitable stand to house the actual aquarium in the very next chapter.

NOVELTY AQUARIUM THEMES

In truth regarding this type of theme, I am not a big fan, but like they say it takes all sorts to make a World, and if such quirky themes brighten up a member of societies life and make them happy, well then alas, who am I to judge.

As mentioned earlier, I remember as a very small boy when introduced to my first aquarium, I saw the wreck of a sunken Galleon that captured my eye and other novelty items, all with bubbles expelling from them in David's Aquarium in his Hallway.

Below are just some of the novelty items that have been popular in the past and still today. However, the world of creative aquarium design with the use of acrylics and polycarbonates, has opened up a whole new world of tropical fish keeping with fish tanks of all shapes and sizes from globes, cubes and tall rectangular designs with curved edges to mention a few.

In the picture below shows also a novelty style aquarium design with two hexagonal towers and joined in the centre by two tunnels. This novelty hexagonal aquarium is suitable for popular common small species of community fish such as;

guppies, platies, swordtails, mollies, tetras, barbs and small catfish with natural or plastic plants.

1/. Hexagonal Designed Aquarium 2/. Wreck of a Sunken Galleon 3/. A Castle 4/. Rock Face and Trees 5/. Old Water Mill – Photographs by Alastair R Agutter

In the 1980's and 1990's the tropical fish keeping hobbyist was seeking larger aquarium sizes and this was a contrast to earlier times where small seemed beautiful.

SMALL AND BEAUTIFUL DESIGNER AQUARIUMS

However, like so many cycles of fashion, small aquariums are again coming back in vogue. A good example of this can be viewed in the set of photographs below of new BiOrb aquarium designs being introduced to the tropical fish hobbyist today.

Regarding small aquariums it may be hard to believe, but they can very often be harder to maintain, as the volume of water is much lower and so any overfeeding, or chemical changes to the water, can rapidly cause an imbalance, leading to stress and illness to the fish.

Today ornate furnishings such as marbled pebbles and plastic plants consisting of many styles and variations are becoming forever more popular as maintenance free items for the tropical fish hobbyist.

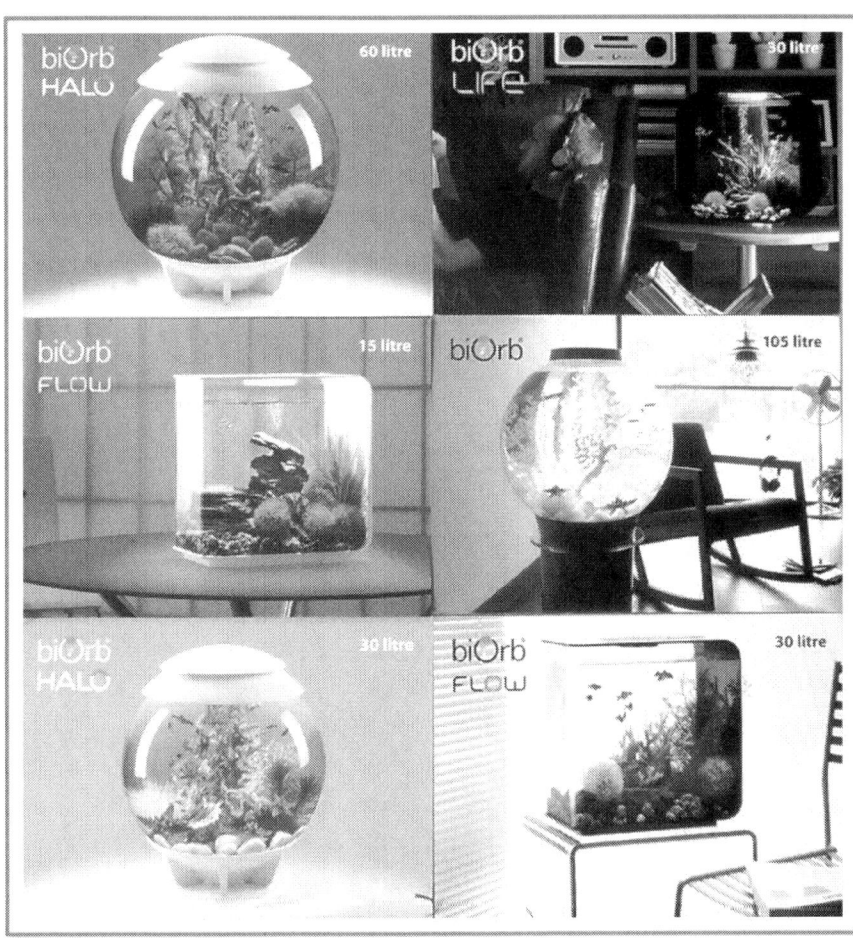

Small Designer Aquariums are certainly back in vogue today for the tropical fish hobbyist created with acrylics and polycarbonates – Photographs by Alastair R Agutter

I hope the chapter just covered, gives you some ideas on the choice of themes and designs for your first Aquarium.

CHAPTER FOUR

The Aquarium Size, Stand and Positioning

There are many Aquarium designs and furniture stands for today's Aquarist and from a considerable number of manufacturers. In fact I like to think a varying range of prices to meet every new Aquarists budget.

Picture of Juwel Aquarium Design and a Collection of Furniture Style Aquariums – Photograph by Alastair R Agutter at Maidenhead Aquatics

Today also with most households being online regarding the World Wide Web and having access to the Internet, it is also much easier to locate new and used aquariums and stands for the home, or the fish house if you do not wish to buy new and in doing so getting yourself a great bargain.

My first ever aquarium purchased for me by Father was secondhand and great value for money. I wanted to discuss this in the book, as I hope folk from all walks of life and especially younger members of our society become encouraged to take up the pastime of tropical fish keeping and also ensuring folk know the hobby of tropical fish keeping is reachable for all.

Regarding this subject area of aquarium stands and sizes, it may be the case in certain instances that appearance is not the main consideration if you are planning to set-up a fish house, or seeking more aquariums and stands, as you extend your hobby and breeding program of tropical fish species.

Regarding Aquarium Sizes, Stands and Positioning, over the years I have had the good fortune to read many tropical fish books from generalized topics surrounding the hobby and pastime of tropical fish keeping, to the more specialized books on specific species of fish and plants. What has struck me from reading these books however, very little is covered or discussed in great depth surrounding the size of aquariums, stands and location. So to me this is a strange thing, as this subject area is surely one of the most important, as the aquarium is the main item and starting point to the hobby.

So in this Chapter, I have decided to go into some considerable detail to assist in the decision making of choosing the most suitable size Aquarium for your needs, as a new Aquarist and one that meets your requirements and expectations.

So to support and aid you, in this section of the book will be found charts, tables and illustrations relating to the topic along with photographs to help in your decision making.

Aquariums and stands come in many sizes and forms as discussed earlier, and therefore another consideration is always the weight of any fish tank to be used. So I have also included in this chapter, guides and tables with reference to the cubic volume areas and weight of Aquariums.

Over the years, I have had the good fortune to design and make some stunning aquarium systems and also been lucky to see some spectacular creations in friends and acquaintances homes, where folk were looking towards designing show case underwater worlds in their lounges, dining rooms, conservatories, kitchens to even loos. Stunning aquariums in cube, rectangular, bow fronted, hexagonal and "L" shaped are just some shapes I have seen over the years.

Today with the advancement of aquariums, glass is no longer the only material used. Acrylic and polycarbonate sheets are now also being incorporated more into aquarium design for aquarists.

A picture of the 1ˢᵗ of a number of new customized Aquariums in construction (36" x 18" x 21") by the Author for breeding Discus (Symphysodon aequifasciata axelrodi) and Angel Fish (Pterophylium scalare) – Photograph by Alastair R Agutter

It also seems a long, long, time ago when you could buy a 3 foot all glass aquarium (36" x 12" x 15") for just $11.00 (£7.50). As glass today has gone up in price considerably due to greater demand surrounding home improvements and solar energy systems. However, if you know of a friendly Glazier, it may be well worth having a chat and seeing if some cheap glass is available to make your own aquarium as another option.

Above is a picture of a recent aquarium I have been making for my specific needs for keeping and breeding Discus (symphysodon), as I endeavour to reverse engineer some strains of the species, to ensure original characteristics and greater size of the fish species is restored. This particular aquarium is deeper in depth and height than most, measuring 36 inches long, 18 inches deep (front to back) and 21 inches in height. As one of the original Discus species namely the Brown Discus (*Symphysodon aequifasciatus axelrodi*) is known to reach over 9 inches in diameter.

Later in this chapter of the book and at the back of the publication in Chapter 17, you will find the "Aquarists Reference Tables" I have compiled to help all Aquarists covering PH, DH, Heater size and Wattage, Gallons (imperial UK and USA), Litres capacity, Square Cubic Foot Weight, the most popular commercial fish tank sizes and optimized aquarium dimensions.

The above points are relevant to this chapter, as it becomes clear based on the theme choice desired and the inhabitant species of fish one wishes to keep. The size of the aquarium therefore, as you can appreciate, does have a significant bearing on this subject area.

The first thing you need to know about Aquariums and their size, is that width and depth, is just as important as the length and height of a fish tank. I am pleased to say that today more commercial manufacturers are making Aquariums that are more optimized for their customers and of the correct size, rather than focusing on the aquarium being just aesthetically pleasing to the eye for commercial reasons and savings on manufacturing costs.

Das Perfekte Aquarium written by Kasper Horst and Horst Kipper in 1978 and the later English version titled The Optimum Aquarium published in 1986 – Photograph by Alastair R Agutter

Surface area in an aquarium optimizes the fish tanks ability to function and greatly aids in the keeping of healthy thriving fish and plants. The study of optimized aquarium sizes was researched thoroughly back in the mid 1970's and 1980's by

German Scientists and Aquarists. One book of particular worth and note for reading with reference to this subject if you can acquire a copy is titled "Das Perfekte Aquarium" written by Kasper Horst and Horst Kipper in 1978 in German and at a later date, an English version titled "The Optimum Aquarium" was published in 1986.

I will now start to explain in this Chapter the science and logic behind aquarium sizes, stands and location and with the aim of not wanting to confuse anyone, as I find it very easy to confuse myself these days, you know the old saying, "age catching up on me" or as my Daughter would say, just becoming an old man. The second thing you need to know about aquariums, is that the smaller the fish tank, the harder it is to maintain a stable equilibrium. One simple example being is feeding tropical fish, for if you overfeed in a small aquarium, you can easily spoil the water, where as in a larger aquarium the risk is greatly reduced or avoided.

I have chosen to cover the three subjects in this chapter in a logical order of relevance, in the hope the information is easy to follow.

AQUARIUM LOCATION

It may be taken as red regarding the most suitable place to locate and position your first aquarium. But we can all at times be guilty of not thinking something through and only after the event can we see the complications or setbacks.

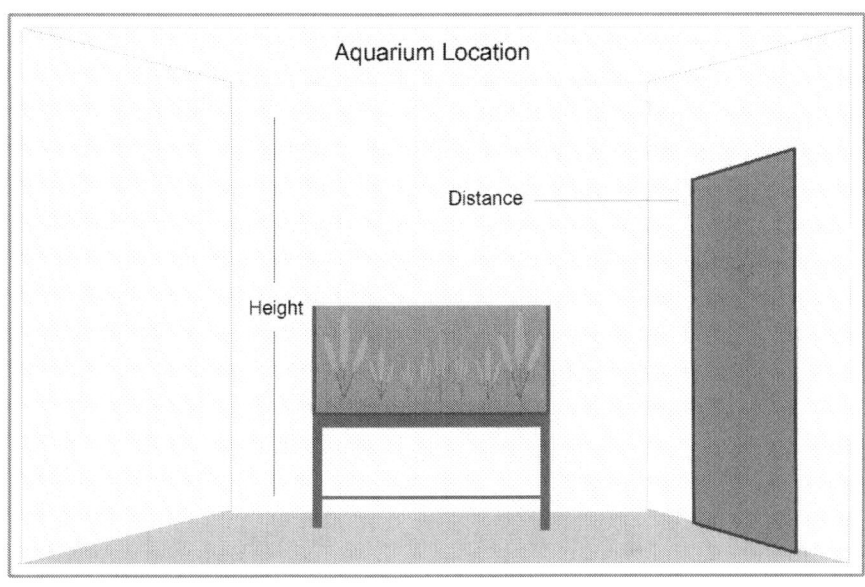

Diagram above shows the consideration required towards the Aquariums actual height, the positioning in a room and suitable clearance regarding doors – Diagram by Alastair R Agutter

So to try and alleviate any problems arising, I have endeavoured to raise numerous valid points to consider from the very start with reference to the aquariums location, its height and practicality regarding doors and other furnishings. To help further in this process,

I have created a series of diagrams like the one seen above throughout this chapter.

The aquarium location may not seem to be one of the most important aspects regarding fish health, but I can assure you it does.

If an aquarium is very low towards the ground, or in a corner, fish can very easily become skittish and nervous. The sudden appearance of a large object in the way of a human being can be daunting and so it is wise to locate your aquarium in a position where your fish can see the arrival of a person and also the departure of one.

This may sound a bit extreme to some folk, but it's like one of the Children creeping up on you when unawares and startling you. Such activity after several weeks on a continued daily basis would leave any human being a quivering nervous wreck.

Diagram above showing an Aquarium positioned centrally that is a practical and desired location for the health of the fish inhabitants – Diagram by Alastair R Agutter

Doors in a room that open inwards near an aquarium can also be a daunting and startling experience for your aquarium inhabitants.

The ideal position for an aquarium when you enter a room via a doorway is to look onto the aquarium.

The fish tank should be positioned in the room centrally along a wall, or if the design is a large cube, such an aquarium needs to be located in the centre of the room, or in the far corner. So the fish are not startled and can see visitors entering and leaving the room.

As the owner of your new fish you will be presently surprised how welcoming your fish become when in a healthy frame of mind, moving up towards the top, front and centre of the aquarium in the hope of some more food.

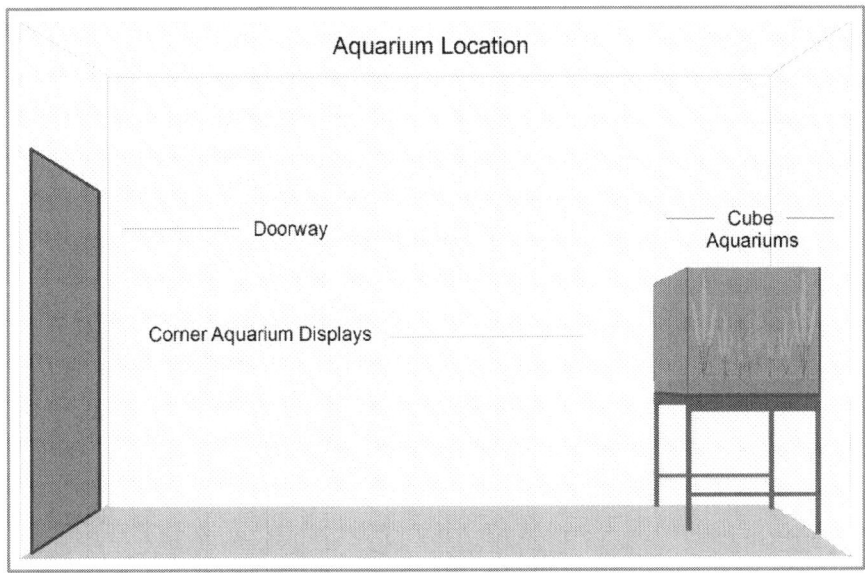

Diagram above showing a Cube Aquarium located in a far corner and well away from a door that would be frequently opening and closing – Diagram by Alastair R Agutter

More evolved tropical fish species such as cichlids and especially Discus (symphysodon) are even far more sensitive to the aquarium location and height. These species are particularly curious and like to see what is going on and at this point, it is well worth remembering these new inhabitants are now part of the family, and so happy healthy fish, means a happy healthy family.

Many diseases manifesting that tropical fish species incur believe it or not are mostly related to nerves, where the fish species are stressed in some way and this so often relates to the location of the aquarium, water quality, temperature or lighting.

One of the most common ailments in fish is "white spot" and this can be triggered from nerves. I find sometimes when acquiring new fish from a retailer they may have the odd white spot, as the tropical fish become stressed in the immediate frenetic retail store environment. But once home and in the correct location and with suitable water conditions and the right temperature, within a day or so, the condition clears up and without any medication, or chemicals.

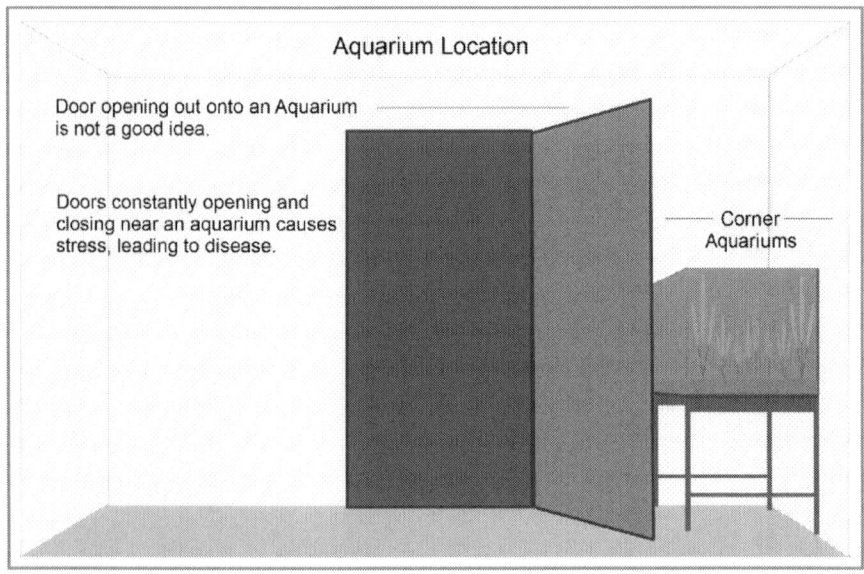

Diagram above showing a door opening inwards onto an Aquarium in a corner that results in very nervous and skittish unhappy fish leading to disease – Diagram by Alastair R Agutter

However, as a new Tropical Fish Hobbyist or Aquarist, I would not advise the purchasing of any fish species with signs of disease, unless you are a very experienced old hand spanning many years and decades who has the confidence to rescue such a species to bring back to full health.

Hallways may not be so practical as a location for an aquarium if the area has a small or narrow walk way. But if the home has a large hallway area, a tropical fish tank in such a location can be a stunning welcoming sight.

The most popular location for Aquariums is either the lounge or dining room. Or if we are talking of a new hobby for a family loved one, such as a Daughter or Son, no doubt the desired place and location by your siblings insistence will be their very own bedrooms.

If the tropical fish aquarium is going to be located in a loved one's bedroom, the same rules apply regarding the location of the aquarium, this being clear of doors and more particularly, in a safe place for knowing siblings as a Parent myself, in their sleep bless them, they can very often lash out from a dream or move around and end up on the floor asleep if the weather is particularly hot and humid.

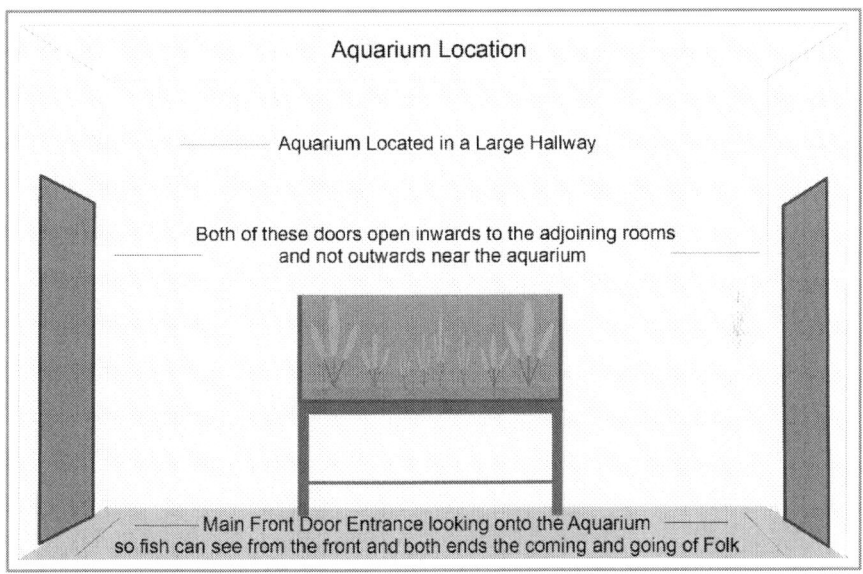

Diagram above showing an example of an Aquarium located centrally in a Large Hallway Area – Diagram by Alastair R Agutter

When choosing the location of the aquarium, always bear in mind the weight aspects of an aquarium filled with water. If the upstairs rooms to the house are floor boards, check to see what way the joists are running.

The ideal scenario regarding floors and joists is to ensure the aquarium stand is located and sits where a number of joists run across the floor. So if you have a three to four foot fish tank for example, you can expect to have at least three to four supporting joists under the floor boards and where they are normally each spaced out about a foot apart in distance under the floor boards.

Now If you live in a modern built home today, there is every chance that the flooring is covered with MDF for example, and this can sometimes make it more difficult and harder with reference to locating the joists. However, locating the joists under MDF can normally be discovered by lightly tapping the MDF flooring. This can be achieved by gently using a small hammer to tap the floor. When tapping the floor the sound changes from a hollow boom to a dampened thud, this will be the indication of a joist being present. Joists can vary slightly in size, but on average they are normally 2 to 2-3/4 inches in width and 8 to 12 inches in height.

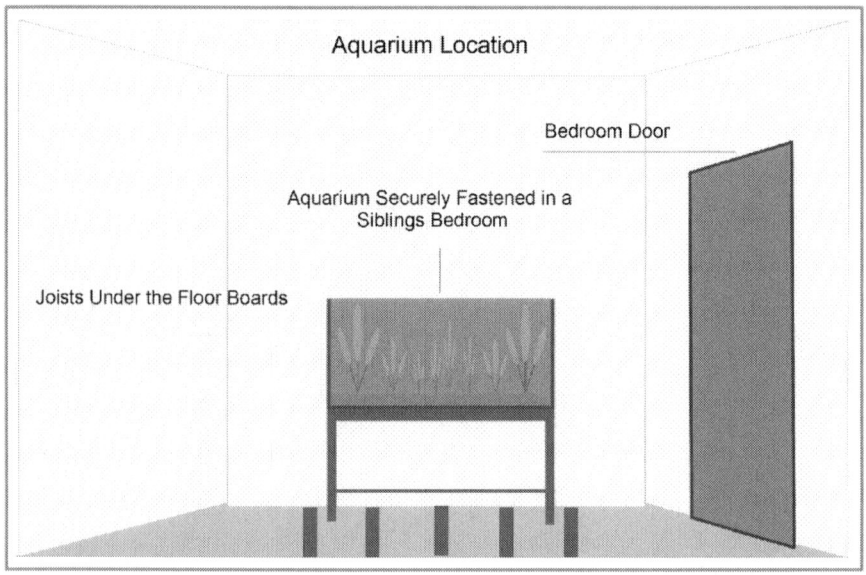

Diagram above showing a 1st floor Bedroom and identifying where the joists run under the floorboards – Diagram by Alastair R Agutter

Please remember that the rule of thumb regarding the weight of a gallon of Water is around 10lbs. The reason I have been a little wooly here regarding weight of a gallon, is that a USA gallon is different to a UK gallon and so there is a slight variation regarding the weight aspect between each.

As you can appreciate several gallons of water begins to mount up regarding the weight aspect of a fish tank and this excludes the actual weight of the aquarium and stand.

On a safety note regarding children and if you do have little ones running around, it is well worth ensuring that the aquarium is fastened securely to the wall and floor. For small children are inclined to grab when beginning to walk or climb, and I would not want any such accident to happen where the aquarium topples from not being secure. Such an event, or accident, could in fact happen and be caused also by yourself, if for example you slip and naturally reach out as a reaction and grab the aquarium. This can sometimes happen for example on a chair changing water, or doing some maintenance to an aquarium. By securing the aquarium, it works as a safeguard from the very outset and well worth considering.

You can easily secure an aquarium via the furniture stand inside the cupboard housing for example, so there are no unsightly visible fixings such as screws, bolts and brackets. If the aquarium stand is of a more traditional and conventional style made of angle iron or timber. This style of stand can be secured by using metal angle brackets that can be easily purchased from your local DIY centre or Ironmongers.

Over the years I have seen aquariums located in more unusual places such as bathrooms, loos and another location becoming forever more popular is the kitchen area of a home.

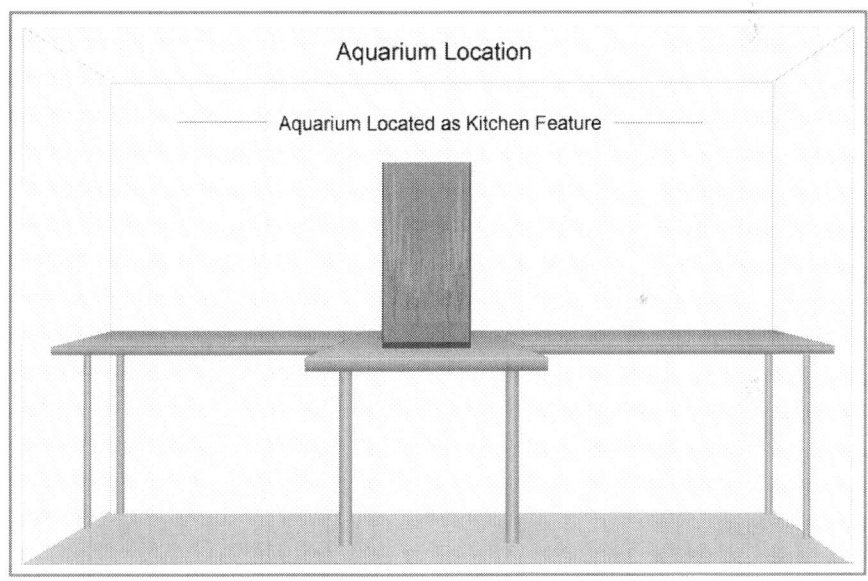

Diagram above showing an Aquarium forming part of a Centre piece on a Kitchen Worktop design – Diagram by Alastair R Agutter

Always remember if deciding to locate an aquarium in one of the above areas, greater caution needs to be exercised as water and electricity simply **do not** get on. Therefore greater insulation will be required regarding Kitchens, Loos and Bathrooms for the protection of sockets, electricity cabling and lighting, for in addition to water in such vicinities, condensation will very often be present.

One friend I knew had an aquarium located in the wall of his lounge and the wall in question adjoined to his garage on the ground floor. The fish tank looked stunning and maintenance was easily carried out by going into the garage area of the home, where the back and top of the aquarium was located and accessible.

Such structural design and changes in lounges, or other parts of the home where load bearing walls come into question, will need to be very carefully throughout, as lintels or RSJ's will be required for these load bearing walls, to prevent any collapse, or long term structural damage to the home in the way of house movement.

Part of the Author's new Fish House under construction for breeding more endangered tropical fish species threatened from Corporate Industrialization – Photograph by Alastair R Agutter

As mentioned earlier in the book, Fish Houses were very much the rage back in the 1960's through to the 1980's that can best be described as a golden era of tropical fish keeping and I hope in truth, we see again those joyous magical days in our hobby of tropical fish keeping, with a massive revival from younger generations especially, who seek to care and want to learn more about our Planet and the miracles of all life we share Mother Earth with.

With the greater diversity in energy solutions today, and more coming soon in the way of advanced insulation materials and more new and innovative solar energy solutions, this provides a window of opportunity for the hobby to grow and evolve again and for good reason, one being the preserving of tropical fish species threatened from Corporate Industrialization.

A green fish house revival using modern day methods of Social Networking to share ideas, and the building of traditional fish houses coming together old and new, I hope will create massive interest again.

Fish houses can be of any size and shape, the recycling of the old humble garden shed, or the family greenhouse can be brought back to life, or even the garage at your home can easily be converted into a fish house, especially as more folk begin to dispense with cars, work from home and cycling becomes a more popular personal health solution and a far more environmentally friendly viable mode of transport.

The building of a Fish house especially for our younger members of society is a great opportunity to learn more about the real world as I call it. Providing free healthy exercise and attaining a "hands-on" experience, learning about tools, methods of construction, materials, electricity, water filtration and more, alas developing life skills.

Fish houses can also be created and designed to meet every Hobbyists budget and ambition. The picture above shows part of a new fish house I am constructing for the purpose of breeding more species currently under threat in the wild.

So I hope we will begin to see momentum again in our hobby, with a resurgence of participation from folk of all ages and especially our younger generation who care about our fragile Planet.

AQUARIUM STANDS

In this next section we now move onto aquarium stands and the importance of substantial frameworks and ensuring their correct location for healthy thriving fish in the tropical fish aquarium.

Today many modern Aquariums designed for the home come with furniture stands and I may well say the larger and more sophisticated models are today meeting the most suitable and desired aquarium stand heights for having healthy happy thriving tropical fish.

A popular modern day style aquarium with furniture stand providing cupboard space to house filters and electrics – by Alastair R Agutter at Maidenhead Aquatics

The first thing to consider when buying an aquarium stand or making your very own, relates to the construction of the aquarium stand and how it must be substantially made.

Another consideration that I alluded to above is also the correct height of an aquarium for healthy happy thriving fish. Aquariums positioned low towards the ground creates stress to the fish, as they cannot clearly see members of the family and visitors entering and leaving the room. For most often all the fish suddenly see is only a pair of feet or legs near the aquarium glass.

Most tropical fish and especially more evolved species such as members of the cichlid family like the security of seeing and knowing what is going on.

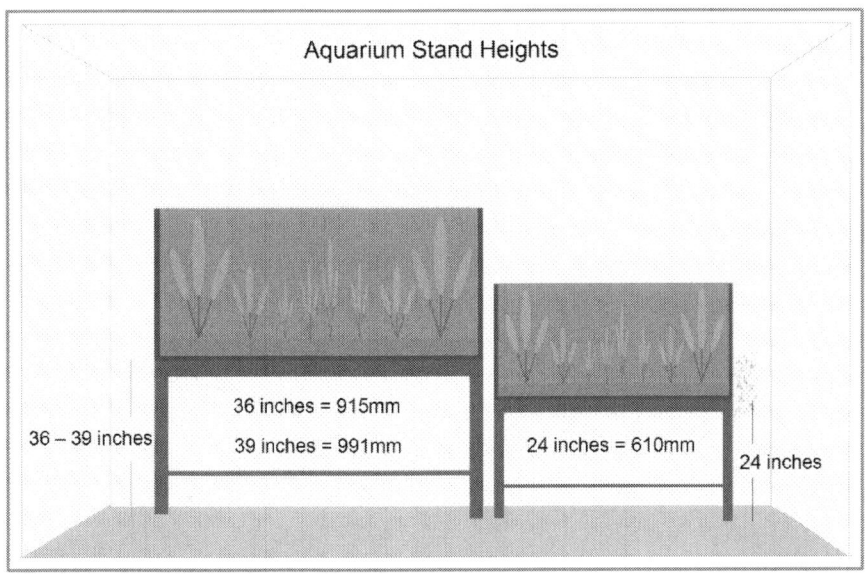

Diagram above showing Aquarium Stand Heights from the Minimum Height to the most Optimal Desired Heights – Diagram by Alastair R Agutter

With the aquarium at the correct height, it's also much easier and better for family members and the tropical fish keeper to communicate between the fish occupants more easily. Now the last such statement made above may sound mad, but I can assure you it isn't. Fish can and will communicate with you and the more observant you become, the more aware you will be of their interaction with you.

The height of the Aquarium stand in the home needs to be no less than 24 inches (610mm) and the optimum height of an aquarium stand is between 36 (915mm) to 39 inches (991mm).

Stand heights for a fish house varies as we are talking about a number of aquariums in one location. Normally a fish house tends to have between two to three tiers of aquariums. The middle or top tier for aquariums is normally for breeding pairs and the bottom fish tanks are normally used as rearing tanks of small fry and the culture of certain live foods such as brine shrimp etc.

In the following diagram is part of the layout to my new fish house that I am currently constructing, as a guide and insight for Aquarists considering the idea of setting up their own Fish House in the Garden Shed, Garage or Greenhouse.

Above picture showing Author's Fish House Breeding Aquariums positioned at the Optimal Stand Height of between 36 to 39 inches – Photograph by Alastair R Agutter

As you can see from the diagram below, it shows one of the phases, where there are six aquariums in two tiers. Three fish tanks on the top tier each aquarium measuring 20 inches long, 18 inches in depth and 21 inches in height. On the second bottom tier are again three aquariums measuring 18 inches long, 18 inches in depth and 15 inches in height.

The aquariums stand has been made from finished and prepared timber measuring 3 inches x 2 inches in thickness at least. Each aquarium stand top can be made from either ¾ inch ply or 1 inch MDF board.

Then between the top of the aquarium stand and the aquarium base, I have used 1 inch insulation polystyrene that you can acquire from your local builders merchants, to serve as a cushion and to allow for any movement or imperfections that could cause damage to the aquariums base.

The actual framework of the aquarium stands in the fish house have been constructed as mentioned by timber and needs to be ideally 3 x 2 inch due to the weight of the aquariums on the structure.

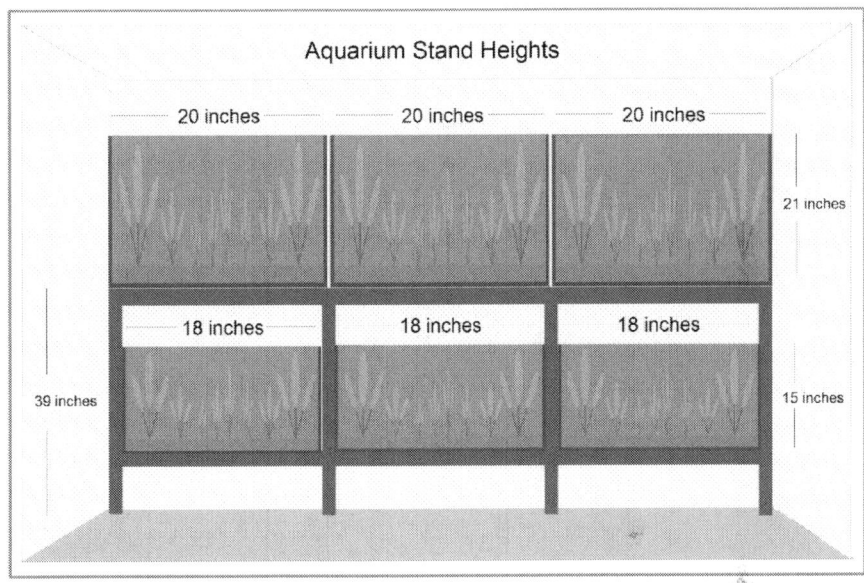

The diagram above shows one phase of the Author's Fish House as an example of what can be achieved and created in a Garden Shed, Greenhouse or Garage. Diagram by Alastair R Agutter

I have cut my timbers so the long sections sit on top of the vertical supports, this ensures there is no weakness to the timbers from different styles or various methods of timber joints that may give way. I then use 2 x 1 inch timbers as further supports in construction and to ensure the cross members are also supported by the vertical uprights with at least 2 x 1 inch of timber in contact.

Below I have created a diagram showing up close how I have made the frame corners with the timbers. All the timber sections joints for the aquarium stands have also been glued in addition to screw fixings using very reliable PVA wood glue that can be purchased from any good ironmongers, builder's merchants or DIY store.

I have used 3 inch screws all drilled and counter sunk for the 3 x 2 inch timbers. Regarding the 2 x 1 inch timbers, I have used 2 inch screws and again counter sunk these to ensure a flush surface. I have also used again PVA glue where the two sets of timbers join each other making the aquarium stand framework.

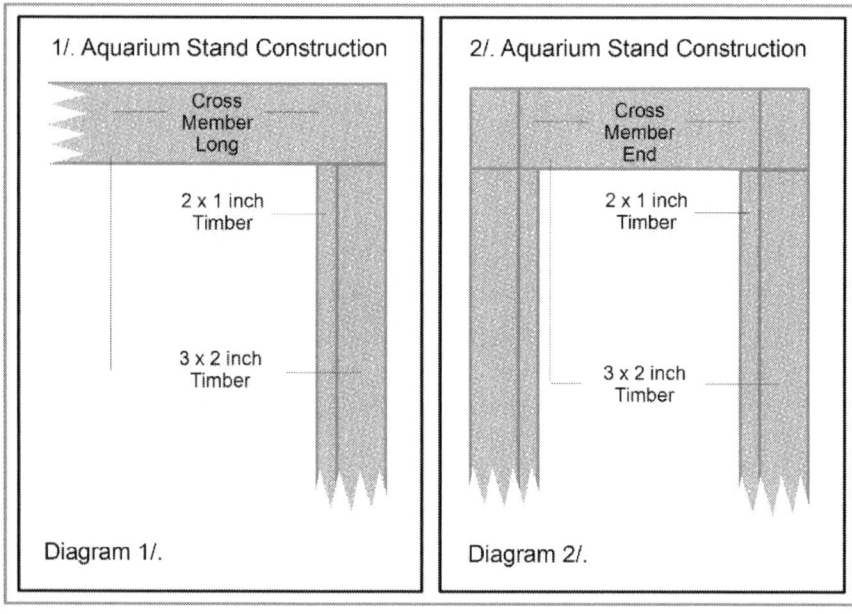

Diagram 1/. Shows the long sections joining the vertical upright of the stand - Diagram 2/. Shows the end section of the stands cross members being supported with 2 x 1 inch timbers also glued and screwed - Diagram by Alastair R Agutter

The above diagrams relate to aquarium stands for the fish house. But the same techniques and methods can be applied for making a single aquarium stand for in the home, finished off with sheet veneer timbers, for making a furniture stand by obtaining some ornate hinges and handles to have a two door front opening.

The following image gives an example where I have created a stand in my fish house showing a naturally planted community aquarium with two doors below the fish tank for storage space. However, I have designed the stand in a way, that should the need arise for more aquariums. I can in fact remove the doors to place two more aquariums for breeding or rearing.

Naturally Planted Aquarium in the Author's Fish House with two hinged doors below the Fish Tank for storage space - Photograph by Alastair R Agutter

I cannot emphasize enough how important it is to have strong sturdy aquarium stands for safety reasons due to the water volume weight in an aquarium.

As a simple exercise to substantiate my advice, if we take an aquarium size of 48 inches long x 12 inches deep and 15 inches high. The cubic square foot capacity equals 5 cubic square feet. Now one imperial UK gallon of water weighs 10lbs and a USA gallon of water weighs 8.34lbs. If we multiply 5 cubic feet by 7.48 USA gallons, this gives us an aquarium size capacity of 37.40 gallons US. Now if we multiply 37.40 gallons by 8.34lbs, we now get a total weight for just the aquarium water of 310.42lbs (140.80 kg) of water, nearly six-hundred-weight.

Now if we take the same aquarium of 5 cubic feet (48" x 12" x 15") for UK imperial gallons and multiply this by 6.23 UK imperial gallons in one cubic foot, this equals 31.15 UK gallons of water and then if we multiply this figure of 31.15lbs by 10lbs per weight of every UK imperial gallon, the total water weight in this instance for the aquarium's water weighs 310.15lbs (140.68 kg), again nearly six-hundred-weight.

This now aptly leads us onto aquarium sizes in the next section and the most suitable for your desired aquarium theme and the type of inhabitants you wish to house.

AQUARIUM SIZES

Today there are many varying aquarium sizes from a multitude of fish tank manufacturers and this excludes the vast potential when we consider custom built aquarium sizes.

A stunning set of Juwel Aquarium designs for today's modern home and for every location. – Photographs courtesy of Juwel Aquarium's and compiled by Alastair R Agutter

Determining an aquarium size might not always be that straight forward if there is a desired location offering a specific amount of space to be utilized.

However, on the other hand the project may be related to a complete aquarium new build to be planned into a new part of the home being refurbished, modernized or completely built as new.

Firstly, I think the best way forward regarding this subject is to discuss the most popular aquarium sizes and their potential regarding certain themes and species of fish and plant life to consider.

Five of the biggest selling aquarium sizes over the past five decades sold world-wide and especially in the USA and UK, has been the following glass aquarium sizes.

- 24" x 12" x 15" (US Gallons 18.70), (UK Gallons 15.57)
- 36" x 12" x 15" (US Gallons 28.05), (UK Gallons 23.36)
- 36" x 12" x 18" (US Gallons 33.66), (UK Gallons 28.03)
- 48" x 12" x 15" (US Gallons 37.40), (UK Gallons 31.15)
- 48" x 12" x 18" (US Gallons 44.88), (UK Gallons 37.38)

Some of the stages showing the construction of an all glass aquarium by the Author – Photographs by Alastair R Agutter

Above is a series of pictures I have taken when constructing all glass aquariums for my fish house, as a visual example before any trimmings and furnishings are applied.

The aquarium under construction in the above set of pictures is an all glass aquarium, but of an optimal size of 36" x 18" x 21" in comparison to the above popular commercial sizes sold over the years. As a result of the change in dimensions, I have been able to gain greater water surface area as well as depth and length.

Today optimal aquariums are more available in the commercial world than ever before for tropical fish hobbyists to buy, and if you are seeking information on traditional optimized sizes first discussed in the 1970's and 1980's by German Aquarists Horst Kipper and Kasper Horst, these sizes are as follows for your reference.

I have detailed both measurements to ensure all aquarists reading this book can easily relate to the dimensions if versed in metric or feet and inches.

PAST OPTIMAL AQUARIUM SIZES by KASPER HORST AND HORST KIPPER

Metric Optimized Sizes

- 70 cm (length) x 45 cm (width) x 35 cm (height)
- 100 cm (length) x 50 cm (width) x 40 cm (height)
- 130 cm (length) x 60 cm (width) x 45 cm (height)
- 160 cm (length) x 65 cm (width) x 50 cm (height)

Feet and inches Sizes (converted)

- 27-1/2" (length) x 18-1/4" (width) x 13-3/4" (height)
- 39-1/4" (length) x 19-3/4" (width) x 15-3/4" (height)
- 51-1/4" (length) x 23-3/4" (width) x 17-3/4" (height)
- 63" (length) x 25-1/2" (width) x 19-3/4" (height)

MODERN DAY OPTIMAL AQUARIUM SIZES by ALASTAIR R AGUTTER

Metric Optimized Sizes

- 45.8 cm (length) x 45.8 cm (width) x 38.1 cm (height)
- 61 cm (length) x 45.8 cm (width) x 38.1 cm (height)
- 70 cm (length) x 45.8 cm (width) x 38.1 cm (height)
- 91.5 cm (length) x 45.8 cm (width) x 38.1 cm (height)
- 91.5 cm (length) x 45.8 cm (width) x 45.8 cm (height)
- 120 cm (length) x 45.8 cm (width) x 38.1 cm (height)
- 120 cm (length) x 45.8 cm (width) x 45.8 cm (height)
- 120 cm (length) x 53.4 cm (width) x 45.8 cm (height)
- 120 cm (length) x 53.4 cm (width) x 53.4 cm (height)
- 120 cm (length) x 61 cm (width) x 53.4 cm (height)
- 120 cm (length) x 61 cm (width) x 61 cm (height)
- 152.5 cm (length) x 45.8 cm (width) x 45.8 cm (height)
- 152.5 cm (length) x 53.4 cm (width) x 45.8 cm (height)
- 152.5 cm (length) x 53.4 cm (width) x 53.4 cm (height)
- 152.5 cm (length) x 61 cm (width) x 53.4 cm (height)
- 152.5 cm (length) x 61 cm (width) x 61 cm (height)
- 182.9 cm (length) x 45.8 cm (width) x 45.8 cm (height)
- 182.9 cm (length) x 53.4 cm (width) x 45.8 cm (height)
- 182.9 cm (length) x 53.4 cm (width) x 53.4 cm (height)
- 182.9 cm (length) x 61 cm (width) x 53.4 cm (height)
- 182.9 cm (length) x 61 cm (width) x 61 cm (height)

Feet and Inches Sizes (converted)

- 18" (length) x 18" (width) x 15" (height)
- 24" (length) x 18" (width) x 15" (height)
- 27-1/2" (length) x 18" (width) x 15" (height)
- 36" (length) x 18" (width) x 15" (height)
- 36" (length) x 18" (width) x 18" (height)
- 48" (length) x 18" (width) x 15" (height)
- 48" (length) x 18" (width) x 18" (height)
- 48" (length) x 21" (width) x 18" (height)
- 48" (length) x 21" (width) x 21" (height)

- 48" (length) x 24" (width) x 21" (height)
- 48" (length) x 24" (width) x 24" (height)
- 60" (length) x 18" (width) x 18" (height)
- 60" (length) x 21" (width) x 18" (height)
- 60" (length) x 21" (width) x 21" (height)
- 60" (length) x 24" (width) x 21" (height)
- 60" (length) x 24" (width) x 24" (height)
- 72" (length) x 18" (width) x 18" (height)
- 72" (length) x 21" (width) x 18" (height)
- 72" (length) x 21" (width) x 21" (height)
- 72" (length) x 24" (width) x 21" (height)
- 72" (length) x 24" (width) x 21" (height)

Some other fine examples of Aquarium design for today's Aquarists seeking modern or more traditional styles to meet home décor themes. – Photographs courtesy of Maidenhead Aquatics and compiled by Alastair R Agutter

Towards the back of the book as mentioned earlier are tables to help you in your tropical fish keeping journey as quick reference guides. But to help you at this stage on the subject of aquarium sizes, if you do plan to make your very own customized aquarium or seeking to retain the services of another, it will be helpful to be able to establish the glass required and most glaziers work in square feet when pricing.

Also you will want to establish the water volume capacity of your aquarium to ensure it meets your needs regarding the theme and type of species you wish to keep.

So I have set out as follows two mathematical calculation formula's to help you establish 1/. Glass square feet requirements and 2/. The Water Volume in the way of the aquarium's gallons or litres capacity.

GLASS SQUARE FOOTAGE MATHEMATICAL FORMULA

Say we plan to build a 48 inch long aquarium and say it is 24 inches in height. OK to work out the square footage for this first pane section being the front glass is to;-

Multiply 48 x 24 equaling 1152, then take 1152 and divide the figure by 144, this then equals 8 and therefore, eight is then the square footage of the first front glass pane of the aquarium. So, if the glazier says your 6, 8 or 10mm glass is going to cost you say around £6.00 or $9.00 a square foot. You then know by multiplying 8sqft x $9.00 for example, once totaled this figure will equal $72.00 dollars and this being for the first front pane of glass to the aquarium.

The same calculation formula can be used for the ends, bottom and sides of the aquarium.

Even the glass ribs can be calculated this way for example.

1-1/2" x 46" = 69" then divide 69 by 144 and it will give you a figure of 0.47 square feet. Multiply 0.47 x $9.00 and this gives you the cost of the glass rib which equals $4.23.

WATER VOLUME MATHEMATICAL FORMULA

Say we take an aquarium that is 48" in length, 12 inches deep and 18" in height (48 x 12 x 18).

In this exercise we are looking for the square cubic feet capacity, for we know that one cubic foot of water equals 6.23 UK Gallons or 7.48 US Gallons.

If we look at the aquarium from the front this being 48 x 18" and calculate the following 48 x 18 = 864 and then if we divide 864 by 144 this will give us the actual square footage of this glass front that equals 6 square feet. We know the depth of the aquarium is only 12 inches in other words 1 foot and so we know the actual cubic square feet of the aquarium equal's 6 square cubic feet. If we then multiply the figure of 6 cubic square feet by 6.23 for UK Gallons, this will give us the gallon capacity of the aquarium and that being 37.38 UK Gallons. If we want US Gallons, we simply multiply 6 square cubic square feet by 7.48 US Gallons, this will provide the figure of 44.88 US Gallons, this being the total water capacity of the aquarium.

Towards the back of the book in the reference tables section, you will find the recommended glass thickness size table in both US and UK Gallon tables for these optimized aquarium sizes.

As I briefly mentioned earlier, aquarium designs today vary considerably and we as aquarists are provided with a plethora of choices. Small aquariums are in vogue as mentioned before, but regarding small aquariums it is obvious we are limited to the types of fish species we can house based on the varying sizes of fish species. The small in vogue aquarium designs are more aimed towards housing some of the smaller species of tropical fish namely guppies, platies, tetras and barbs. However such species in numbers and especially the vibrant colours of tetras in shoals can provide a stunning scene in your new miniature underwater world.

Rift Lake Malawi and South American Cichlids will require far larger aquariums as these species will grow to a considerable size and are also territorial.

The smallest standard size aquarium for housing some cichlids needs to be a minimum of 24 inches (24" x 12" x 15"). Aquariums of this size can house a small number of cichlids such as Kribensis, Ramirez, Firemouth and Blue Acara's. The two latter species, especially the Firemouth Cichlid are not suitable as community cichlid species.

I have seen Blue Acara Cichlids housed in large community aquariums seemingly getting on well with the other inhabitants. But if a pair exists and breeding comes into play, their natural disposition will dramatically change, where they will become very aggressive in the community aquarium towards all other species in the fish tank.

To house Cichlids of a notable size such as 3 inches plus, they need an aquarium of no less than 36 inches (three-feet) in length. If the cichlids in question are Discus or Angel Fish they will need an aquarium that is of a minimum size of three feet in length, but also a greater height of water no less than 15 inches. For these species can grow considerably in size and will appreciate the security provided by the greater depth of water.

There can be some exceptions to the above rules if we take Angel and Discus fish as examples with reference to breeding the species. In most cases the aquariums housing the breeding pairs are what are commonly known as "sterile" aquariums, in other words bare bottom fish tanks, where they only house the selected breeding pairs. Space being a premium and wanting the species to focus on the job in hand, cichlids in breeding may be housed in aquariums say 18" x 18" x 18" or as seen in the picture below two of my breeding bare bottom aquariums of 21" x 18" x 21" regarding an Angel Fish breeding project.

Two of the Author's deep water tanks for his Golden Marble Angel Fish to help preserve the species by writing and recording the events in captivity – Photograph by Alastair R Agutter

The sterile type aquariums as seen in the picture above are commonly used in the world of commercial breeding for ease of maintenance and high volume water exchanges that is required.

Regarding size and safety, the normal rule of thumb regarding glass aquariums is; any fish tank up to 18" x 12" x 15" needs to have a glass thickness minimum of 4 mm. Aquariums up to 24" x 12" x 15"; needs to have a glass thickness minimum of 5 mm. Aquariums 24" x 12" x 18"; these fish tanks need to have a glass thickness of no less than 6 mm ¼").

All, all glass aquariums made over the past several decades from 24" x 12" x 18" up to 48" x 12" x 18" have most often been made from Pilkington 6 mm (1/4") float glass.

Aquariums with greater depth from three foot onwards (36" x 18" x 18") to 72" x 24" x 24", have normally been made from 10 mm (3/8") plate glass. These aquariums of such a larger size also have additional features to them regarding the aquariums ribs, with reinforcement cross rib structures all made from 10 mm plate glass.

Some other exceptions to the rule regarding glass thickness is where in the past aquariums were constructed from angle iron aquarium frames and very often the glass was around 4 mm in thickness, or as I recall known as 32 ounce and this measurement was based on the square footage weight of the glass. Another example and exception to the rule was the emergence of the first cube aquariums back in the early to mid-nineteen-eighties. These fish tanks were normally 20" x 20" x 20", or 22" x 22" x 22" and made from 6 mm thick Pilkington Float Glass.

I do know of other instances also where aquariums of certain sizes mentioned above have been made using thinner glass, I have in fact done so myself in the past on certain occasions. But in those instances, such aquariums were used in breeding programs and away from the general public, or young members of the family for safety reasons.

When writing this book in a "claims" culture society today sadly, I have to ensure the information I provide is both accurate and safe on the grounds of Health and Safety.

Personally speaking today if I were to acquire a new aquarium for in the home, I would plum for an optimal sized aquarium dimension and with the assurance that I purchased an aquarium with an 8, 10 to 13 mm thickness of glass, dependent on the actual size of the aquarium itself in question.

Today from technology and materials, the world is your oyster when it comes to design opportunity and potential. If I had a long lounge for example, I think I would consider an "L" shaped aquarium to go around the back of an "L" shaped settee, or a rectangular aquarium to go the complete length of a wall. The magical height I recommend would be 21 inches and a depth of around 18". Aquariums with this height are pleasing to the eye and the depth offers greater water volume and security for the fish, especially if your inhabitants are quiet large such as Discus, Angel Fish or Oscars for example.

One of the Author's Natural Aquariums with Angel Fish 39" x 18" x 21" and a self- sustaining environment using his Polyatomic-ion Biological Reactors – Photograph by Alastair R Agutter

I hope the picture above provides an insight to the benefits of an optimized aquarium size. For as you can see the Angel Fish in the aquarium above (39" x 18" x 21") are well at home in their environment and all at the front of the fish tank waiting for me to get my priorities right and feed them, rather than take their photo's (fish selfies).

You can see with the height of 21 inches in the above aquarium, the adult Angel Fish (Pterophylium scalare) have sufficient water to move up and down, this provides security for large species such as these. These Angel Fish in question have not yet fully grown and the Black Velvet or Ghost Angel Fish as they are commonly called, which is the fourth fish to the right in the picture. When she displays her fins fully already from top to bottom, the length and distance from the top of the Dorsal Fin, to the tip of the Anal Fin, is already over 10 inches in height and will exceed to 12 inches in the coming months.

To summarize and help in your decision making, regarding aquarium sizes and the most suitable species. Small aquariums up to 24" x 12" x 18" are suitable for small species namely Platies, Guppies, Tetras, Sword Tails, Mollies, Barbs and small Catfish such as members of the corydoras family.

Medium Aquariums 36" x 12" x 15" to 48" x 12" x 18" are more suitable for all the fore mentioned species, Gourami's, and also small to medium size members of the cichlid family such as Firemouth, Blue Acara, Convict, Kribensis and Ramirez cichlids etc.

For Malawi theme medium size aquariums of 36" x 12" x 15" can house smaller member species such as Melanochromis Auratus and Pseudotropheus Elongatus, but these species will grow in size and this is worth bearing in mind.

For much larger members of the tropical fish community you need to be looking at aquariums of 48" x 18" x 18" and larger through to 72" x 24" x 24" plus in size.

In the sections of the book (chapters 11 and 12) covering fish behaviour and the identity of fish, will be found more detailed information on each selected species covering their characteristics, natural location in the wild, which family members of fish species they are from, their diet and expected maximum growth.

CHAPTER FIVE

Aquarium Substrates and Furnishings

One of the biggest debates and bones of contention over the years has surrounded substrates, especially when it comes to successfully growing tropical fish plants in an aquarium full of tropical fish species.

A selection of Aquarium friendly Substrates from 5mm White Gravel, 10 mm Marigold Yellow Chippings, Fine Sand and a Chemical Free Soil for Plants – Photograph by Alastair R Agutter

So I hope this chapter will be informative for our new tropical fish keeping hobbyists especially and also helpful to our existing fellow aquarists with regards to finding further answers.

For our new aquarists, I hope this subject section of the book is both logical and timely, coinciding nicely as a valuable reference to your chosen desired Aquarium Theme planned and also sheds some detailed light on the subject.

AQUARIUM BACKGROUNDS

Aquarium backgrounds can very often be the last consideration to most tropical fish hobbyists taking up the pastime for the very first time. However, it may come as a surprise to some, but backgrounds are a critical consideration in tropical fish keeping and I will explain why.

From Jack Wattley, Dr. Eduard Schmidt-Focke, Dr. Herbert Axelrod, Heiko Bleher, Eberhard Schulze to Bernd Degen, myself and others. The colour of backgrounds over the years has posed some really big searching questions, to seek out and find some serious and convincing answers regarding the physical and mental well-being of Marine life species.

From breeding some of the most difficult species in the World you consider everything in the process to find success. The colour of Aquarium backgrounds has been high on the list of priorities by mentioned notable colleagues and friends above who have all asked the same question.

The more we examine our own behaviour and characteristics, the more we will understand our fellow creatures that we share this World with. Just think about it for a second. When we acquire a new home, one of the first things we do is decorate and the very reason being is for our own mental frame of mind and to a degree, for our subconscious human condition in the form of security regarding our family and cosy familiar surroundings.

When we take the above on board as aquarists, the picture becomes far clearer regarding how we care for our new family members. Just like us, they seek security and routine, in other words the reduction of chaos and confusion in ones lives, so then the home provided is an optimal environment for healthy thriving fishes.

I often hear of couples struggling to start a family, very often this has nothing to do with any genetic incompatibility, but very often as a result of career workloads and lifestyle that is not conducive for a new family addition to the existing unhealthy environment.

Tropical fish species are no different and backgrounds play a significant part in having healthy thriving fish that will eventually want to breed, if the environment and conditions are correct.

Over the years I have found various colours deliver differing results in the rearing and breeding of tropical fish species. Very light, pale colours are not favourable to the tropical fishes disposition, or are multi-coloured backgrounds depicting artificial reefs or rock and plant landscapes.

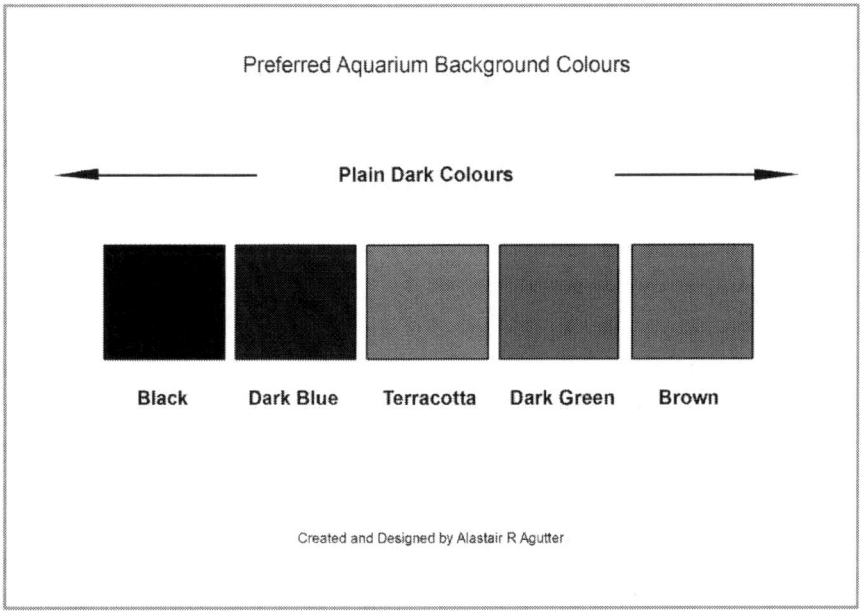

Diagram showing the most popular and desired colours for Aquarium Backgrounds for Healthy Thriving Tropical Fish – Photograph by Alastair R Agutter

Breeders have found pale light colours result in very poor reproduction cycle results. I have found also like other breeders over the years, plain darker backgrounds are the most desired by the fish and in fact help to bring out the tropical fishes colours, as they naturally and instinctively send instructions to the body from the brain to camouflage themselves in the event of predators or for courting purposes.

The background colours I have found to be the best for breeding, rearing and keeping healthy thriving fish to be plain Black, Terracotta, Dark Blue, Brown and Dark Green. The latter colour is seen in the following picture that in fact compliments the naturally planted aquarium environment.

Rummy Nose and Cardinal Tetras in full vibrant colour in a naturally planted aquarium with a dark green background enhancing the landscape – Photograph by Alastair R Agutter

You can also see that the rummy nose and cardinal tetras are exhibiting very bright vibrant colours from such an environment and not enhanced from the light system that is used to assist in plant growth, this being an eco-friendly low wattage white light method and not Grolux.

There are various methods to use when applying a background to an aquarium. First we need to consider if just the back of the fish tank is to have a background. If an aquarium is located in a hallway for example with two approaching doors either side it is wise to leave both ends clear so your fish inhabitants can see the coming and going of visitors and where they will not be spooked by the sudden appearance of a human, if each of the aquarium ends vision is blocked off by a background.

However, if you have a corner aquarium such as a cube you may wish to have two sides of the aquarium's walls covered as backgrounds if these are panes facing the walls. If you have a number of aquariums side by side you may seek to block both ends as well as the back of the aquarium with a background.

If you plan to have a sterile aquarium environment for exotic species such as Discus (*symphysodon*) or for breeding purposes, you will no doubt want to block off both aquarium ends, the back of the aquarium and the base of the aquarium with a desired colour scheme.

If you have acquired for example a fantastically new designer aquarium, you will no doubt want to avoid painting the aquarium's background glass and so in this instance, I recommend visiting the local art shop and acquiring some heavy back mounting board card for the job. This card can be lightly glued in one or two places at the edges and bottom of the aquarium glass. Cello tape will not suffice, as it will become damp or wet and eventually breakdown and fall off.

The other option is to paint (externally) the back, bottom and sides of the aquarium subject to what sections are to be covered. Today fortunately health and safety is very much to the fore regarding paints in the home surrounding child welfare and so acrylic paints today have little fumes when applied to glass externally and does cover well and dries quickly, allowing you to apply a second or third coat of paint a day or so later.

Diagram above showing Ethafoam and Polystyrene to be used as a cushion for the base of the Aquarium to prevent cracking of the glass – Photograph by Alastair R Agutter

When painting my aquariums, I tend to leave them to dry in a shed, garage or well ventilated part of the house for around 3 to 4 days as this ensures the paint has properly hardened off. The importance of the paint being dried is especially relevant if you are using a sterile aquarium design, where the base of the aquarium has also been painted and where you do not want any paint to be tacky where it may stick to the ethafoam or polystyrene sheet that cushions the base of the aquarium to the stand.

Luxury aquarium designs with cabinets will no doubt have a layer of polystyrene or ethafoam already supplied to cushion the glass aquarium base when placed and housed onto the aquarium stand.

The ethafoam I use, can be purchased from your local DIY superstore, the ethafoam material is laid on floors before the laminated flooring is applied and placed on top to work as a cushion and commonly known as underlay.

Above is a diagram showing two photographs of both materials ethafoam and polystyrene, both of which are available from your local DIY superstore in the flooring section regarding the ethafoam. For the polystyrene sheeting, this can be obtained in sheet form for a few pounds or dollars from your local Builders Merchants, where the material is normally used for wall or loft insulation.

If you are using a modern style furniture based aquarium with a stand and you are supplied without any polystyrene or ethafoam. I would plum for using ethafoam in this instance. For the ethafoam material is quiet thin, normally around 5 mm in thickness and will therefore allow the furniture stand cabinet to sit properly and still disguise the ethafoam sheet.

Polystyrene sheets are much thicker in size measuring normally 1 inch (25 mm), but they are ideal in fish houses and for large aquariums. The sheets are normally 8' x 2' (2400 x 610 mm). These large thick sheets can be cut very easily just like the Ethafoam, by using a Stanley Knife. These polystyrene sheets will cushion very well the big heavy aquariums, or aquariums in a line on racks in a fish house, or commercial outlet.

In a fish house for example, overtime it is particularly relevant to have sound aquarium stand cushioning such as the thick polystyrene sheets. As timber stands will age and will therefore generate some movement. There is always a degree of movement in timbers through cold, damp, dry, winter and summer seasons, where wood expands and contracts. Also overtime timbers contract from age, as more water moisture is removed from the timbers as they continue to season each year.

Newly purchased commercial pine often used today to build Aquarium frames for a fish house can often retain water moisture up to as much as 40%. After around 2 years through proper ventilation and as the timbers begin to season, can see the water content in the timber reduced to about 20%. A slower process then begins afterwards and continues over many years and with each year passing, more moisture is gradually removed from the pine timbers.

It is always important for the timbers to retain a degree of water content. Otherwise, the timbers will eventually simply disintegrate one day. For maintenance purposes when referring to a fish house, or a large aquarium custom timber made stand, it is worthwhile every five or so years, to apply some linseed oil (from your local Ironmongers) to your timbers, to give them a degree of protection and to help with the retention of water (moisture) in the wood.

Parts of the Author's Classic Fish House made from Pine Timber and now seasoning after time and maintained with Linseed Oil – Photograph by Alastair R Agutter

You will note from the pictures above the dark green background of the aquariums. This is my personal preference regarding aquarium backgrounds in a fish house for the best results in rearing and breeding.

If I were to consider a new aquarium in the home, terracotta would be my first choice as a colour for the background, as it always looks classy. I distinctly remember many years ago back in the 1980's the Juwel Aquarium range made from gold frames had a terracotta background and they really did look stunning when set up as a naturally planted aquarium, Eberhard had a great Juwel show tank at his Highgate Aquarist Shop.

A Terracotta coloured background in a Naturally Planted Aquarium can look stunning. Photograph of Author's Terracotta background tank in 1988 – Photographs by Ian Russell

Above is a set of two photographs of one of my Natural Discus Aquariums back in the 1980's with a colour picture showing the terracotta background, where you can see one of my strain 7 turquoise discus breeding pairs and in the black and white picture, one of the parents in the same aquarium guarding her Discus eggs on the bogwood in this natural environment.

Now after discussing aquarium backgrounds we move onto the aquarium substrates choices available to you for consideration.

AQUARIUM SUBSTRATES

As mentioned at the beginning of this chapter, substrates have been a bone of contention for many decades with regards to what is best to use and also of course there is always personal preference with reference to appearance.

I am pleased to say a great deal has changed over the years regarding substrates from when I began tropical fish keeping back in 1967. One subject area being and where there is more notable discussion today is with regards to sterile aquariums, where no substrate material is used on the actual aquarium's bottom.

Today gravel comes in many different colours and sizes for the tropical fish hobbyist. White, Red, Brown, Black, Mottled, Yellow, Natural, in fact you name it, I am sure you can get it.

One of the key factors about any gravel you intend to use is to make sure it is thoroughly washed before placing the gravel in the aquarium. So when I use gravel for an aquarium, I tend to wash small amounts of the gravel at a time in a bowl and then using my hands in a sweeping figure of eight motion to thoroughly stir up the gravel in the water, to make sure the gravel is sufficiently clean. I then drain off the dirty water from the gravel and again pour in more fresh water to repeat the process again.

Picture from one of the Author's Aquariums clearly showing how gravels can and will discolour after several weeks and months by algae and sediment waste – Photograph by Alastair R Agutter

I normally wash and rinse each amount of gravel in the bowl about seven times, until the water in the bowl after washing and stirring the gravel becomes clear. If I am honest, washing gravel can be a time consuming and laborious process, but well worth it at the end of the day, to remove any unwanted dirt, sediment, waste and pests that maybe in the gravel.

The actual size of most coloured gravel granules on the market for the tropical fish hobbyist is around 5 to 6 mm in diameter, and when first installed into an aquarium can look stunning. However, regardless of the type of filtration that will be covered in the book later in some detail, nature will begin to take her course regarding the gravel, where waste sediment and algae will build up discolouring the gravel substrate in the aquarium.

Earlier is a picture of some white gravel in one of my aquariums succumbing to this natural process caused from sediment, waste and algae and where the picture clearly shows the discolouration even after a few months?

The above aquarium houses Malawi cichlids for the purpose of this book, but even so, regardless of these species being vigorous eaters and very messy.

One of the Author's Aquariums showing how the natural coloured gravel is blending in with the natural discolour changes from algae and sediment waste – Photograph by Alastair R Agutter

Any aquariums substrate will eventually discolour from nature's underwater world of biological processes.

Again it is down to personal preference, but I tend to stick with a more natural coloured gravel as a substrate, as pictured below, for I find these natural processes and changes tend to blend in with natural gravel, and after time as algae's form in the substrate and across certain ornaments and filters, the aquarium starts to exude an authentic and established appeal that is very pleasing to the eye by most who view such a tropical fish and plant underwater world landscape.

Even if you are using under gravel filtration or external filtration methods the gravel substrate will discolour over time and this is worth bearing in mind, when you are choosing your aquarium gravel as a substrate.

In addition to gravels, today as a substrate aquarists have available to them decorative pebbles to place in the bottom of an aquarium on the gravel floor or even sometimes used without any gravel present. However, as a maintenance consideration, pebbles on their own will collect sediment and waste between the pebbles, thus causing a cleaning nightmare. If you do find pebbles appealing, I would suggest you place them on top of some gravel.

One of my favourite pebbles available on the market today for the tropical fish hobbyist is a marble pebble in white and they do look stunning, and if I were to use gravel with the marbled pebbles, I would be inclined to compliment the pebbles with a white or black gravel substrate.

Pebbles again will need to be washed several times to make sure they have no dust or dirt on them, before placing in the aquarium. If you do plan to use pebbles, please be ever so careful when placing them in the aquarium, to avoid cracking the aquarium glass base and this can happen at times from dropping an object such as a pebble or a large rock, when creating the picturesque landscape in an aquarium.

If you plan to create a naturally planted aquarium using live plants, the gravel substrate does become a serious consideration, as you ideally need to ensure that your plants will survive and thrive in such an environment.

Plants in an aquarium around the roots especially, do need food obviously and in addition to various fish waste, minerals in the form of trace elements from the water, they also require oxygen (O_2) and carbon dioxide (CO_2).

I have found over the years, if a too finer gravel is used for the aquarium substrate for the plants and without any assistance in the form of substrate enhancements, fine gravel can serve to the detriment of plants, as the roots are unable to receive the vital nutrients and food from fish waste (nitrate), from a lack of water circulation, which is vital for ensuring these nutrients and trace elements required to feed plants can get to their rightful destination, and this being the plants root systems. Very often also, the water temperature in the gravel can be much lower, and this will also inhibit the growth of your aquarium plants and serve as a negative.

Now there are several ways to address this issue and if you are a gardener, or have gardening experience, this will help you greatly as a new or existing aquarist. As you will already be familiar with the world of plant food, composts and suitable substrates, that can help increase oxygen and carbon dioxide delivery to the plant roots so they survive and thrive.

The bottom line is like the fish, plants need to be fed and cared for and this information will be covered in greater detail in the following section of the book titled "Growing and Keeping Healthy Aquarium Plants" in Chapter Six ".

Regarding this topic and subject area of substrates and plants, you now have to consider your desire and commitment to the hobby. Now do not be alarmed, for as I said from the very beginning, I want your tropical fish keeping experience to be one of great joy and enjoyment. So you have to ask yourself now, can you devote that little extra time and effort to your hobby with regards to preparation and feeding of plants?

At this point and on this topic, I would be failing in my duty as an authority on the pastime if I did not introduce you to successful ways of growing plants in an aquarium and the substrates required to achieve this. However, some of these methods may not be used by others in the hobby, but these techniques I am about to explain are based on many years of research and firsthand experience where such methods work.

In other words "I do practice what I preach" and my naturally planted aquariums are; well I must say, they are a sight to behold, where there can be found healthy plants growing, and very happy super large fish for their age, in aquarium environments of crystal clear water.

The following diagram I have created shows an aquarium with my substrate design for growing healthy thriving plants. But, and here is the big but, this method is not designed for under gravel filters. This I will explain clearly later in greater detail in the filtration section of the book, so please do not worry at this time.

Thriving plants in an aquarium has been as mentioned earlier a big conundrum over the years for the everyday tropical fish hobbyist and dedicated aquarist. So being me I asked why?

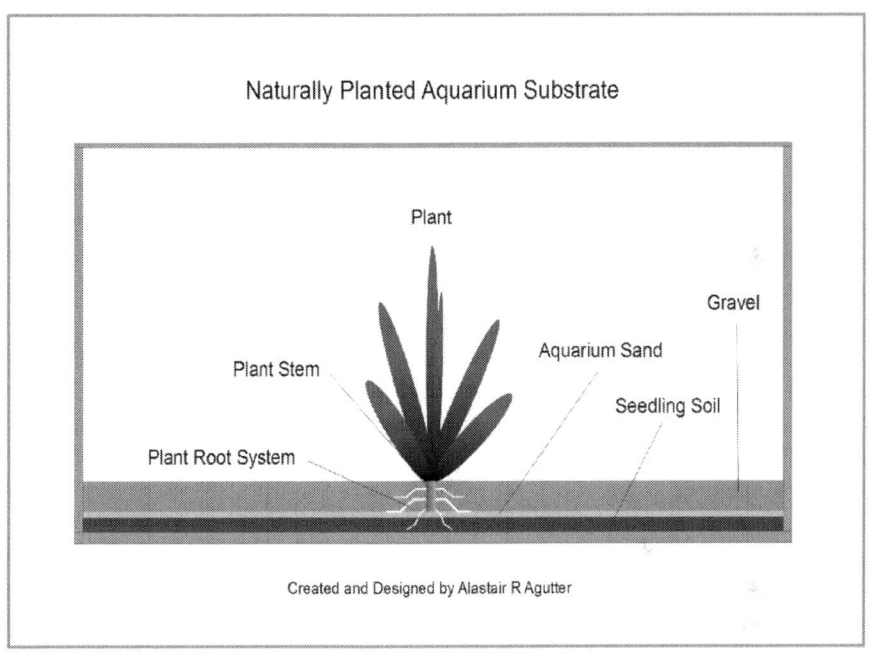

A Naturally Planted Aquarium Substrate Diagram showing a proven method developed and used by the Author for healthy thriving plants and tropical fish – Photograph by Alastair R Agutter

To have healthy thriving plants in a tropical fish aquarium, the substrate needs to be alive and thriving in both a biological and natural sense. In the depths of the substrate we need oxygen, carbon dioxide, nitrate, metal trace elements, bacterial micro-organisms and a compatible temperature with a source to deliver these critical elements, for roots to grow and in turn delivering healthy thriving plants foliage in the tropical fish aquarium.

The commercial world of Aquatics regarding substrates are getting to grips more from greater understanding today in the 21st century of tropical fish and plant husbandry and as a result of such advances, more new products are being developed and released each year for the tropical fish hobbyist. This is very encouraging as there is nothing more despairing than planting out an aquarium using gravel only, to see plants dwindle and fade over the course of several weeks and months.

Below in the photograph is a small selection of products available today for the modern aquarist who is seeking success with a naturally planted aquarium for healthy thriving aquatic plants.

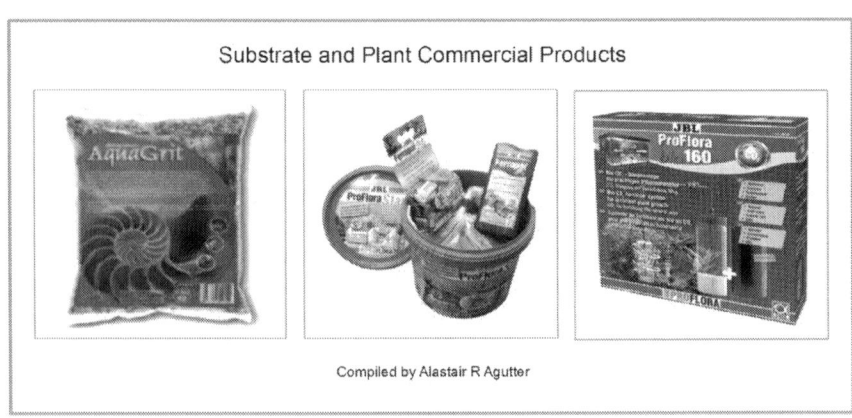

More advanced products are being developed for today's Aquarist. Left Aqua Grit, Centre JBL ProFlora Products, Right Co2 Diffuser – Photographs compiled by Alastair R Agutter

I do not expect my fabulous readers or fellow aquarists and owners of this book to be as sad as I am, in relation to becoming consumed in this topic of natural activity regarding substrates and plants for nearly 50 years.

So to grasp the overall activity surrounding this topic, I have created the following diagram to hopefully explain some sound logical points that we have to consider and get a visual idea of what is actually going on and happening as a cycle in the aquarium.

Light is also critical for thriving plants for photosynthesis and this process is to convert light energy into chemical energy that can be later released to feed plant life and organisms. This energy is stored in carbohydrate molecules such as sugars, which are then in turn synthesized from carbon dioxide (CO_2) and water delivering in most cases a waste product in the form of oxygen (O_2). This subject will be covered in greater detail in the lighting chapter of the book.

My First Aquarium Collectors Edition

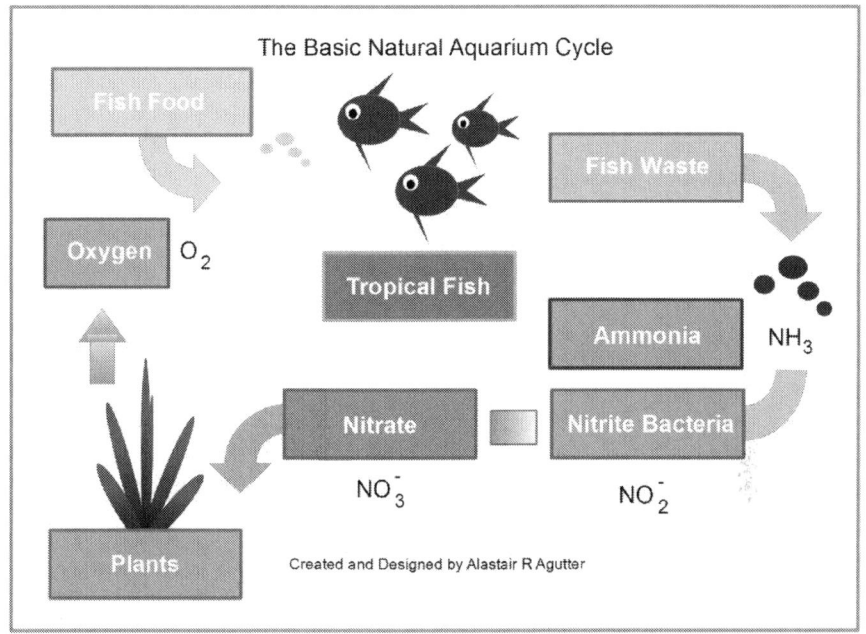

A diagram showing the basic natural aquarium cycle in a tropical fish tank as a visual idea surrounding this topic being discussed – Created and Designed by Alastair R Agutter

Above as promised is a visualization of the basic cycle that takes place in a naturally planted tropical fish aquarium and of course these events take place in the wild and this is the very reason why we endeavour to create a naturally planted aquarium based on factual knowledge and as a result, where we are in fact trying to replicate these conditions found in the wild, we then seek to apply them to our very own tropical fish keeping creation.

By looking at the above diagram we can clearly see that there is a cycle and a series of processes that are relevant to substrates, in relation to ammonia (NH_3), nitrite ($NO-2$) and nitrate ($NO-3$) that need to be broken down, most often in the substrate by micro-organisms and plant life.

Earlier in this chapter and section is displayed a diagram I created, showing how I set up my substrates and where these conditions are complimented, in the form of filtration with my **Polyatomic-ion Biological Reactors.** These reactors I have invented and created are for the sole purpose of a filtration method that would deliver circulation to the plants, but at the same time, reducing and preventing damage to the root systems of plant life. In the chapter of filtration, I will go into greater detail of the subject and even show how to build and make your own Polyatomic-ion Biological Reactors and other filtration systems for healthy thriving fish and plants.

When enjoying my tropical fish keeping as a young boy in the late 1960's, I was fortunate to live near the coast. So I earned my pocket money even at the age of 9 and 10 years, from bait digging when the tide was out. I use to dig up lug worm and rag worm, selling them to the local bait shop to give myself an income to buy tropical fish keeping equipment. For me our local estuary was part of the World's largest Marine University on the planet for getting to know and understand our World. From such experience, it fueled my curiosity to learn more about our environment.

One thing you learn about bait digging in silt and sediment, it can be sometimes life threatening if you do not learn to respect Mother Nature, for within 24 hours from heavy storms; sand bars, creeks and streams, can be changed forever, or be even gone for all time. In such a terrain bait digging especially inshore, the silt and sediment can be very soft and within a few seconds, you can quickly see your wellington boots or waders rapidly being consumed from the soft substrate below ones feet.

But what you do learn from bait digging in such an environment is the abundance of micro-life in the silt and mud in addition to worms, crustaceans and mollusc's. You also get from such an environment a highly trained nose, to recognize the many smells and odours including decomposition, ammonia, stagnation and more.

When you then couple gardening experience taught to me by my Grand Father, this is a pretty good grounding to understand what goes on beneath the substrate surface.

Microbiology and Biochemistry fascinates me and hopefully God willing, if the human journey is allowed to continue, evolve (knowledge) and survive, I am confident there will be many "WOW" factor moments, as we discover more about Quantum Mechanics and Natural Branching and thus in turn learning more from Nature and hopefully. Just maybe one day, learn to co-exist with all our other fellow life forms.

One thing you learn from the Sea, Lakes, Estuaries, Creeks, Streams and Rivers is sedimentation build up and this process has been in existence for millions of years. The recent flooding in Britain on the Somerset levels is a prime example of silt and sediment build up.

In our naturally planted tropical fish aquarium just like in the wild, we will get deposits of waste and sediment build up from a collection of different properties. These namely being; fish waste (excretion), dead plant life, uneaten food, dead micro-organisms and algae to mention some of the main players and protagonists, regarding fish and plant health.

As plants grow in a substrate, they will shed leaves as we often see throughout seasons in gardens. Some aquarists tend to as part of their maintenance program remove such elements, but as we all know in gardening and below the water surface of ponds, lakes, streams and rivers, this material eventually breaks down and serves as a food source, in the form of compost for plants and micro-organisms that help breakdown matter and chemical toxins.

Primitive plant entity forms such as Algae also play their part in the filtration and substrate process, for attaining an eco-balanced environment within the naturally planted tropical fish aquarium. On the substrate floor I leave the algae, as it helps filter the water and this becomes more apparent when you consider the popularity of moss balls available today for the aquarist, as these plant forms breakdown waste matter and filter.

These elements of waste and sediment even in our naturally planted aquarium, serves to help grow a microscopic biological culture of life form entities, that can also thrive in the substrate below, therefore creating movement to help transfer chemicals and other trace elements to the plant life root systems in this environment.

Also as like in the garden above water, regarding fellow creatures and especially our feathered friends, sometimes you will see birds and other wild life eating leaves and other dead vegetation, as this forms part of their natural diet.

Very often in the naturally planted aquarium, you will see a great variety of fish species having the occasional peck at plants and dead plant vegetation, as this food source serves to help in the fishes balanced diet (roughage) and constitution. In fact, if you get the time to read some of the ingredient labels on the packaging containers of the most popular tropical fish foods available for aquarists to purchase today, from flake to pellet foods, you will often find in the food recipe, various plant and vegetable food forms.

So as you can see and have read, if we remove dead vegetation and other natural materials that are being broken down in a naturally planted tropical fish aquarium, we could well be doing a great disservice to the plants requiring this material, that will eventually become a food supply and serve to help fish health.

All these points written and covered in the previous pages, including the reasoning and explanations, have been as a result of studying the subject for many decades, to deliver the optimum aquarium.

It was in fact in the mid 1980's I realized and discovered from research in the wild, that waterways had an exchange rate to the power and factor of 10! This meant for example, a 100 gallon aquarium needs to ideally filter 1000 gallons an hour. Hence my passion in the 1980's, to create and develop the **"Power Vain Filtration System"**, a trickle filter method to deliver such a requirement in very large aquarium systems and for extremely difficult and volatile species to reproduce in captivity.

So my following method of a substrate is one that is proven and works. The substrate concept has in fact been thought out and developed over many years and decades by myself and today, seeing such a fully functioning environment, exceeds all my wildest expectations and hopes and very surprisingly also, the natural cycle and method becomes established very quickly over a short period of time, around 2 – 3 months for a 50 gallon (220 litres) plus size aquarium. In just three months there are clear signs of how plant life begins to benefit from such an environment, with new plant leaves emerging and others beginning to grow vigorously. Another confirming factor is when I see my Clown Loach busy at work on the bottom, digging around in the substrate enthusiastically for morsels. Clown Loach as a fish species is a good indicator to the quality of water, for these fascinating and beautiful fish are very vulnerable, when it comes to poor water in the form of toxins (Ammonia, Nitrite and Nitrate).

So please let me introduce you now to my substrate method and some background information. I first applied this method back in the 1980's, when I had to import from the wild Heckel Discus (*symphysodon heckel*), these species I had to acclimatize regarding the water over a considerable period of time. For in the wild regarding these species, the water quality can be very acid with a PH range varying between 4.8 to 6.8 in different regions of South America and lacking many mineral and trace elements resulting in a low general hardness (DH or GH) of water. To combat the difference between my local water and the water from the wild, I deployed in the substrate Irish Peat Moss, to bring down my local water hardness. Then eventually over time using my trickle filtration system and introducing certain substrate material, I then began to raise the PH level of the large aquarium holding the 30 Heckel Discus, so the fish started to become accustomed to my local water. This was achieved with a water acclimatization process, so the Heckel Discus became accustomed to my local water quality that I describe as in the safe zone between 6.8 to 7.6 ph.

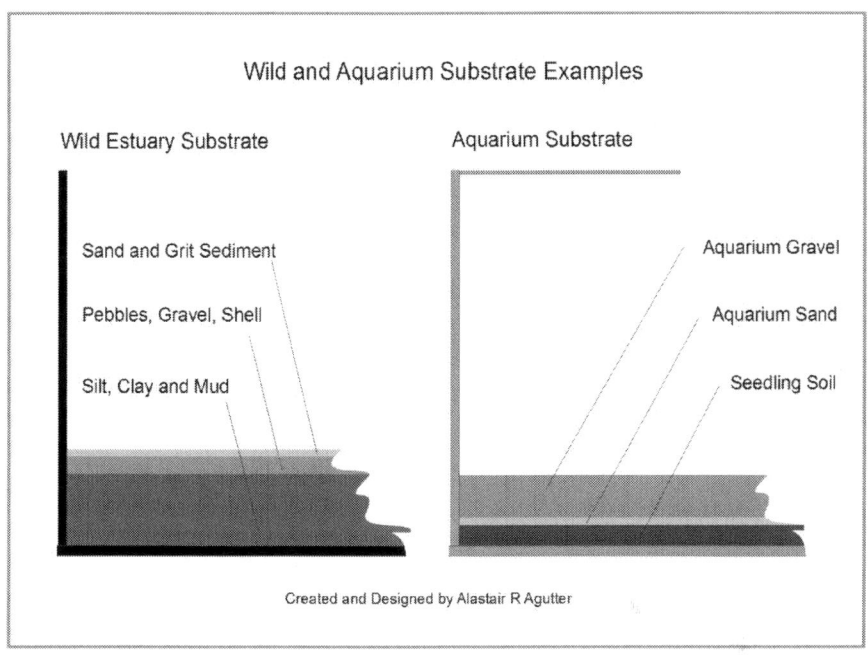

A diagram showing a typical Wild Estuary Substrate and the Author's Naturally Planted Tropical Fish Aquarium Substrate – Created and Designed by Alastair R Agutter

Today fortunately, we do not have such a problem for most tropical fish species including Discus purchased by the Aquarists. As most species purchased today are tank bred, and I like to think from my humble endeavours and others recording our work over the decades, we have had a positive impact on marine animal welfare and fish husbandry. Resulting in the availability of most species today for the tropical fish hobbyist being tank bred from commercial breeders in Holland, Germany, Asia, USA and Britain, by using local tap water for an unlimited safer water supply.

Above are a set of substrate diagrams, one being the normal substrate habitat of Wild Rivers and Estuaries, the other being my method for a Naturally Planted Tropical Fish Aquarium substrate.

The flow of water and the substrate can have a bearing on the Marine environment ecology, and this can vary greatly due to the location and geology of the landscape. A River and Stream system will be different to an Estuary, or a set of spring fed lakes for example. Temperature in relation to tree, animal and plant vegetation life forms will also have a bearing on the Marine environment and its chemical make-up.

A waterway receiving large deposits of plant, leaf and tree vegetation will very often become brackish and resulting in softer water. Whereas Rivers and Streams fed by a landscape of Rocks, Cliffs and Mountains can produce more neutral to alkaline water conditions, especially if the substrate is chalk based. Chalk Stream examples can be found in Hampshire in Britain with the Rivers Test and Itchen. These flowing Rivers are crystal clear, with thriving plant life and some of the World's finest Brown Trout and spring run Salmon.

So the substrate I am about to finally introduce you too, was deliberately engineered so the water quality did contain a fair degree of mineral content to help feed the plants and a 7.2 to 7.4 water PH, this being comparable to my localized tap water. So then in the future when I do decide to carry out water changes to the aquarium, the water chemistry would be similar or the same as my tap water and therefore causing least or no stress to my tropical fish at all.

So the first substrate I use and place in my aquarium is seedling soil. In fact I use a John Innes seedling soil No 1, as it emits little or no chemical compounds, such as toxins that could affect fishes health, or worse still, poison them.

Or if the soil is too rich based like compost, this could cause a significant and dramatic change in the water chemistry namely PH and GH.

The depth of the soil I place in the aquarium is around 1 to 1-1/2 inches in depth (25 to 35mm). The soil is evenly laid out across the aquarium bottom. The coverage is exactly the same at the front of the aquarium, as it is to the back of the fish tank.

Once I have levelled the soil across the base of the aquarium, I then gently tamp the soil down and then take a leaf out of an old Aquarists diary in the 1950's, where he used to use old rusty nails and screws to increase the iron content in the water for the plants and the fish. So I collected together around 30 to 50 old rusty screws and nails, placing them gently across the surface of the soil in the aquarium. This will provide over time a regular amount of iron content in the water, as found in the substrate to many parts of the River Amazon in South America, where the fish and plant life is especially abundant and thriving.

Next, I then put in a large builders bucket, or large bowl, a good few large handfuls of fine sand and wash this thoroughly, until there is no discolouring to the water. You will find that you will need to wash and rinse through the sand about six to seven times, before the water in the bucket or bowl becomes clear.

Once the sand is clean, I then gently place a thin layer of sand in the aquarium over the soil, with an even coverage of sand around ½ to ¾ (15 to 18 mm) of an inch deep.

This beds down the soil in the aquarium as found in the wild, where the mud and clay is divided by sand, grit and silt before contact is made with water flow on the Sea or River bed.

A picture showing a Bowl of Fine Sand and a Builders Bucket with Natural coloured Gravel all to be washed and rinsed thoroughly at least 6 to 7 times – Photograph by Alastair R Agutter

My next step is to empty into a builders bucket about one third deep the first batch of gravel for the aquarium. This is a natural coloured gravel and slightly larger in size, around 8 to 10 mm in diameter on average and I will explain why later. Again as mentioned earlier in this chapter, I wash the gravel thoroughly, by using my hand in a figure of eight motion. Then once the water is discoloured, I drain off the water in the bucket from the gravel. I then begin the process again by adding new water to the bucket containing the gravel and washing again.

Make absolutely sure the gravel is washed at least six to seven times. Then the water should start to become clear even after washing the gravel in the bucket.

I then start to place gently into the aquarium my first batch of washed gravel over the top of the sand and only a thin layer of gravel at this time, about 1 inch (25 mm) deep.

Once I have a good coverage of washed gravel around 1 inch (25 mm) across the surface of the aquarium over the sand and evenly laid out. I then position my Polyatomic-ion Biological Reactors onto the gravel and in the desired position within the aquarium.

In the filtration and products chapter as mentioned, I will discuss making a Polyatomic-ion Biological Reactor, but at this stage I do not want to confuse the issue, for the intention may be to use another form of filtration such as an external Canister Filter, or a trickle filter system.

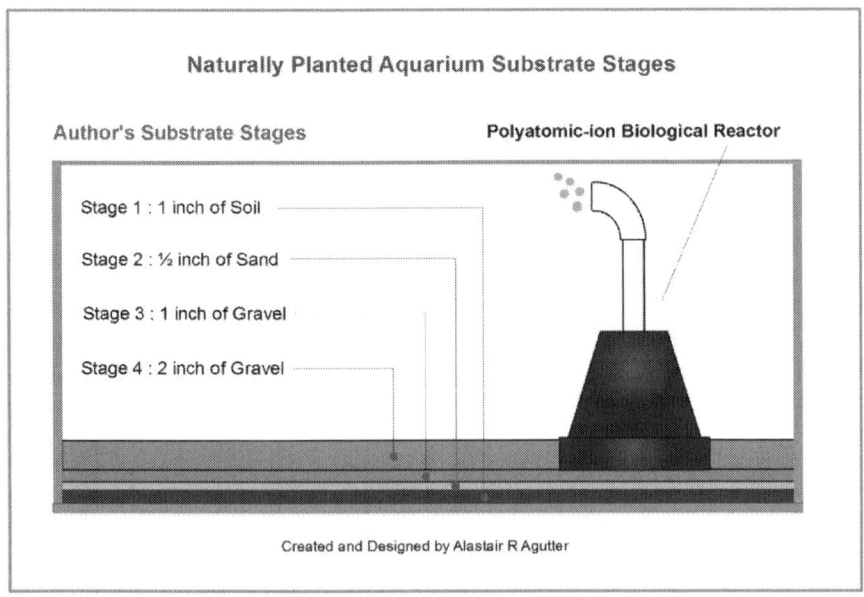

A diagram above, showing in more detail the stages and measurements of substrate for the Author's Naturally Planted Aquarium Method. – Created by Alastair R Agutter

Once I have positioned my Polyatomic-ion Biological Reactors in the desired position in my aquarium. I then again start washing more natural coloured aquarium gravel, as I had done before.

On this occasion, I then gently place enough washed gravel around the Polyatomic-ion Biological Reactors and across the rest of the aquarium surface, so I now have an additional coverage of gravel of a further two inches in depth. Please see diagram below.

As mentioned earlier in the book, I have a personal preference for an aquarium height to be around 21 inches. Perhaps when we look at the substrates ideal total height that measures 4-1/2 inches there is without doubt some sound logic behind the suggestions.

You need a substantial degree of substrate for plant life to root successfully and grow.

The Author's Naturally Planted Aquarium Method in real life and the finest evidence and endorsement one could ever wish for from the experts, a pair of Angel Fish (Pterophylium scalare) Spawning in crystal clear water. – Photograph by Alastair R Agutter

Some exceptions are as we know relate to certain Algae and moss forms that can grow directly onto rock or substrate surfaces.

But the most decorative plants in the form of foliage do require a substrate of a suitable depth for root systems to attain those vital nutrients and chemicals as food.

I hope the photograph above dispels any doubts regarding my Naturally Planted Aquarium method including the use of my Polyatomic-ion Biological Reactors, showing the finest proven example and endorsement regarding how successful the system is, with a real pair of experts in the form of Angel Fish (*Pterophylium Scalare*) happily spawning and a species well known by dedicated aquarist experts as being one of the hardest cichlids to breed in captivity, and if conditions are not right they will not spawn!

In the next part of this chapter we begin to discuss aquarium furnishings and this aptly coincides and relates to discussion in the book earlier surrounding aquarium themes. There are many styles and choices available to us as discussed and coupled with a desired theme or design, unfortunately that word "practical" often tends to raise its head regarding our lifestyles.

If for example you lead a very hectic or busy social life, you may opt and seek to acquire plastic plants, as a more maintenance free and lighter touch approach to tropical fish keeping.

Whilst plastic plants have been around for many decades surrounding the world of Tropical Fish Keeping, designs today are more eco-friendly to the fish where many plants are being made from silicones and so the plants are more pliable and less rigid, reducing the risk of damage to any of your fish inhabitants, where they can very often swim into rigid plastic plants and objects injuring themselves, especially if a squabble ensues in the aquarium.

Of course if a decision is made to opt for plastic or silicone plants in your tropical fish aquarium, the criteria and requirements for gravels and substrates become less of a priority with regards to creating a substrate environment for real tropical plants to grow and thrive.

By using plastic or silicone plants you can enjoy the many gravel colours and types available to you for your tropical fish aquarium. Certain gravel types may also fall into line with your planned styles and colours for your aquarium to coincide with reference to your home décor colour schemes and even furnishings planned for the aquarium itself.

But regarding gravel substrates in general before we move onto aquarium furnishings. If you do plan to start a small aquarium for the very first time and just seek to dip your toes into the water of Tropical Fish Keeping as a new pastime, or do not have the confidence to explore my methods for a naturally planted aquarium environment. You can attain substrates today that are slightly further enriched with clay material such as "aqua grit" for example to help assist plant growth and this will be covered in more detail in the following chapter.

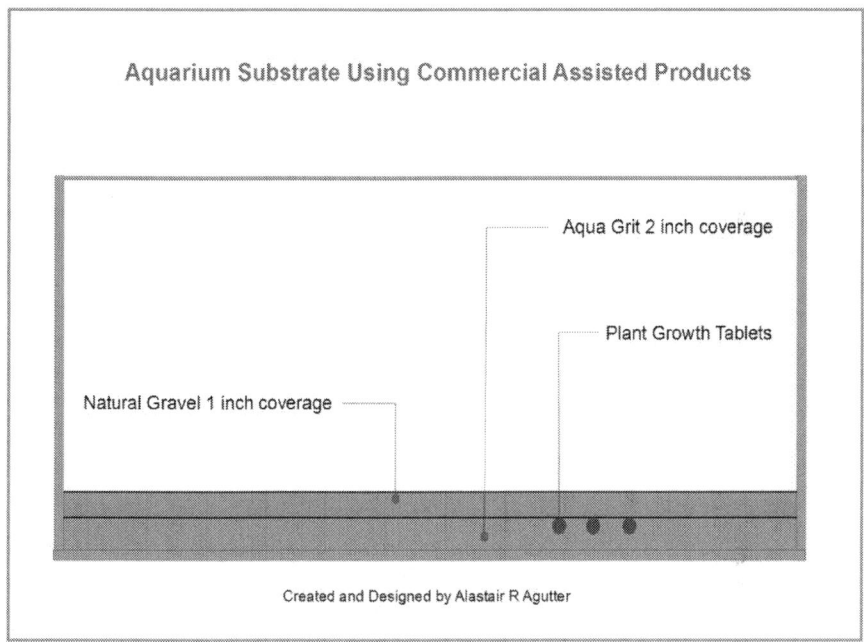

A diagram showing a typical substrate using conventional aquarium gravel, aqua grit (clay based) and plant fertilizer tablets – Photograph by Alastair R Agutter

But in the meantime, the above diagram shows a typical tropical fish aquarium substrate using "aqua grit" and plant food tablets in the substrate.

Regarding substrates in a sterile aquarium scenario before we move onto aquarium furnishings, we of course do not require a substrate. However there can be occasions in a sterile aquarium, where we do require plant life for decoration, or for a specific purpose regarding water quality changes and spawning by certain species, where plants can be potted. This subject area will be covered in the following chapter.

AQUARIUM FURNISHING

So far we have discussed a Naturally Planted environment in relation to substrates and where living tropical aquarium plants are used. But an aquarium's landscape can consist today especially, of many offerings from the commercial world.

A picture of one of the most popular aquarium furnishings for more than five decades the sunken Galleon Wreck – Photograph by Alastair R Agutter

Some of the most popular and main furnishings on offer for the Aquarist are rocks and bogwoods. Other furnishings include more novelty type objects, some like the sunken galleon wreck pictured above, a product that has adorned the Aquarists aquarium now for more than five decades.

Below is another set of photographs showing more novelty furnishings for today's aquarist and many of the pieces popular over many years and decades.

My First Aquarium Collectors Edition

A collection of pictures showing some of the most popular novelty furnishings over the years and decades for the tropical fish hobbyist and aquarist – Photograph by Alastair R Agutter

The treasure box has always been a favourite with many of the younger tropical fish hobbyists, where an airline can be connected to discharge bubbles, and where the lid will occasionally lift. Other items pictured above include; the water mill, a bridge, a castle and a magical wonderland. The last picture shows a segment from a set of wall caves that can be compiled and positioned on the back of an aquarium, using rubber suckers for small rock dwelling cichlids.

When introducing furnishings into an aquarium of any size, I would always urge with a word of caution.

Sadly when water conditions become perfect and food is in abundance in a tropical fish aquarium, the world of specie hierarchy begins and there will be fighting as a pecking order is established across all the species introduced into your aquarium and even between different species.

At such times of squabbling and fighting, your fish will on occasions dart quickly, so they can escape an attack. When such an event happens, very often a fish may swim into an object in the aquarium.

Therefore alas, our tropical fish members of the family are no different to our Children when young, and so safety has to be a main priority considered when purchasing aquarium furnishings.

Please always ensure when purchasing any item for the aquarium, there are no sharp edges on the object(s) that could cause any members of the aquarium great harm.

Even bogwoods can sometimes have sharp pointed edges. In the past when using bogwood as seen in the picture below, I have cut off these potentially dangerous hazards with a hacksaw and sanded the edges when the bogwood is relatively dry before placing the object into the aquarium.

A set of four stunning pictures showing the potential of using rocks, bogwood, mosses and plants in a tropical fish aquarium – Photographs compiled by Alastair R Agutter

Bogwood is very much described as it is a "bogwood" and therefore needs some vigorous cleaning by using hot water and a kitchen nylon saucepan brush, before placing the bogwood in the aquarium. For very often, you can purchase bogwood that still retains hardened clumps of earth, or sediment, and where we have very little knowledge of what organisms may lurk, or are being harboured within this earth.

Bogwood as a furnishing in an aquarium can look absolutely stunning and has always been one of my favourite objects for medium to large aquariums and can be a worthwhile addition by the aquarist to achieve a fabulous underwater world to behold.

When I look at the above four picture landscapes, it gives me hope for the future of the human race, for such majestic scenes clearly demonstrates how beautiful and creative we can sometimes be.

1/. The first picture top left shows how black granite rock has been used and blends in with the small aquatic plants and mosses.

2/. The second picture shows how a landscape has been built up and created with small rocks and bogwoods for mosses and algae to become established, with small plants serving as a backdrop and white gravel to the forefront with a carpet of small green foliage.

3/. Picture three is without doubt one of my very favourites, as it displays a long established underwater tropical world, where the bogwood branches have amassed over time a carpet of algae and moss, with towers of green algae ascending and pieces of small grey slate scattered across the substrate. A landscape so like the wild in many parts of the world's streams, rivers and lakes when been blessed by the Sun's rays in summer.

4/. Picture four is a clearer image of bogwood with fine spreading branches into the water and complimented with a carpet of fine plant life and a small roaming shoal of Cardinal Tetras (*Paracheirodon axelrodi*) members of the Characin Family.

Aquarium furnishings can have practical uses as well as being appealing to the eye, the imagination can very often inspire – Photographs compiled by Alastair R Agutter

1/. The above first picture shows how you can use artificial Coral as a furnishing even in a Malawi Aquarium with bright vibrant coloured cichlids. As you can see this man-made coral is now becoming established as algae forms on the surface and the material used, has no sharp or pointed edges.

2/. Picture two shows a potted amazon sword plant in a bare bottom aquarium, to help neutralize the mineral content in the water and to provide a spawning surface (leaves) if so desired. This breeding pair of Angel Fish decided to spawn on the inverted flower pot to the left where the eggs are clearly visible in the picture.

3/. Picture three shows one of my Polyatomic-ion Biological Reactors and where I have cut in half a moss ball and placed it above the dome to further help purify the water.

4/. Picture 4 shows another one of my Polyatomic-ion Biological Reactors for purposes as a spawning substrate for my Discus (symphysodon), but in this case working hard as a filter providing crystal clear water in a juvenile rearing tank where these fish are fed 4 to 5 times a day on a specially prepared high protein beef heart, liver, spinach and broccoli food I make myself.

This later picture listing and explanation takes us nicely onto aquarium furnishings regarding water chemistry and toxicity.

As many of you know not all items or objects can go into an aquarium for fear of poisoning, or altering the water chemistry, leading to stress and eventual death of our new beloved family household members.

Any piece of bogwood or gravel mentioned earlier must be thoroughly washed. Rocks also need to be washed and of a geological density to prevent any emission of toxins from rock material of a softer and more porous nature.

Safe rocks to use in an aquarium are granites, marbles, quartz and slate. However before using any quartz stones, or rocks, again please check to make sure there are no sharp edges.

Natural grey and black slate roofing tiles can also be used. Many commercial breeders use such substrate furnishings when breeding many varieties of cichlids, including Angel Fish and Discus. Very often if you come across Discus, or Angel Fish Books and articles on cichlids, will be present frequent pictures of cichlid eggs on pieces of slate, positioned at an angle up the side of an aquarium and with the parents aggressively guarding their young.

No Rocks or Substrate material must ever be used if they are lime based, such as man-made concrete objects as these will contain lime poisoning the fish.

Porous materials such as chalk is not suitable in the aquarium as a furnishing rock or object because of the calcium elements and deposits present in the rock, as this will affect and increase the PH and GH (General Hardness) or DH (Degrees of Hardness) of the water.

Sometimes chalk is used, but only in small amounts and in small granular or pebble form in a well-managed environments, say for use in a trickle filter, if the local water is too soft and acid. Chalk will help raise the PH and General Hardness to a more neutral, or alkaline level.

Terracotta in the form of flower pots and ornaments is fine in an aquarium and the slightly porous rough surface of this material will encourage the rapid growth of algae and moss, giving a more established and authentic look. Terracotta is also an ideal material if you are seeking, or planning to use something like a terracotta sculpture in the aquarium for example.

Smooth glassware and ornaments are again safe for in the aquarium, but just be mindful and careful if and when placing such objects in the aquarium, for the collision of glass on glass is not often a very good thing.

In the next chapter, we will of course continue to refer to substrates, as we discuss healthy thriving plants. Where I hope, I will able to provide further answers, if certain topics of interest have not yet been covered in this chapter.

As we also move onto the next chapter, again we will begin to understand how critical water chemistry and water quality is for our plants to survive and thrive in addition to our tropical fish.

CHAPTER SIX

Growing and Keeping Healthy Aquarium Plants

Today as aquarists, we are very fortunate to acquire and read books and many articles dedicated to aquarium plants and covering a wide and varied plethora of plant species, one book in particular is written by Peter Hiscock titled Mini Encyclopaedia of Aquarium Plants, and a worthwhile read and investment for any tropical fish hobbyist.

The leaf colour variations from old and new growth leaves of plants in a Naturally Planted Aquarium with healthy thriving plants and fish – Photograph by Alastair R Agutter

Taking up the hobby of tropical fish keeping regarding plants in an aquarium is something to learn and enjoy. Over time from first-hand experience, you will find how very quickly you learn of the species and the plants that appeal to you, for developing magnificent planted aquarium landscapes in your home or fish house.

To get you started in this new found hobby and pastime regarding this chapter section of the book covering aquarium plants. We just need to cover and familiarize ourselves with some fundamental biology cycles.

If you do have a passion for gardening, or you do have an interest surrounding the pastime as a gardening enthusiast, such knowledge will serve you well regarding your new tropical fish keeping exploits.

As I have said before in the book, I want your new pastime of tropical fish keeping becoming a joyful experience and a great process for learning. So in this chapter, I will cover the topic in a practical and easy way.

I must confess at first, when it comes to marine animal welfare and plant life in an aquarium, my style and methods are to help and enhance the natural environment for all inhabitants in an aquarium, rather than focusing on cosmetic design as a priority. For plant cycles do have a significant purpose with regards to the co-existence of other inhabitant life forms and I will explain why!

Whether you seek to be a marine landscaping master of plant life, or a more laid back tropical fish hobbyist seeking a natural underwater world, to grow any aquarium plants successfully is only ever achieved when the substrate, filtration and water quality is right, thus ensuring the process cycles of plant and other marine life forms can be achieved and are executed successfully.

In the photograph above shows one of my naturally planted aquariums and in the picture, you can clearly see new plant growth and other leaf vegetation in decline (brown leaves). If you are like I and are a big fan of the Autumn Season (The Fall), such a look and landscape may also appeal to you with the changing colours of the leaves in your aquarium.

What I can advise, this decaying leaf material serves many purposes and none more so than serving as compost overtime when naturally broken down, or as food in the aquarium for microscopic organisms and plants.

But even decaying leaves can serve as a food source of nourishment in the aquarium for current fish inhabitants, serving as part of a balanced diet (roughage). Decaying or declining leaves, can also frequently serve as a place of refuge (protection) as a spawning substrate or for young fish, escaping predators within the aquarium.

Three great examples showing how Aquatic Plants serve as great contributors to the Marine Environment 1/. Oxygen 2/. Roughage 3/. Protection – Compiled by Alastair R Agutter

On the next page the following diagram takes us through the basic biological process that takes place within a plants life. Our objective is to create and replicate these conditions, so these processes work in an aquarium environment to achieve healthy thriving plant inhabitants.

Aquatic Plants in the aquarium environment are providers rather than consumers of material, or elements, and as is well known, plants generate oxygen that can help more evolved species, such as fish regarding the respiratory process. Plants also greatly aid and assist micro-organisms and bacteria as a food source in addition to oxygen.

The following diagram shows how important Algae can be, even as a very basic form of plant life, as these species can become providers in the way of Oxygen being a waste by-product after the Photosynthesis process.

Today as mentioned earlier in the book, mosses are becoming a popular plant life species in aquariums, as they do help the aquarium environment by filtering out or absorbing various elements including metals, nitrates and toxins. Algae in years gone bye has often been deemed as a pest rather than an asset. Algae can often serve as a food source for numerous critical bacterial life entities and even fish to form part of their diet, especially fry.

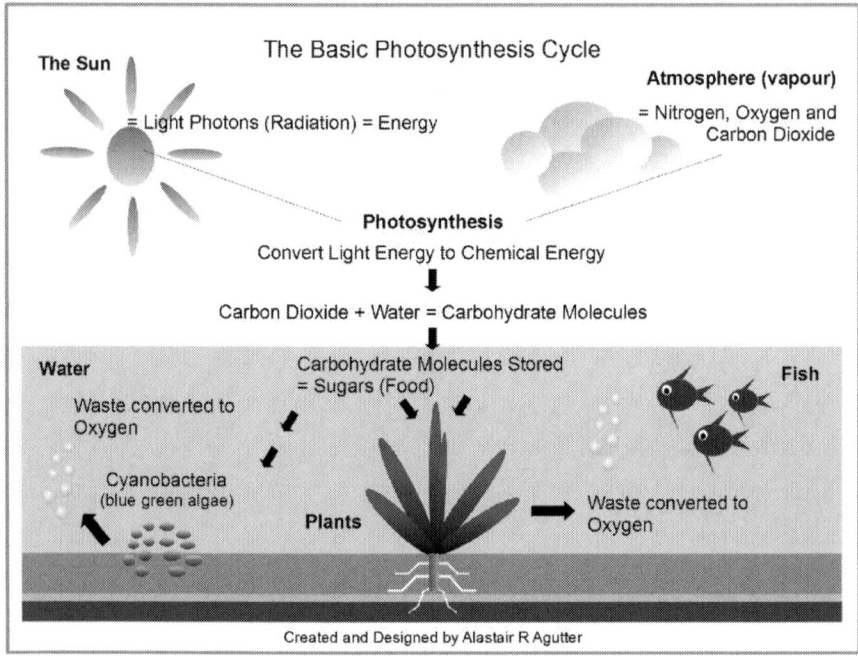

Diagram above showing the basic cycle of Photosynthesis where light as energy is converted to chemical energy to provide Carbohydrate Molecules – Diagram Created by Alastair R Agutter

The process of photosynthesis is performed differently from one plant life species to another. However, the process of photosynthesis always begins when energy is received from light and is absorbed by proteins known as reaction centres that contain green chlorophyll pigments.

Now, as we know throughout seasons, the growth and colouration of plants leaves do change and within this existence of plant life and these cycles, are many other life form entities that help serve the process of plant life development. All plant leaves have a cell structure (membranes) and within these is another world and hive of activity of bacterial life forms and all dependent on oxygen to breakdown and process matter.

As gardeners and observers of our wild, we recognize the changing seasons and where certain tree and plant forms send their solar arrays in the form of leaves into autumn and winter month's periods of dormancy. Here we witness the majestic variation of colours throughout our wild, as the tree and plant leaves become regulated in respect of the amount of light trees or plants in those periods are able to receive to make food. Chlorophyll is critical for the photosynthesis process (absorbs energy) and in autumn and winter month's trees and plants is less able to generate or store (chloroplasts) so much food as this process is greatly restricted as a result of greater periods of darkness, thus in turn reducing the light intensity from the electromagnetic spectrum and where across such a spectrum, blue and red is the most intense and green is far less so.

It may seem strange to discuss the cycles of plant and tree life when we are providing artificial light for our aquarium. However, that is not strictly true. Years ago in the Science community it was believed plant energy was transferred by a process of plant or tree membranes in the form of leaves and stems once light is received to the leaves containing the chloroplast cells in the plant leaves tissues. However, the Science Community is now beginning to understand the photosynthesis process of energy and how it is distributed throughout a plant or tree life form is by way of waves. When any wave is involved from our understanding and the definition, we then know electromagnetic energy forces are at work in conjunction with photons and atmosphere. So even if we regulated our artificial light in an aquarium for 12 hours a day for example, our aquatic plants have other ideas when measuring light as they encompass atmosphere, electromagnetic waves and sub atomic atom particles.

This I have studied and noticed for some years now in naturally planted aquariums and where even fish species know a specific time of a year in a plants life seasonal cycle. Please let me explain!

Thankfully, I have always been very successful in growing Amazon Sword Plants and in South American Themed Naturally Planted Aquariums, this is critical when wanting to breed Angel Fish in captivity, as these plants are their most favourite as a spawning surface.

In the months of spring in Britain where I live, from March to May Amazon Sword Plants begin to develop new shoots, but a considerable amount of energy seems to go into the root system of the plant. Regarding the fish such as Angel Fish from the Native region of South America where Amazon Sword Plants exist, they tend not to spawn, if at all, during these months. But when we come to the autumnal months later in the year July, August and September, the leaf growth of Amazon Sword Plants becomes very noticeable, and this is a time when my Angel Fish begin to start frantically cleaning the Amazon Sword Plant leaves and begin to spawn.

I have also noticed with Vallisneria that this plant in the months of July, August and September vigorously grows, and when some of these months are some of the longest for daylight hours. This only further confirms to me, we still have much to learn about our pastime and fellow creatures regarding cycles and events that they seem to clearly understand and we have yet too!

The following diagram covers our understanding of the plants biological anatomy as we begin to discuss their needs within the aquarium, and the vital signs to look for, when purchasing plants and their suitability regarding aquarium theme conditions.

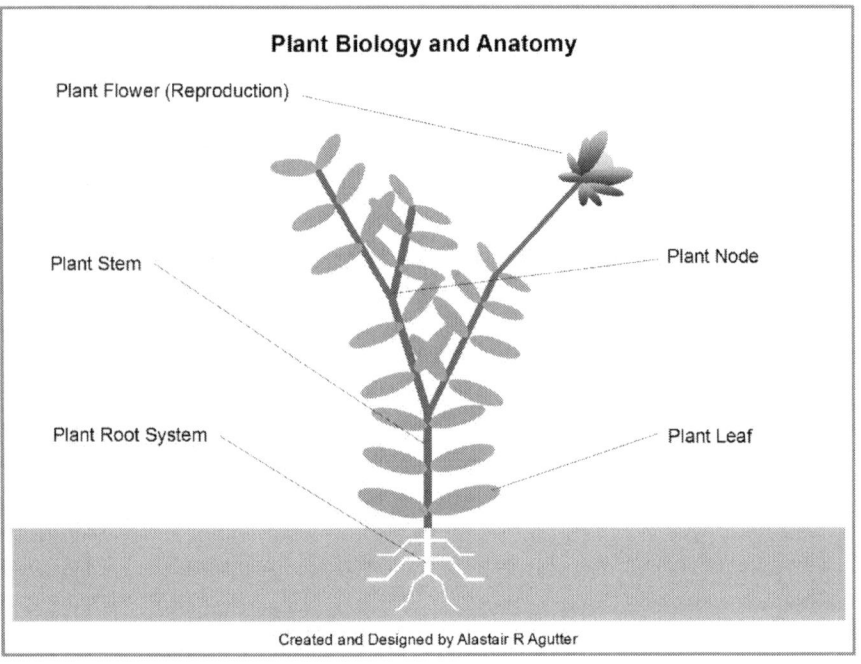

Diagram above shows the basic anatomy of a plant consisting of 1/. Stem 2/. Roots 3/. Nodes 4/. Leaves and 5/. Flower for reproduction – Diagram Created by Alastair R Agutter

As discussed already in the chapter and book, plants acquire most of their food through the process of photosynthesis, where light energy is converted to chemical energy, Carbon Dioxide (CO_2) and Water (H_2O) to Carbohydrate Molecules (sugars) that are stored or transported around the plants system using water for plant growth.

In the diagram above, we have broken down the plants anatomy, where we see the stem structure, plant leaves, plant nodes, plant roots and the plants reproductive mechanism in the form of a flower.

Roots are not only the securing mechanism of plants above and below water. But they also greatly assist in attaining nutrients and foods for the plants growth.

Healthy aquatic plants will always have healthy white roots. If you find plants being sold that have roots of a brown colour, please do not buy, for they are in decline and this can be confirmed if you are able to touch these plant roots with your fingers. You will notice a soft slimy texture and this is the sign of bacteria eating the plants root system as it goes into decline and breaks down.

Photograph showing how Healthy Aquatic Plants should look displaying lush green leaves and where you can actually see them oxygenating the water – Photograph by Alastair R Agutter

The above raised points on plant roots, can also be applied here regarding leaves and stems of aquatic plants in general, for they should **NOT** be slimy and should have fresh lush coloured leaves and of course mostly of a bright fresh green, as seen in the photograph above. However, as we know many plant species are of a different leaf coloured variety, but in the main plant leaves and stems should be clean and crisp to the touch.

So, how do we achieve the objective of growing healthy thriving plants in a Tropical Fish Aquarium environment?

Well, the first plus in our favour is "evolution" in the form of Quantum Mechanics and Natural Branching. For such topic areas have taught us that plants are adaptable.

Today we need our aquatic plants to be adaptable in view of the different environments we seek to place them, in relation to tropical fish keeping.

If we take a leaf out of our Horticultural friends in Gardening ideal conditions for healthy thriving plants is good soil, plenty of sunlight and plenty of rain.

Well, the reality is, we can achieve all of this by careful planning and this relates to aquarium themes again and substrates. Plenty of water, well that is a given considering our tropical fish aquarium plants are submerged. Plenty of sunlight, well we can certainly assist here with artificial light and finally good soil, the latter takes a little more time and thought, but we can achieve this also.

Even with suitable conditions as a tropical fish hobbyist, or as a budding gardener, we all know some folk strike out. Now this I believe relates to the touch, or should I say the human touch.

Over the years, I have watched numerous folk potting up plants. Some force the poor thing in so hard, the plant must feel it has been placed in a pair of concrete boots. Or other times with a member of the fairer sex and with other things on her mind (time to pick up the kids from school), plonks a plant in a pot in such a way with just a sprinkling of soil, it looks as if she is waiting for the plant to top up the rest of the pot with soil and tamp itself down.

PLANT ROOT SYSTEMS

This leads us nicely onto plant roots in greater detail. Plant roots do carry and take in from the surrounding soil and substrate mainly nitrate compounds from the aquarium water. In old money fishes waste and dead vegetation, that we would often describe in gardening terms as manure, or compost.

Also within the aquarium water are common metals and trace elements, some of these are; Iron (Fe), zinc (Zn), potassium (K), copper (Cu), chlorine (Cl), lead (Pb), sodium (Na), tin (Sn), calcium (Ca), phosphorus (P), magnesium (Mg), manganese (Mn) and iodine (I).

Many of the above metal trace elements are digestible for plant species through water and soil substrates and some metals are of particular importance regarding successful plant growth and health. Iron, potassium and zinc for example are three very popular metals that are greatly welcomed by most plants above and below water.

All aquatic plants whether from light energy converted to chemical energy or metal trace elements and compounds within the water and substrate, all need to be transported to the aquatic plants leaves, stems and roots by way of water. In the aquarium above and below the substrate for healthy thriving plants requires movement, and to assist in this process, some of the players are fish and bacteria.

Chemical changes take place above and below the substrate in an aquarium and this is often seen when testing water where changes can then be seen in black and white regarding PH, Nitrate and GH tests to mention a few.

Also within the aquarium above and below the substrate are toxic chemical and gas exchanges from methane, hydrogen to carbon dioxide. Other chemicals can also be a factor within and above the aquarium such as sulphur and nitrous dioxides. Such latter chemicals mentioned can also have a bearing on plant, fish and bacteria life forms in the aquarium affecting water chemistry where toxicity can build up such as Carbon Dioxide that is focusing very much in the news today, regarding climate change across our seas and rivers around the world.

Surprisingly enough and this is one of the reasons why you can enjoy this pastime of tropical fish keeping, is that Mother Nature will always have your back if you try. The secret to healthy plants and fish in a naturally planted aquarium is balance.

If we consider and relate this to the wider world, we can quickly see evidence all around us of the impact and damage caused when we do not respect Mother Nature and balance, leading to failed crops, natural disasters, species extinction and disease.

As a tropical fish hobbyist the subject of Maths becomes a great friend and this is worth bearing in mind regarding our younger aquarists still at school, for many of the questions we have to ask ourselves to attain answers, especially when quantifying volume mass, can only accurately be achieved from and by the use of Maths.

Whether we have potted plants in a sterile aquarium without a substrate or a naturally planted aquarium with a substrate, we do need circulation. In the chapter on filtration, we will discuss how we can establish currents and flows, for both sterile and substrate aquariums, where we establish movement within the aquarium above in the water and below in the substrate. We will also see how some forms of filtration are not conducive to aquatic plants in an aquarium.

Assuming we have a filtration system set up to accommodate healthy thriving plants we will now begin the object of growing healthy thriving plants in the aquarium.

I have found when using potted plants in an aquarium it is wise to use terracotta garden pots. They are favourable for the plants, as the terracotta helps retain the temperature of the substrate in the flower pot. One of the set-backs to growing healthy thriving plant is when there is a too greater differential between the temperature in the substrate and the aquarium water. One method is to use under gravel heating by laying in the substrate a heated cable design. However, such heating methods do come at a considerable price and if there is a failure with the under-ground heating product, replacement will require the removing of the existing product that is faulty and this will entail the disruption of the substrate and plants.

Today, I still use combined heater thermostats that I will cover in greater detail in the aquarium heating chapter of the book.

So let's assume we have the right filtration and the correct heating for the job in hand regarding the propagation of healthy thriving plants. Both heating and filtration will be covered in the respective chapters of the book, so please do not worry as the information will be available.

POTTED AQUATIC PLANTS

As mentioned, I use terracotta pots as this helps with the retention of water temperature and therefore assisting in the healthy growth of the plant roots by residing in a substrate that has the same, or a similar, or only a slight variation in substrate temperature by one, or two degrees.

On the next page is a picture showing one of my Angel Fish breeding tanks with potted amazon sword plants for spawning purposes. These plants thrive when individually potted. I normally use flower pots from 3 inch to 6 inches in size.

With larger more aggressive cichlids for example, I tend to use 5 and 6 inch flower pots, to prevent pots from being knocked over when amazon sword plants are being cleaned by the breeding parents, or in the event of a husband and wife family feud, that does happen occasionally, if one parent is not pulling their way, regarding the care of their siblings, or domestic cleaning of the aquarium.

Photograph above showing a young Amazon Sword Plant in a Terracotta Flower Pot and used as a spawning substrate for the breeding pair of Angel Fish – Photograph by Alastair R Agutter

The above picture shows a young Amazon Sword Plant growing in a Terracotta Pot that will eventually become a spawning substrate option for the young breeding pair.

The method I use to pot the Amazon Sword Plants and in fact any other species of plant is similar to pond keepers when planting Water Lilies in a pond.

If you are a Pond Keeper, this process should be familiar to you with regards to potting. When potting Water Lilies, the roots are placed in the soil and the rhizomes sit just above the soil and then the surface area of the pot is topped up with gravel.

I will now take you through the process of potting aquatic plants and the following diagrams and photographs will serve as aids and as visual guides and examples.

1/. Soil or Aqua-Grit in Pot ¾ full and Roots in Soil 2/. Amazon Sword Plant in Terracotta Pot 3/. Soil ¾ full and Topped Up with Gravel – Photograph and Illustrations by Alastair R Agutter

1/. The first process is to establish the right type of pots to be used. This can be of glass, terracotta and other hard material that does not expel any toxins in the water. You can in fact use glazed ornate pots, as long as they have been properly kiln fired.

2/. Next we need to consider is the size of pot. For a pot being too large, once the plant is sown in the vessel, the whole furnishing may be too tall with regards to the water height in the aquarium. For example if you have a 6 inch high pot with a 13 to 14 inch Amazon Sword Plant and the potted plant is being placed in an aquarium with a maximum depth of 15 inches, the pot will not only look out of place, but will not serve the purpose of healthy plant growth, to help provide oxygen as a provider and removing any toxins and metal trace elements from the water (deionization).

3/. We also need to ensure the pot we plan to use is not too small, where the pot could be easily knocked over in the aquarium by very active larger fish species such as certain cichlids. A too smaller pot may again look out of place, or look rather strange if the plant is of a substantial size (looking top heavy).

4/. Once we have determined the type of pot(s) we plan to use for our plant(s), we need to ensure the pot itself is thoroughly clean and this can be achieved in the sink with hot water and using a new, or clean grease free saucepan, or plate brush.

5/. If you are using a terracotta flower pot, you do not need to block the hole at the base of the pot, for this will further serve as an aid where gentle movement of water will feed through the substrate.

6/. We now have to decide on the type of substrate we are going to use for planting. I use as mentioned earlier in the book under the substrates section a John Innes Seedling soil, as this soil is very low of any possible fertilizers that could poison the fish. Or you could use pond soil for planting lilies from your local Garden or Aquatic Centre. Or you may wish to invest in a substrate such as Aqua-Grit, a clay based gravel substrate for your plants.

7/. The soil substrate is where we are going to gently place the roots of the plant. So the soil or grit placed in the flower pot needs to be gently placed in the pot and only very gently patted down. Do not fill the pot with soil or grit up to the top. Allow for the soil or grit to only come three-quarters of the way up the pot, leaving around 1 to 2 inches free at the top of the pot, to eventually place on the top area our decided aquarium gravel.

8/. Once the soil has been gently placed and patted down in the pot. The next stage is to get the plant you plan to use and gently wash the plant leaves and roots in warm tap water and only using your fingers and thumbs, to gently rub up and down the leaves, and by using your fingers to gently wash and separate the roots, so they are free of any unwelcomed hidden guests in the plant, such as snails eggs, that will not only devour your plants when hatched, but also plague your aquarium.

9/. Next is to make a small hole in the soil so the roots of the Amazon Sword Plant can be located, and then gently firm round the soil at the base of the plant.

10/. Once the Amazon Sword Plant is positioned in the soil upright and in the correct position in the pot, you then need to grab a good handful of gravel and place in a bowl, or bucket, and give the gravel a good wash and rinse in warm water, continue this process until the water is clear. Gravel normally needs to be washed through about 5 to 7 times, or until clean.

11/. Once the gravel has been washed thoroughly, gently distribute the gravel around the Amazon Sword Plant over the soil and continue until the gravel is near to the top of the pot, as seen in the above diagram.

12/. Remember to allow for water displacement in the aquarium as you very slowly lower the pot into the aquarium to the chosen position. If the aquarium is full of water, you may have to remove some of the water from the fish tank to allow for the potted plant when being added to the aquarium.

I know at this stage of the chapter and earlier in the substrates chapter, some Aquarists maybe concerned or hesitant regarding the use of soil with the possibility of any toxins, or chemicals in this substrate soil. But this will be covered later in the filtration chapter, where all will be explained on how we combat any such scenarios ☺

If as a new Aquarist you are concerned regarding acquiring the correct soil type for your potted Aquatic Plants, you can use a clay based material such as "Aqua-Grit" as an alternative and accompanied in the substrate material one or two plant food tablets, as displayed in the following diagram.

1/. Aqua-Grit in Pot ¾ full and Roots in Aqua-Grit 2/. Amazon Sword Plant in Terracotta Pot 3/. Aqua-Grit ¾ full, two Plant Food Tablets placed in the Aqua-Grit and Topped Up with Gravel – Photograph and Illustrations by Alastair R Agutter

As potted plants become established in an aquarium after a few weeks, there will be distinct signs of growth, as your plants begin to benefit from the environment regarding artificial light, suitable water conditions, nitrates and metal trace elements in the soil and in the aquarium water.

By this time also after several weeks, there can be found life and activity in the potted plant soil and gravel substrates, as a bacterial world and culture begins to get to work. From such activity and movement within the potted plant substrate by these forces, this allows for vitamins, chemicals and foods to be absorbed and digested by the potted plants roots system and in turn, repaying the environment by expelling oxygen as a by-product into the aquarium's water.

At Night as Plants expel Carbon Dioxide, an Air Stone in the Aquarium just below the Water's surface assists with a gentle flow and an Oxygen supply – Photograph by Alastair R Agutter

As we know, at night there is a chemical reversal to a degree, where plants expel Carbon Dioxide (Co2) into the water and atmosphere. However, this can always be compensated with the presence and use of an air stone in one of the far corners of the aquarium, towards the top of the fish tanks water surface. The air stone will greatly aid fish with oxygen and especially at night time, but also the air stone can further aid plants with gentle movement in the water, as these gentle flows and currents of water helps the plants collect more food resources from the water, be it chemical, trace elements, or nitrates.

On a personal note, these days I use air stones for all my aquariums, positioning them towards the top of the aquarium around 2-1/2 to 4 inches below the water's surface in the far corners of the fish tank to create a gentle movement of water and serving as a further aid to plants and fish encouraging healthy growth. Air Stones also helps the fish tank environment with increased oxygenation, thus assisting natural bacterial cultures in the substrates and filtration systems in the aquarium breaking down waste matter.

AQUATIC PLANTS IN THE AQUARIUM

One of the biggest conundrums for the Aquarist over many decades has been as mentioned earlier in the book the successful keeping and growing of Aquatic Plants in an Aquarium with Tropical Fish. Very often after several weeks and months, Aquatic Plants purchased gradually decline and die, as a result of the conditions.

We would naturally assume if the water quality is right in an Aquarium, plants will thrive and grow. But the reality is, plants require more than just good water and as all great Gardeners know, the whole process begins with tender love and care. We are all familiar with the coined phrase "green fingers" with regards to gardening, where it often appears some folk have a gift for Gardening and others sadly do not. But like life and the path of learning, it is sometimes the little things that play a big role and are of great importance. Within any substrate housing plants, exists life in some form, be it bacterial, chemical or other. All such life entities require oxygen and chemicals at some point and so we need a substrate that can allow for movement for these entities to thrive and assist the plant.

Very often when gardeners do not have much luck with regards to growing plants in pots, normally comes down to the fact that the soil in the pots is too compact. This prevents movement and oxygen in the soil substrate that is critical. Another consideration is the substrate itself. Is the soil suitable for the type of plants being grown and can such substrate material being used, provide the nutrients that potted plants require.

When potting plants, or placing them directly into the aquarium substrate, never press down too hard, or compact the substrate in anyway. When soil or sand substrates are being used in addition with gravel or grit, simply lightly tamp down the substrate at every stage, so it is firm but not hard.

If we step back for a minute, it will be obvious that a substrate consisting of only gravel, or grit, is not going to be the perfect medium for many aquatic plants, the few exceptions being surface species, such as mosses, or floating plants that produce few, or no root systems.

If you are a Gardener, you know the impact short and long-term when a substrate is deficient. Plants and shrubs begin to quickly decline in growth and size and eventually die over a period of time if no action is taken to enrich the soil.

Unlike conventional Gardens, where we have no substantial providers of nutrients for plants from having a considerable animal presence, in our Aquarium we do have the support of our tropical fish producing waste (excreta) that becomes nitrate material.

This process from fish waste by-products as a benefit to aquatic plants will not be instant, as the material has to be broken down and then be able to eventually find its way to the plants root systems in the substrate.

Gravel or Grit alone does not constitute a good anchor material initially either, again it is only over time from sediment, waste and root systems does such a substrate begin to thrive and support itself from such a structure.

For the successful growth of aquatic plants, we need good food and water movement. As a Gardener we know as mentioned earlier certain substrates alter the chemistry of the environment conditions. A very peaty soil base will produce a more acid type soil. Whereas, more clay based soils will produce a more neutral to alkaline substrate condition.

In the Great River Amazon, can be found as mentioned earlier, many large iron deposits throughout the larger River and Estuary waterways, this condition to the environment has come about due to erosion and thus the River or Estuary system bed coming into contact with geological minerals such as iron.

In certain regions the iron mineral content in the River Amazon tributaries and streams, can be cancelled out with reference to water chemistry, by the heavy presence of dead vegetation deposits. In such wild environments, where there is a presence of both natural materials in the form of dead vegetation and minerals, water stream or river conditions are normally producing a neutral water quality, with a PH range of between 6.6 to 7.0 ph.

If a river or stream environment in the wild has an abundance of dead vegetation over many years, such as dead trees and leaves etc. The water conditions in these regions, is normally very soft and acid reaching as low as 4.6 ph. in some parts.

As we explore such thoughts and facts, we can quickly see like our fish species, not all will fit. This is the case regarding plant species from different regions of the World. Water temperatures and water chemistry conditions will have a bearing also in addition to oxygenation and sunlight on whether plants thrive or die.

At this stage again on reading this material do not begin to get disheartened or confused, for my objective of this book is to make your tropical fish keeping experience enjoyable and fulfilling.

As in life there are many variables and all will eventually become clear, but this part of the book reminds me of an editorial written in "Tropical Fish Hobbyist Magazine" back in August 1972, when Neil Pronek (Editor) said at the beginning and introduction of the magazine, "Sometimes we as publishers of aquarium literature do a disservice to beginning hobbyists by making things look too easy." In defence to Neil, I think he was being a little harsh on himself, for even in my professional life as a Computer Scientist surrounding the development and programming of the World Wide Web, you can often read countless articles online and in magazines about "How Easy" this and that is, or can be done. The real truth at the end of the day, as in all walks of life, experience does count, as well as time served as a tropical fish hobbyist, where such years past, provides an invaluable timeline of knowledge.

In this section of the book regarding the planting and growing of healthy aquatic plants, as like our aquarium themes, we have to consider the availability and the type of aquatic plants we can use and successfully grow along with our fish inhabitants in the aquarium.

One thing we do know and learn regarding visual impact is that any composition comprises of a number of factors. Regarding an Aquarium, we have to consider the type of plants, their suitability and their location in the aquarium.

The following diagram I hope helps to give you an idea on the various sectors that need consideration and attention. As we consider these areas in the aquarium, we also need to think about the more generalized categories of aquatic plants at this stage and these are;

1/ Tall Plants, 2/ Medium Plants, 3/ Short Plants, 4/ Floating Plants

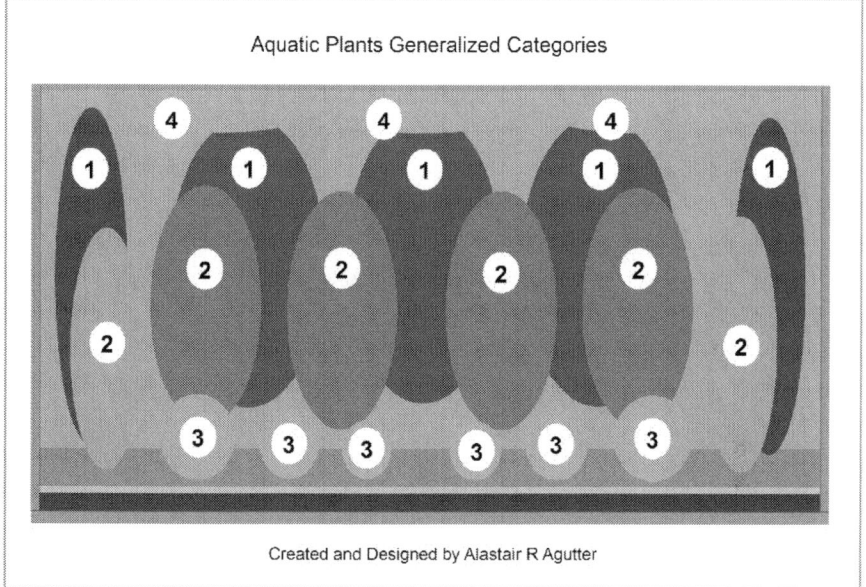

Aquatic Plants Generalized Categories 1/. Tall Plants 2/. Medium Plants 3/. Short Plants 4/. Floating Plants – Diagram Created by Alastair R Agutter

To create a visual masterpiece in your aquarium with aquatic plants can best be achieved when we do consider a 3D approach where from the scene we create provides some visual depth that the eyes can explore. To achieve this goal successfully, we need to consider plant growth and aquatic plant species regarding those that would look best towards the front of the aquarium, to the sides, middle and to the back of the fish tank.

As like in gardening our plant species can help us get an indication to the type of environment they prefer. The normal rule of thumb found in Gardening and covered in my book "Gardening for Beginners" is that light coloured leaved plants prefer more Sunlight whereas darker green leaved plant species prefer more shaded areas in a garden. Two good examples of this so as to prove my point is; when you look at the Hydrangea Shrub, that has light coloured leaves and prefers dry more alkaline soil in a sunny position in a Garden. In comparison to the Rhododendron Shrub, that has dark leaves and likes more acid peaty type soil and prefers a position in the garden that is more shaded.

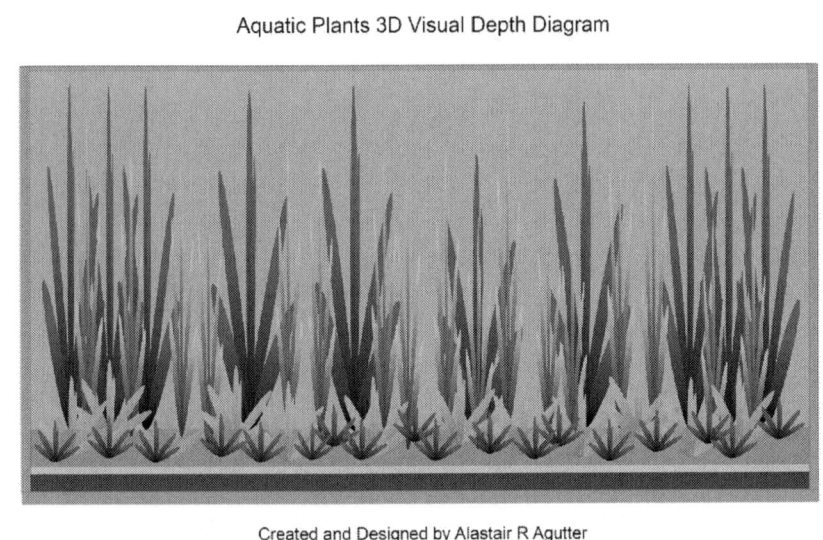

Aquatic Plants 3D Visual Diagram to aid in planning, by considering taller growing plants towards the back of the aquarium, medium sized plants in the middle to centre and short plants front and centre of the Aquarium – Diagram Created by Alastair R Agutter

So regarding the planting of an aquarium, to create a majestic aquatic underwater world scene, leaf colouration of plants as well as growth of certain aquatics plants is also relevant regarding the visual creation of depth to an aquarium. Tall darker leaved aquatic plants would give greater visual depth to an aquarium scene if placed towards the back of the aquarium. Whereas smaller lighter coloured leaved aquatic plant species, would be better and well placed if they were towards the front and middle of the aquarium.

The best method I have found for planting out an aquarium is to fill the fish tank to around half to three-quarters full of water. This gives me a sufficient amount of water in the aquarium when planting to get a good idea of how the plants will look in the aquarium when completed. It is far more manageable to plant out when the aquarium has only this amount of water present.

The next thing I do is to start making small wells in the gravel at the back of the aquarium for the tall plants first. I then place each plant gently in each hole (well) created, to ensure each of the plants roots begins to make contact with the thin layer of sand. So this will ensure in a matter of a few days and weeks, the roots of the plants begin to grow and make contact with the soil substrate, so the plants can receive nutrients from the soil and begin to establish firm anchor holds in the soil, sand and gravel substrate.

A diagram showing the Aquarium filled half to three-quarters full of water before beginning to plant out in the Aquarium starting at the back first – Diagram Created by Alastair R Agutter

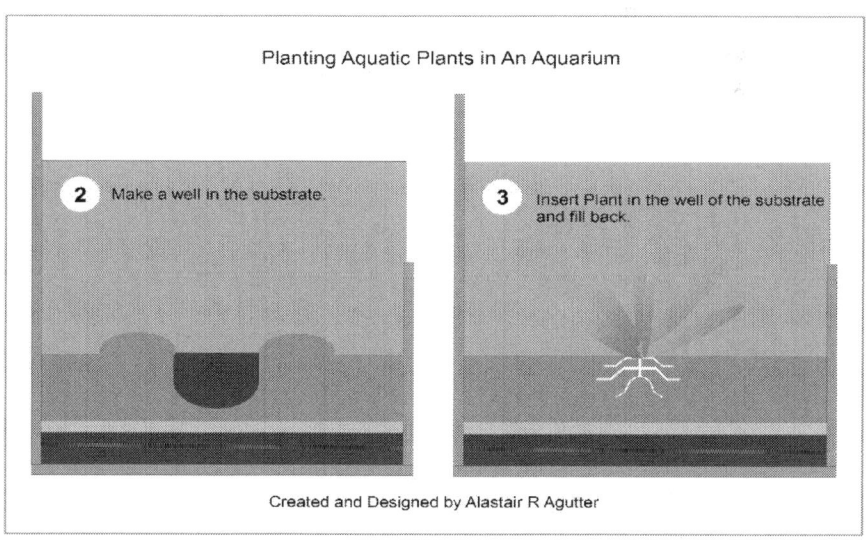

Diagram 2 shows the well (hole) in the gravel to place the Plant. Diagram 3 shows the plant in the gravel where the gravel has been filled back around the Plant. – Diagram by Alastair R Agutter

Once I have placed the plant in the well created, I gently fill back the hole around the Aquatic Plant making sure the roots are covered. I repeat this process with each individual plant I plan to use at the back of the aquarium.

Next, once I have repeated this process regarding the plants at the back of the Aquarium, I then begin to make wells (holes) across the centre of the substrate in the middle of the fish tank for our medium height aquatic plants.

On the following pages are a selection of popular aquatic plants to familiarize Aquarists with and many I use myself. All these Aquatic Plants are still available today for the tropical fish hobbyist and these particular plants should be freely found in all good tropical fish stores and pet centres for a few dollars or pounds.

Aquatic Plant Fact File:

Name of Specie: *Elodea Canadensis*

Summary *Description: Elodea is commonly known as Canadian pond weed and very often found to be a floating plant. Most Elodea plants acquired are female when found in Western Europe and Eurasia and very rarely flowers as a perennial. Elodea can be planted in a pot or substrate in bunches of five or six strands for best effect, but very often fairs better as a floating plant. The plant is ideal to be used as a background display.*

Propagation: *Cuttings from the Plant*

Average Height: *18 to 22 inches*

Native Region: *North America, Europe*

Temperatures: *48 – 68 degrees Fahrenheit*

Aquatic Plant Fact File:

Name of Specie: *Cabomba Caroliniana*

Summary Description: *Cabomba has been a very popular aquatic plant for countless generations in ponds, tropical fish and cold water aquariums. Very easy to maintain and very adaptable for varying water quality and thrives in bright light conditions. The plant is ideal to be used as a background display.*

Propagation: *Cuttings from the Plant*

Average Height: *18 – 22 inches*

Native Region: *Central and South America*

Temperatures: *70 to 82 degrees Fahrenheit*

My First Aquarium Collectors Edition

Aquatic Plant Fact File:

Name of Specie: *Cladophora Aegagropila (Moss Balls)*

Summary Description: *Moss balls are becoming forever more popular with today's Aquarists as they greatly contribute towards making stunning underwater world displays and also serving as a water filter by removing microscopic elements. The algae moss balls are slow growing around 3 to 5 mm a year and can be propagated easily by cutting and separating parts of the balls and rolling them around in your hands for a few seconds to form a sphere. Moss Balls are ideal aquatic plants that can be used in the foreground of aquariums, especially in designer aquariums with white marbled pebbles further complimenting them.*

Propagation: *Cut into small pieces*

Average Height: *3 to 4 inches*

Native Region: *Europe and Asia*

Temperatures: *38 to 86 degrees Fahrenheit*

Aquatic Plant Fact File:

Name of Specie: *Echinodorus (Amazon Sword Plant)*

Summary Description: *The Amazon Sword Plant is without doubt one of my favourite Aquarium Plants and has been a great servant over the years, especially when breeding numerous difficult and complex fish species, none more so than Angel and Discus Fish. Echinodorus family of plants consists of over 35 species discovered to date and an ideal background plant in an aquarium with large broad bright green leaves spanning out. I have experienced Amazon Sword Plants flowering, producing beautiful white and yellow flowers under Halogen Light (12 to 14 hours) conditions with a large headroom area in the aquarium condensation sector and a slightly soft to acid water of around 6.5 ph.*

Propagation: *The Main Plant Produces Runners*

Average Height: *18 to 22 inches*

Native Region: *South America*

Temperatures: *72 – 88 degrees Fahrenheit*

Aquatic Plant Fact File:

Name of Specie: *Cryptocoryne Undulata*

Summary Description: *Cryptocoryne is a very attractive Aquatic Plant species comprising of over 60 family members discovered to date and has been very popular with Aquarists over the decades. Cryptocoryne (water trumpet), are one of my favourite aquatic plant species and can look spectacular as background or middle planted displays in an aquarium, especially when being complimented with an ornate piece of bogwood as part of the landscape. Another similar species is the Aponogeton Family of Plants, with over 40 varieties from Africa, Asia and Australia.*

Propagation: *Main Plants Produce Runners*

Average Height: *10 to 14 inches*

Native Region: *India, Asia, New Guinea*

Temperatures: *70 – 86 degrees Fahrenheit*

Aquatic Plant Fact File:

Name of Specie: *Hygrophila Difformis (Water Wisteria)*

Summary Description: *Hygrophila Difformis has always been commonly known in the aquatic world as wisteria. The leaves of this plant are very light bright green and they are a fabulous plant for protecting new born fishes. They grow well in bunches in the aquarium with an iron based substrate and I have found these aquatic plants will also grow well as a floating plant, giving protection to small fry, especially live bearers. Ideal when planted in the middle section of the aquarium, or towards the back, providing your aquarium landscape with some depth and good coverage.*

Propagation: *Cuttings by removing stems and leaves from main plant*

Average Height: *14 to 20 inches*

Native Region: *India, Thailand, Malaya, Asia*

Temperatures: *72 – 86 degrees Fahrenheit*

Aquatic Plant Fact File:

Name of Specie: *Vallisneria*

Summary Description: *One of my favourite plants are the members of the Vallisneria family, commonly known as eel grass, and is one of the most popular aquatic plants in tropical fish keeping. Vallisneria can look stunning in any aquarium. Very often one of the very first plants Aquarists acquire to use at the back and sides of a fish tank.*

Propagation: *Vallisneria propagates in numbers by producing runners (small plants) from each main plant, as seen in Gardening with Strawberry Plants.*

Average Height: *8 to 16 inches on average.*

Native Region: *Europe, Asia, Africa and North America*

Temperatures: *48 to 86 degrees Fahrenheit.*

Aquatic Plant Fact File:

Name of Specie: *Myriophyllium Tuberculatum*

Summary Description: *Red Myriophyllium displays leaves of a brown to red colour in nature and this depends on the water quality and aquarium conditions. The leaves of this plant are very fine and lace like, the plant needs to be in a debris free water environment ideally for the plant to thrive. Grows well in bunches of 5 to 6 strands plus and requires good lighting of around 10 hours a day at least. Myriophyllium is an ideal display plant positioned towards the back, sides, or in the middle of the aquarium.*

Propagation: *Cuttings from Main Plant*

Average Height: *16 to 18 inches*

Native Region: *Brazil and South America*

Temperatures: *72 – 86 degrees Fahrenheit*

Aquatic Plant Fact File:

Name of Specie: *Rotala Rotundiflolia*

Summary Description: *Rotala is a very attractive plant with small delicate leaves and when planted in bunches in an Aquarium can contribute greatly to make a stunning scene. The ideal position in the aquarium for this plant species is towards the back or used in the middle to form plant displays.*

Propagation: *Cuttings from Main Plant*

Average Height: *18 to 22 inches*

Native Region: *Southeast Asia*

Temperatures: *66 – 86 degrees Fahrenheit*

Aquatic Plant Fact File:

Name of Specie: *Alternanthera Reineckii*

Summary *Description: I think Alternanthera Reineckii is one of the most attractive of aquatic plant species with varying leave colours. This plant is easy to care for and maintain if given plenty of sunlight and grown in bunches in the centre, middle, or sides of the aquarium to form a stunning show piece. When mineral content is present in the water such as iron, this plant will particularly thrive and reward you with a series of varying green and pink coloured leaves.*

Propagation: *Cuttings from Main Plant*

Average Height: *16 to 20 inches*

Native Region: *South America*

Temperatures: *70 – 86 degrees Fahrenheit*

In the previous few pages, I have provided a little insight into some of the very many aquatic plants available to the Aquarist today. The following photograph shows how I have used these plant species in a naturally planted aquarium, to try and give an idea of how an aquarium environment can be transformed with a few plants that will benefit the fish in the short, medium and long term.

Creating a magical Naturally Planted Underwater World from a few Aquatic Plants – Photograph by Alastair R Agutter

Now as you can see from the picture above when it comes to a naturally planted aquarium, it is what it is, a "Naturally Planted Aquarium." I must say in real life, the scene is stunning with happy fish and plants in crystal clear water.

In fact regarding this aquarium, I currently have three breeding pairs of Angel Fish, all arguing over territory with regards to spawning on the Amazon Sword Plants, which is now a frequent occurrence by different Angel Fish pairs every week.

This Naturally Planted Aquarium is one I made myself and measures 21 inches in height and so you can see how tall the Amazon Sword Plants have become in just 6 months from purchase, when they measured around 8 inches originally and now some of these plants are 20 – 22 inches in length and beginning to reach the water's surface as they further grow and arch.

As mentioned earlier in the book when setting up a naturally planted aquarium and after placing the substrate in the aquarium, I then fill the fish tank to around half to three-quarters full. I carry out this process of filling the aquarium with water 24 hours before I begin planting in my aquarium, as this gives me time to check to make sure, pumps, heaters and filters are working correctly and also allows me to make any adjustments.

The water I use to fill my aquarium is tap water, good old fashioned H2O from the tap, the local authority water supply. For my medium and long term objective is to acclimatize my fish and plants to this water source, so I have the water in abundance and on tap, please excuse the pun!

When I fill my aquarium with water I DO NOT use any chemicals, or de-chlorinators. Filtration over a 24 hour period will completely remove any chlorine in the water and in many respects when setting up a new aquarium, as is the case with water changes, the small amount of chlorine in the water works as an antiseptic, removing any common unwelcomed entities from the aquarium that could harm the fish.

When filling an aquarium with water, I carry out this process by using a small saucer placed on the surface of the substrate as seen in the following diagram as this prevents from the velocity of the water entering the aquarium disturbing the aquarium's substrate floor. To fill the aquarium, I use a hose pipe that has a splitter, so you can connect one hose section to the hot water and the other to the cold water.

Our tropical fish aquarium will eventually have a water temperature range between 70 to 86 degrees Fahrenheit dependent upon the species of fish we seek to keep. The rule of thumb to ensure your hot and cold water when mixed entering the aquarium is around the right temperature, is to see if the water is lukewarm to the touch, as this test normally delivers water temperatures of around 68 to 76 degrees Fahrenheit dependent upon the time of year. Please let me explain, in cold winter months, warm water is often lower in temperature, as you have acclimatized yourself to colder weather conditions and so the water seems hotter. In the hot summer months, warm water to the touch could mean around 76 to 78 degrees Fahrenheit.

In the book later under Aquarium maintenance and care, we will cover these areas in more detail, as well as in water and filtration chapters.

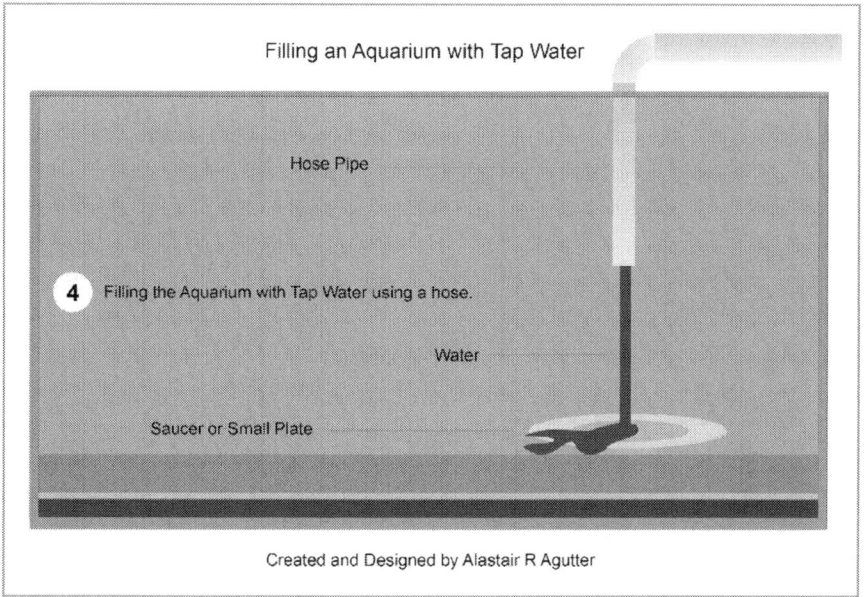

Filling the planned Naturally Planted Aquarium with Tap Water using a Hose with a splitter for connecting to the Hot and Cold Water Taps – Photograph by Alastair R Agutter

Before placing your aquatic plants in the aquarium, always remember to give the aquatic plants a good thorough gentle wash in warm tap water, using a clean grease free bowl or bucket, as this will remove any unwanted guests along with any plant fertilizers, that have been commercially used to grow these aquatic plants and others in volume that could harm your fish.

Such concern regarding plant fertilizers is justified, for I have read most recently (2016) a good number of reports highlighting problems, including customer feedback reviews on Amazon and other sites surrounding aquatic plants purchased, where such plants from not being washed have harmed or killed their fish from plant fertilizers.

So finally in this chapter, another valid point is for Aquarists to ensure when buying aquatic plants they come from a reputable and legal commercial operation. Unless aquatic plants are being swapped or sold to members through their local Aquarist Club, where they will know in most if not all circumstances, the plants have been meticulously grown and cared for by the hobbyist.

CHAPTER SEVEN

The Aquarium Filtration System

Water as we know is essentially the product for creating all life on Earth and throughout the Cosmos, and in an environment of tropical fish keeping it is paramount, therefore we try and establish the best water quality possible for our new family members.

Water is Key to all life and our Survival, we should respect her power and complexities at all times, as we journey into our new pastime as Aquarists – Photograph by Alastair R Agutter

If you are a big fan of survival programs on television such as "Bear Grylls Survival", you can easily see and appreciate how critical water quality is, and also how dangerous it can become. Water filtration survival techniques are one of the first things you are taught in the forces and where you quickly learn of the many ways and mediums that can be used to achieve fresh clean water for survival.

Our forefathers the Victorians understood all too well the need for good quality water and how powerful and important it was. Even still today, some of the finest Victorian Engineering feats in History by these grandmasters of the industrial age are still in use today in many parts of the World either pumping, transporting or filtering water.

Most of us acquire water from our local water authority, where the water is in abundance "Out of the Tap" and the key to one of the greatest secrets in commercial tropical fish breeding is to have an unlimited supply of quality water and in great volume.

Immediately when water comes out of our tap, the water begins to deteriorate and breaks down, unless it is filtered. One of our greatest aims here is to try and acclimatize our tropical fish to our local tap water supply, so there is in place a water resource in abundance for our tropical fish keeping needs to have healthy thriving fish and plants.

So where do we start with regards to filtration?

Well, in tropical fish keeping today, there are essentially four types of filtration; 1/. Internal Box or Container Biological Filtration, 2/. Undergravel Biological Filtration, 3/. External Canister Biological Filtration and 4/. Power or Gravity Fed External Sump or Reservoir Biological Filtration.

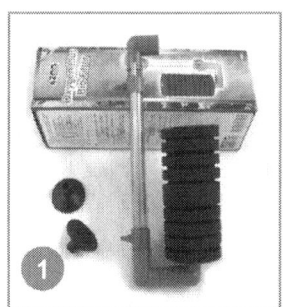 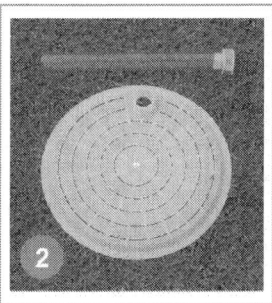 

1/. Internal Biological Sponge Filter 2/. Undergravel Filter 3/. External Canister Filter 4/. Internal Polyatomic-ion Biological Reactor 5/. External Large Sump Type Filter 6/. Internal Power Head Pump – Photographs Created and Compiled by Alastair R Agutter

Now these above methods of filtration differ considerably and this is where some filtration methods may suit some environments and not others.

Today's Aquarist's choice of filtration is determined by a number of factors, some of these relate to the size of the aquarium planned, the type of species to be kept, the number of species to be kept and even if aquatic plants are to be used.

At this stage of the book again, please keep an open mind with regards to the topic of water filtration, for the variations will be clearly explained along with their uses, as we continue through this chapter of the book.

INTERNAL BOX FILTERS

Internal box filtration can come in many varied forms, shapes and sizes for the aquarium today.

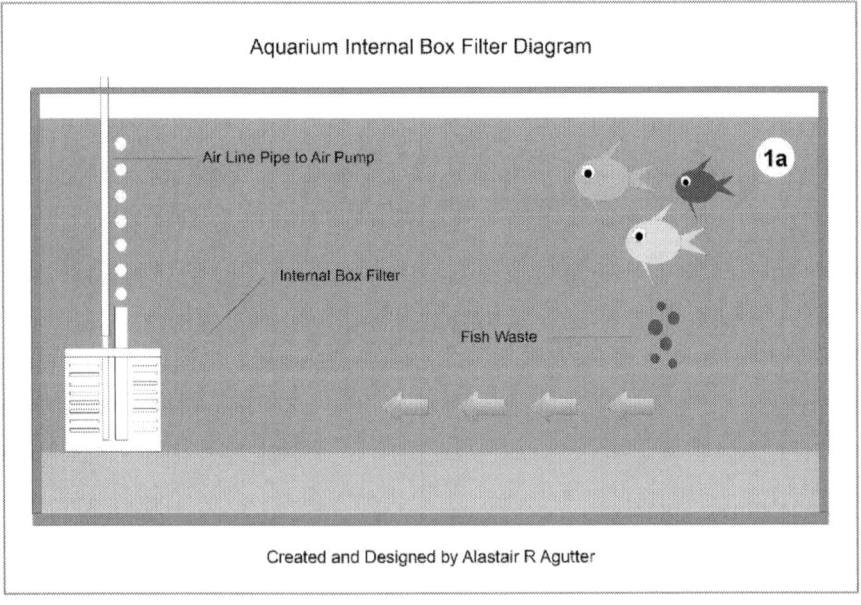

Early Internal Box Filter Powered by an Air Pump – Illustration by Alastair R Agutter

Very early forms of box filtration is less used today, that consisted of very small triangular corner, or square box shaped units, housed in the corner of an aquarium and powered by an air pump. The contents of the filter device to aid in the purification (filter) of the aquarium water for the fish tanks inhabitants, material wise was a small amount of cotton wool (filter floss) and activated charcoal or carbon.

The filter floss from the internal box filter would create a biological bacterial culture to breakdown harmful toxins and bacteria in the form of Nitrites, Nitrates and Ammonia from fish waste (excreta). The activated Charcoal or Carbon is to help reduce metal trace elements also in the water and to aid in the elimination of any poisonous toxins that could harm plants and fish life.

Above pictured is a diagram showing the early form of box filters used by aquarists in the past? Whilst these box filters of days gone bye worked considerably well, after several weeks or months the filter floss mostly and occasionally the charcoal had to be replaced. Now in a naturally planted aquarium, obviously this can cause disruption to the fish and chemically balanced environment.

These internal box filters would work for aquariums in the past of between 18 to 36 inches. In larger aquariums, more than one of these internal box filters would be used and powered by an air pump with two outlets, or using an air pump with two non-return adjustable valves, that could then regulate the air flow to the filter.

Internal box filters of the past would provide a steady air flow to filter the water and display a serene series of bubbles being expelled from the internal box filter as seen in the diagram above.

Internal Box Filters operate like many filters, by using the forces of gravity and vacuum. Air is pumped into the base chamber of the box filter where there are small holes in the plate to draw down the water from the box filter section holding the filter medium. The drawing down process of particles and waste through the water into the filter box section holding the medium is achieved by pumping air into the base chamber, where the air then rises, causing a vacuum by dragging the water with it and escaping through a short exit filter pipe aperture, where bubbles can be seen escaping in the diagram above.

I am sure these Internal Box Filters can still be purchased today and can be a handy item in the aquarist's toolbox regarding quarantine of fishes in a small aquarium, or as a filter in a small rearing fish tank, to prevent the baby fry from being eaten by parents, guppies, platies and swordtails initially come to mind.

In such a scenario as mentioned above, ensure water from the main aquarium is used in the fry tank initially, as this water will contain an established biological bacteria culture that will soon establish itself in the new internal box filter. In fry tanks, you will have to do small water changes to prevent any ammonia build up from overfeeding and fish waste excesses that could harm the fry. Water changes temper these chemical changes and imbalances.

The water transfer flow for the filtration of the water in an aquarium from these small internal box filters is around 4 to 5 litres of water an hour, around 1 to 2 imperial gallons. This is important to remember the volume transfer of filtered water and this will become all clear as we progress through this chapter and other parts of the book, namely water conditions and quality.

In the next section below we cover a similar process discussing internal sponge filtration and the benefits, accompanied again with a diagram.

INTERNAL SPONGE FILTRATION

Internal sponge filters are very much a very useful friend and piece of kit in the aquarist's tool box.

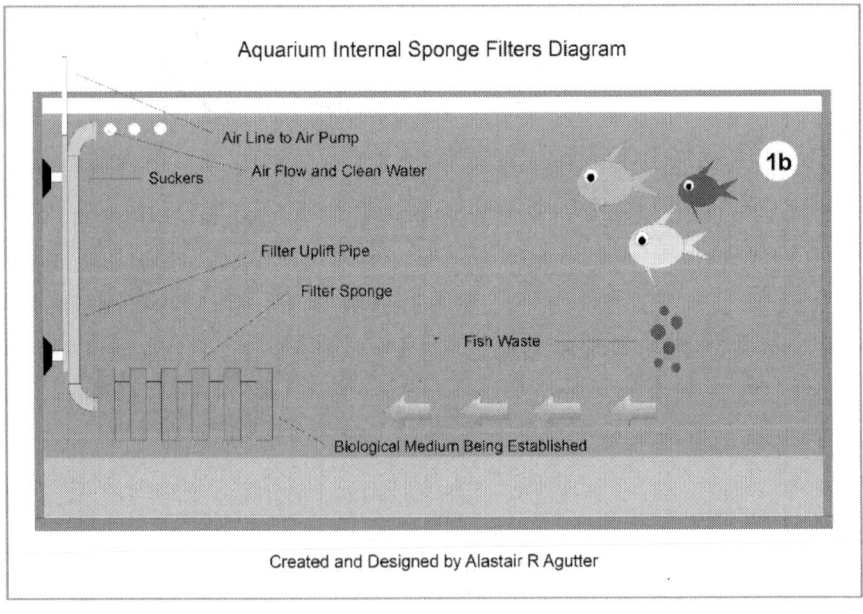

Aquarium Internal Sponge Filter Powered by Air Pump – Illustration by Alastair R Agutter

Many tropical fish hobbyists and commercial breeders use these sponge filters, as they provide a steady flow to purify the water and very safe in breeding tanks for difficult species spawning and the rearing of baby fry.

The picture below, takes us back over 25 years. The black and white photograph shows a home-made sponge filter used in one of my Discus (symphysodon) breeding fish tanks.

The other object in the picture is an Oxydator, a German invention that can assist in providing a high content of oxygen in the water by using the chemical Hydrogen Peroxide.

Author's Breeding Pair of Red Discus over 25 years ago spawning in a breeding Aquarium filtered by a home-made sponge filter for water quality – Photograph by Alastair R Agutter

Internal Biological Sponge Filters can be deceiving regarding the impact they do have on filtering an aquarium. If you take the home-made sponge filter in the picture above, the circular sponge in length measured 4-1/2 inches and the diameter across the sponge measured 2-3/4 inches. If we use "Pi" by multiplying 2-3/4 inches (2.75) by 3.14159 it gives us a figure of 8.639 and then if we multiply 8.639 x 4-1/2 inches (4.5), it gives us a total of 38.87 square inches. When you look at the sponge filter medium in these terms, you can quickly see the actual impact size of the amount of filtration coverage and where it shows that it is of a considerable surface area size.

Internal Biological Sponge Filters have always been great value for money in past years and still so today. They are simple to install and often come with two suckers, so you can attach the internal sponge filter to the sides or back of the aquarium easily.

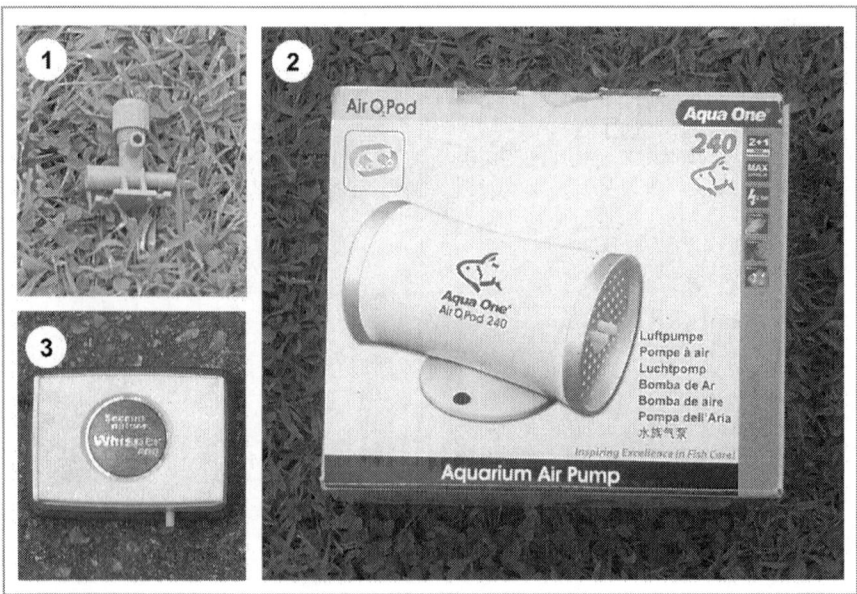

Pictures above show 1/. Air Line Non Return Valve, 2/. 240 Litre an hour Air Pump, 3/. Whisper Single Outlet Air Pump – Photographs and Compiled by Alastair R Agutter

Once the Internal Sponge Filter is positioned correctly in the aquarium, you can then attach an air-line pipe to the biological filter. Then connect the other end of the air-line pipe to a non-return valve, so the air flow to the filter can be regulated. Finally, then connect from the non-return valve to the air pump by using more air line.

All biological filter mediums need an active biological culture functioning to break down fish waste and matter. Most dedicated aquarists and commercial breeders will place a biological filter in an established aquarium for a few days and then transfer the entire internal sponge filter or just the sponge to the new aquarium to be used for rearing fry for example and siphon water from the main aquarium to the new fish tank, so the water is already biologically active along with the filter deployed.

UNDERGRAVEL FILTERS

Undergravel filters have been used in the hobby of tropical fish keeping now for a good number of decades and still used today by many aquarists.

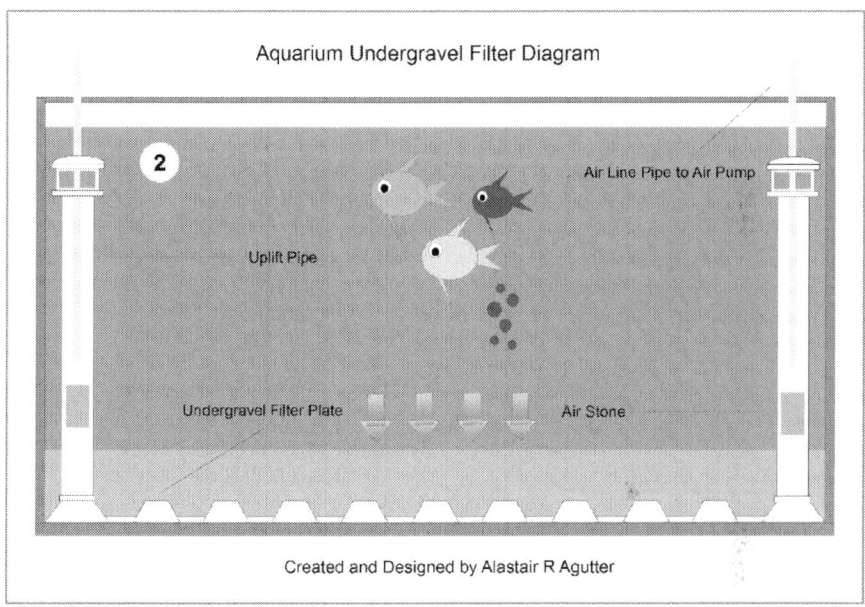

Undergravel Filter with two uplifts powered by an air pump – Illustration by Alastair R Agutter

However, in more recent years from advancements in the pastime, there has been a clear realization other methods of filtration besides Undergravel filtration is more favourable, especially concerning a naturally planted aquarium.

As you can see in the diagram above undergravel filtration works where waste from fish is drawn down through the aquarium's gravel substrate to try and filter out these bye-products mainly created by fish.

Now if the gravel substrate is too shallow when the waste material is drawn through the substrate, this filtration process will not be efficient or effective.

The minimum depth of any substrate using undergravel filtration needs to be at least 2-1/2 to 3 inches deep. However, this will still not ensure you have a filtration environment that is effective and safe for your tropical fish.

To help prevent a build-up of toxins and chemicals including Carbon Dioxides and Methane in addition to Ammonia, Nitrites and Nitrates you need the presence of plants to help breakdown these chemicals and toxins as a result of fish waste and uneaten food.

But to have healthy thriving plants to breakdown these chemicals, gases and toxins they need to be living in a substrate environment that supports them.

As pointed out earlier in the book, just using gravel is not good enough for growing healthy thriving plants. Plants need to a significant degree, a combination of sands, grits, gravels and organic mediums such as compost and soils to grow remain healthy and thrive.

Plant root systems serve as anchors, as well as complex structures to retain and remove materials from the substrates that can be converted to food for plant growth.

For this environment to be optimal for healthy plant growth, so aquatic plants do serve a positive in the aquarium, plants prefer and require a serene, steady and very gentile flow of water. However, with undergravel filtration, the draw down through the substrate of water bringing waste product material can be very fast, as water will always find the quickest route.

This flow rate with undergravel filters can be considerable, and DOES damage root systems, leaving other areas of the substrate experiencing a build-up of waste matter and dead vegetation, where these areas are NOT being filtered and as a result, creating in certain areas a toxin and chemical build-up in the substrate (stagnation), that will be detrimental to the health of your tropical fish.

Furthermore with dead spots in the aquarium and no flow, comes with it when only using gravel, a drop in temperature in the substrate that also damages plants and root systems.

This area of filtration over the years has given me cause for considerable thought with regards to how we overcome such issues as undergravel filtration is still used today.

So the coming filter system methods to be covered, is where we discuss canister filters and also polyatomic-ion biological reactors that I developed to help overcome such problems for delivering optimal aquarium environments for plants and fishes in a naturally planted aquarium.

EXTERNAL CANISTERS FILTERS

In the early to mid-1970's external canister filtration came to the fore in the aquatic world very significantly. More and more articles were being written and more international tropical fish shows saw many more retailers promoting canister filtration, especially models from Eheim.

So far regarding filtration, we have discussed biological filtration methods inside the tropical fish aquarium. Now for the first time we begin to discuss the method of filtration outside the aquarium and it may come as no surprise the concept of external filtration began far earlier than the birth of the canister filter itself. In fact I remember the first filter I owned powered by an air pump in 1967 for "My First Aquarium" was an external filter.

Eheim External Canister Filters – Photo's Courtesy of Eheim, compiled by Alastair R Agutter

The above picture shows the famous and well-known brand of German Company Eheim, who are renowned for external canister filters of superb quality and at this point, I must confess I have a particular affinity for Eheim, as they have become a reliable old friend over many decades for efficiency.

The German Company of Eheim was founded by Gunther Eheim an Engineer back in 1949. In 1962 Eheim helped change the World of Aquatics, with the development of a centrifugal pump with magnetic transmission and a year later in 1963, saw the release of the first ever mechanical suction filter. By 1971 over 100,000 Eheim filters were in use world-wide.

Since those ground breaking days in the 1970's of aquatic advancement by Eheim in Germany, we have seen emerge many more brands of canister filtration including Fluval and others, to meet every Aquarist's budget today.

These systems are very special for many reasons and from such technology advancements by Eheim in the early 1960's today we see even more filtration system descendant methods.

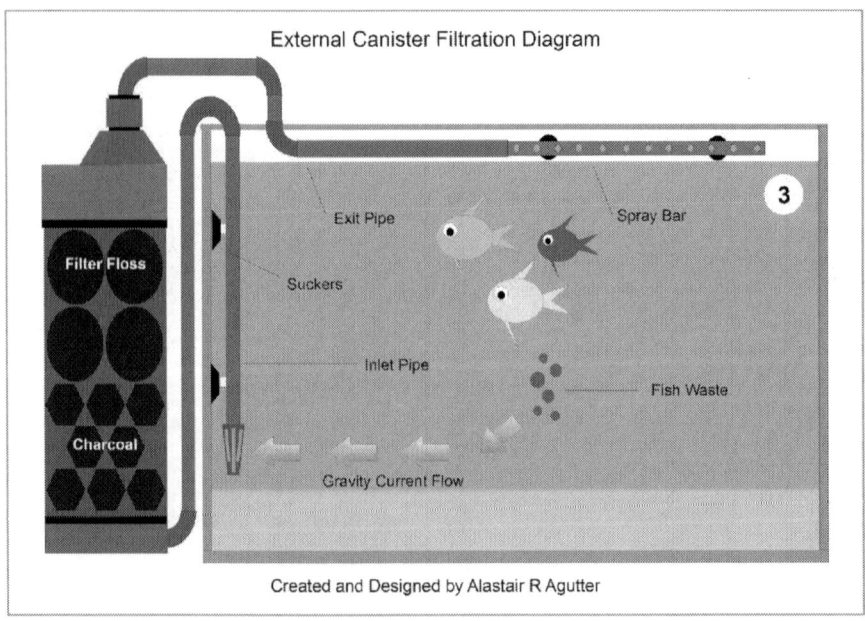

Diagram above showing how an External Canister Filter is Set-up and Works for the Aquarist's Aquarium – Illustration Created and Designed by Alastair R Agutter

External canister filters over the years, have very much been the stars of the show surrounding tropical fish keeping filtration. External Canister Filters can be very versatile pieces of equipment for creating biological mediums outside of the tropical fish aquarium. Canister filters can also alter the chemistry of an aquarium if required, by making adjustments with the use of specific medium placed inside the filter canister(s).

The above diagram shows the traditional medium used, this being Activated Charcoal and Filter Floss. How I set-up my canister filters in the past was by using a series foam sheets consisting of coarse, medium and fine grade foam and cut into circles. The circular pieces of foam are then placed in the filter canister as follows. The first circular piece of foam being placed in the canister is the coarse foam and then the second and next piece of foam placed in the filter canister is the medium foam and then finally, the last circular piece of foam being the fine.

Canister sizes do vary depending upon the model you have purchased, where you may find you have enough space in the canister to place 2 circular pieces of coarse foam, 2 circular pieces medium foam and finally, 3 circular pieces fine foam for example.

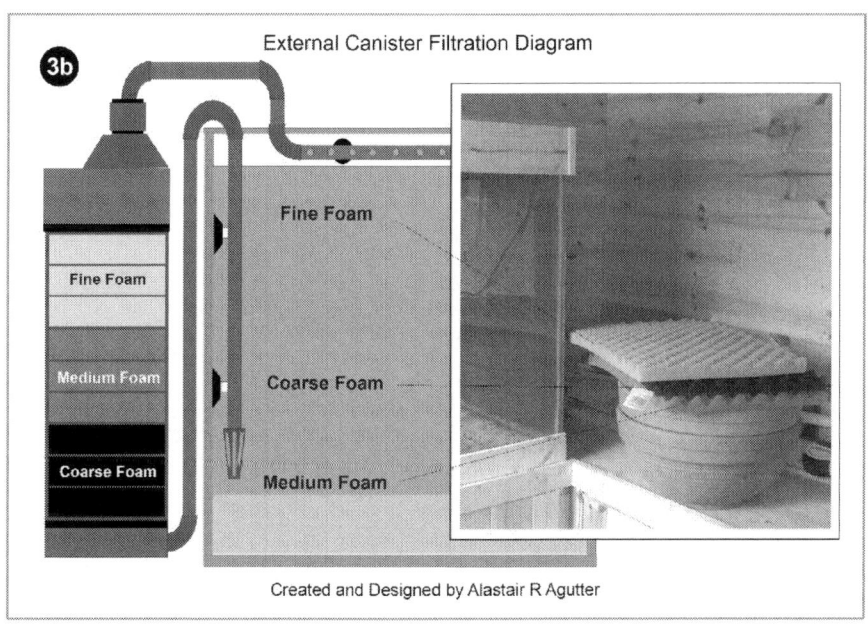

Diagram above showing how an External Canister Filter is Set-up using custom-made Circular foam discs, cut out from foam sheets – Illustration and Photograph by Alastair R Agutter

This method of using foam will create a biological bacteria culture in the filter canister that is stable and not chemistry altered and this is particularly important regarding certain difficult species of fish with reference to their reproduction. So by placing a series of different grades of foam in the filter's canister ensures any waste material is completely broken down and the only substance leaving the outlet of the external canister filter is good clean clear water (H2O).

This above diagram example accompanied with a photograph is showing the type of fine, medium and coarse foam material I use for my internal and external filters, including canister filters as and when required. This foam material can be purchased in all good comprehensive tropical and cold water fish shops, pet stores or large aquatic centres. For it is very often the case, that this foam material is available in the above stores, as the medium is used for large sumps and pond filtration systems regarding Koi Carp.

At this point regarding external canister filters, we have not discussed the flow rate yet, but as you can see on the outlet section of the external canister filter is attached a spray bar, that is positioned just above the water's surface to evenly distribute the water to avoid a heavy turbulent flow in the aquarium. By positioning the spray bar in such a way it helps introduce oxygen into the water.

Regarding flow rate of water filtration, we have already discussed a little about the exchange rate in the Wild which is on average 10 times. However in an aquarium environment we have to consider a number of factors to determine the ideal flow rate for particular filtration methods that serve as optimal conditions for the health of plants and fish.

Commercial manufacturers of filtration devices and especially canister filters boast a wide and varied range of flow rates with regards to the Litres or Gallons filtered per hour.

However, filtration is not that straight forward, regarding the bigger filters and the faster flow rate per hour of filtration they offer, will it necessarily make an aquarium more efficient. Some conditions including specific foods and waste materials being broken down in certain circumstances if drawn through the filtration system too fast, will not filter the water properly, but in fact pollute the aquarium water further. This is because the biological system hosting the bacterial culture does not have sufficient time to break down this waste in the form of chemicals and toxins (oxides) as they are passing through the filtration systems biological culture.

Another consideration and valid point that substantiates my findings, is when you look up close at different materials (waste) that need to be biologically broken down, it is a given and you do not have to be a rocket scientist to realize, hat certain elements that need to be broken down will take longer than others.

Another consideration regarding filtration is equilibrium and this relates to inhabitant numbers in the aquarium. If for example you have 20 fish in an aquarium, the waste volume to be broken down by the bacterial culture will be greater than if you only have 10 inhabitant fish in an aquarium.

Sometimes therefore the filtration rate as advised by manufactures of canister filtration in relation to aquarium size might not be appropriate or in fact correct.

As we progress through this chapter and section of the book, eventually all will become clear and more so, as we now move onto another form of filtration.

POLYATOMIC-ION BIOLOGICAL REATORS

It may come as a surprise to some, but the title above is the correct definition as we explore the world of micro-biology and filtration.

1/. Polyatomic-ion Biological Reactor in Action, 2/. Oxygen Saturation from Optimal Conditions, 3/. Angel Fish Spawning and Breeding –Photographs Compiled and by Alastair R Agutter

I created and developed the Polyatomic-ion Biological Reactor after considering and studying for many years filtration for an aquarium and a subject that has always been one of the biggest posing problems and questions in the aquatic world.

The above set of photographs shows the Polyatomic-ion Biological Reactor in action, producing crystal clear water, and oxygen saturation as seen on the amazon sword plants in the second picture and finally, Angel Fish successfully spawning in such an environment and one of the hardest species to breed in captivity.

By studying the wild and natural environment surrounding River and Stream systems purification and filtration, has allowed me to breakdown such an environment in component form, to establish what is required and how we can achieve this in a tropical fish aquarium.

Concerning the Wild's water system environments, these have a natural water exchange rate of 10 times an hour on average and will be covered more in the book later. However, over the years having a continued growing respect for the mind blowing wonders of Natural Law, in the form of Natural Branching and Quantum Mechanics, such rules are not set down in stone. For one thing you learn from Natural Branching and Quantum Mechanics in a mathematical sense, and one thing that Albert Einstein battled with for more than 20 years, in relation to establishing some mathematical formula surrounding the understanding of Quantum Mechanics. I discovered that the answer to this question in mathematical terms is "QM = I" with regards to Quantum Mechanics. What this means is that in Natural Law, surrounding Natural Branching and Quantum Mechanics, the answer in fact is infinite! In the World of Science and Technology, we call it "Work Arounds" and this following simple example explains.

The beginning of all life in vegetative form began with the seed, and from such a seed came grass. From grass evolved plants and then eventually trees. Plants on land evolved and adapted creating new plant species in water that we describe and call today "Aquatic Plants" and such plant species have morphed as I say, and become into being as a result of the differing landscape environments. From plants we see first-hand clear "work arounds" in the form of climbers, regarding species such as Wisteria and Clematis, where for the continued evolution and the survival of the species, has allowed these plants to adapt by becoming climbers and using other forms of plant and tree life as hosts. Climbing plants can also ascend up buildings and geological rock formations such as cliffs. This is a clear example of "work arounds" in Quantum Mechanics and Natural Branching, almost subconsciously possible as to where we coined the phrase "no such word as can't" comes to mind.

On the following pages I show you two diagrams of the Polyatomic-ion Biological Reactor in detail and how it works. The flow rate in the aquarium using a Polyatomic-ion Biological Reactor(s) only powered by an air pump, completely defies the rules of the past in relation to the volume of water exchange often recommended and again shows how Natural Law in the form of Quantum Mechanics can defy all human thought and logic. But believe me there is logic (higher intelligence) here and this can be found as we explore further our world and look at things in more finite detail.

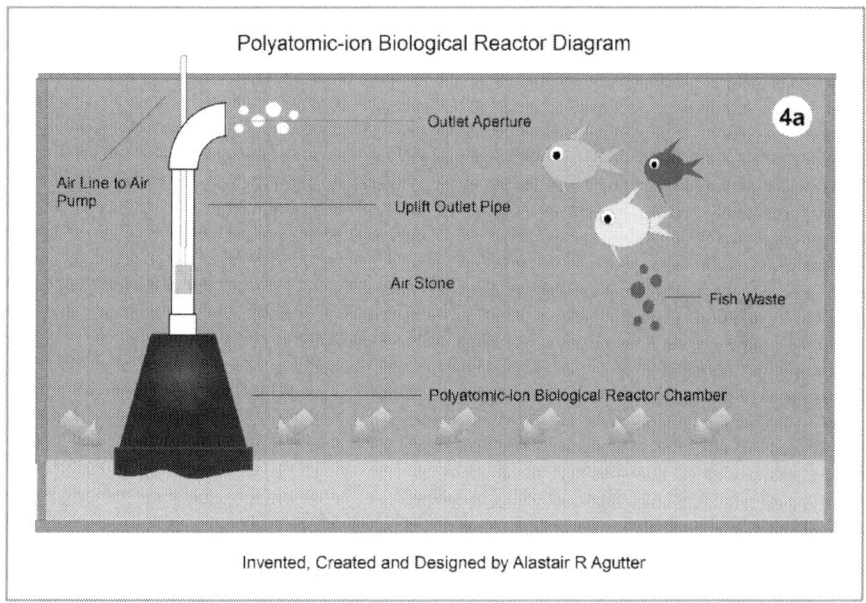

A Diagram showing the Polyatomic-ion Biological Reactor in action and how it works creating natural currents in an aquarium - Invented, created and developed by Alastair R Agutter

The above diagram shows how the Polyatomic-ion Biological Reactor works and functions in an aquarium, creating gentle flow and natural currents.

One of the most important aspects of the filter is how the flow rate behaves in the aquarium, as opposed to a canister, or an undergravel filter. The movement of water with a Polyatomic-ion Biological Reactor, shows how there is a very gradual draw of water at an angle in the aquarium and replicating a characteristic found in the wild, regarding the natural movement of water. You will note if you view a river or stream in the wild, objects such as dead vegetation and weed, tends to roll over and bumps along the bottom of the stream or river bed, as the objects travel down-stream.

This means plant life rooted in the aquarium is experiencing a similar activity found in the wild, where waste and nutrients are passing by the plants very gradually and where sometimes, dead vegetation, nutrients and waste is collecting near the neck base of plants allowing them to absorb and digest these vital nutrients and minerals from the water and thus in turn, chemical energy is converted into carbohydrate energy (sugars), by the process of photosynthesis.

You will note also with Polyatomic-ion Biological Reactors, they are not covering the whole of the aquariums substrate surface, and therefore allowing greater areas to be dedicated to plants, this prevents root systems being damaged by undergravel filtration methods. This method also diminishes a great variation in temperature as you find with an undergravel filter system substrate consisting of only gravel.

With Polyatomic-ion Biological Reactors, the substrate that provides a natural bed environment is by combining gravel, grit, sand and soil to help retain temperatures, as found in gardens where the soil is warm when heated by sunlight from above in summer months, with the retaining of this heat for several months, even when temperatures begin to drop, hence fog. Whereas, when only gravels are used in a substrate of an aquarium, heat loss is fast and gravels alone are unable to efficiently provide heat retention.

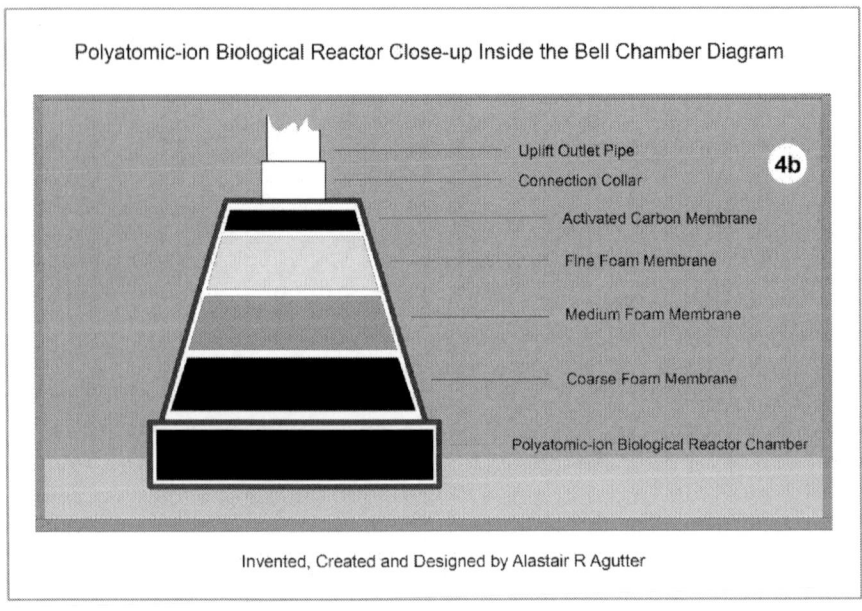

A Diagram showing the Polyatomic-ion Biological Reactor inner workings and components in the actual chamber - Invented, created and developed by Alastair R Agutter

The diagram above shows up close workings inside the terracotta bell chamber of the Polyatomic-ion Biological Reactor. I have used terracotta as a material, for it is slightly porous that will encourage algae growth and this will further help filter the water. Also, clay based objects such as terracotta is perfect for retaining heat, thus ensuring the environment inside the reactor bell chamber is the same as outside.

As you can see from the diagram above, the Polyatomic-ion Biological Reactor sits in the substrate just above soil, sand and a thin layer of 10 mm gravel in a naturally planted prepared aquarium substrate. Then lastly, further gravel is added and then built up in the aquarium around the Polyatomic-ion Biological Reactor(s) to a recommended depth in total of around 3 inches as covered in the plant and substrate sections of the book.

Within the Polyatomic-ion Biological Reactor's Bell Chamber as seen in the diagram above, it shows the filtration membranes for creating an effective biological culture, to remove ammonia, nitrites, nitrates and other toxins from the water and with the additional aid of an activated Carbon or Charcoal membrane.

At the base of the Polyatomic-ion Biological Reactor Bell Chamber is the first medium, this being a coarse foam membrane. The second level in the bell chamber is a medium foam membrane. The third level in the bell chamber is a fine foam membrane and finally the fourth and last level in the bell chamber consists of an activated carbon or charcoal membrane.

This layout and method provides an environment to create a biological bacterial culture that begins to breakdown matter starting in the coarse membrane first and then onto the second chamber with a medium membrane and finally a third chamber with a fine membrane as any waste materials and toxins work their way through the system. Each chamber and level provides finer membranes with an active biological bacteria culture breaking down waste into even finer modules. Until eventually at the very end of the biological process in the Polyatomic-ion Biological Reactor Bell Chamber, all waste is removed and any remaining metal trace elements or toxins, not removed by plants, is finally reduced, or eliminated, by the presence of an activated carbon or charcoal membrane.

In filtration we naturally assume the more water filtered the better, and many commercial manufacturers of filters do tend to emphasize these features of performance when selling their wares.

But filtration does not only relate to filtered water exchange rates, but also coverage efficiency with the bacterial culture community created. If for example a filter canister area of bacteria is say 6 inches in diameter and filtering 120 litres of water an hour. Then you have a canister filter with a bacteria culture area of say 12 inches but filtering at the same rate of 120 litres an hour. We can see that there is a different flow rate through the mediums and bacterial cultures. The second medium even though passing the same volume of water is in fact processing the water more efficiently as the flow rate across the larger medium is half as fast.

So then regarding filtration flow rates we see another dynamic aspect exists in the way of calibration adjustment to meet the environment and in this instance determining the optimal rate flows and bacterial culture processing rate exchanges for our aquarium.

The following picture shows one of my Naturally Planted Aquariums of 67 UK imperial gallons (304.58 litres) with two Polyatomic-ion Biological Reactors operating. The air pump in question powering these two Polyatomic-ion Biological Reactors processes 60 litres an hour and so this means by using two non-return valves and adjusting these for an equal air flow output to each of the Polyatomic-ion Biological Reactors, there is a filtration process flow rate being carried out of 30 litres an hour with each.

A Photograph showing Two Polyatomic-ion Biological Reactors working in one of the Author's Naturally Planted Aquariums delivering optimal conditions - Photograph by Alastair R Agutter

This means the process rate to replace all the water in the aquarium is at a rate of 5 hours 7 minutes approximately, to exchange just once. So this figure certainly contradicts the flow rate found in the Wild, where the average exchange rate is 10 times per hour. But this is where it gets further interesting, for the water quality and conditions in my naturally planted aquarium are optimal, even down to the nitrate levels, where I get a frequent reading of "ideal conditions" as seen in the following picture.

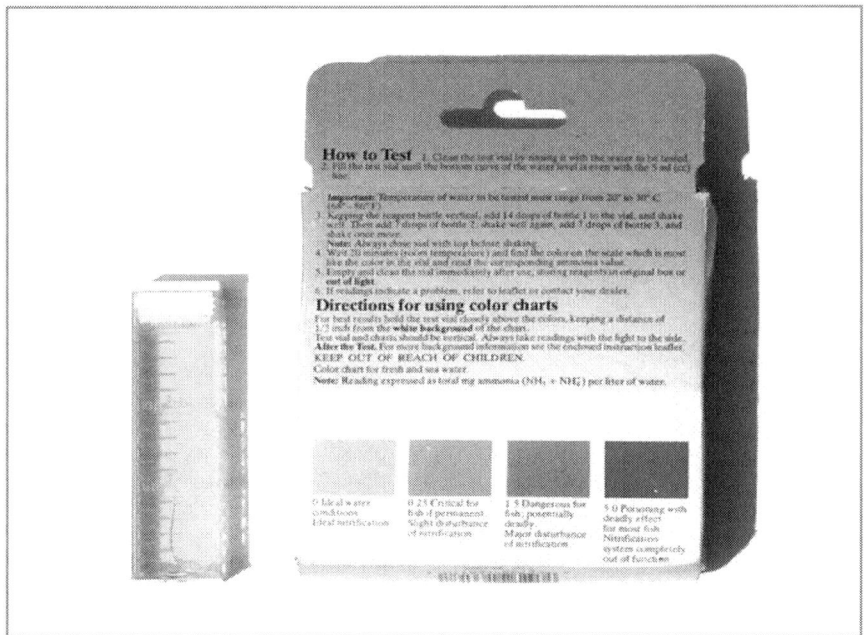

A photograph above showing a Nitrate Test Result for the Author's Naturally Planted Aquarium using Polyatomic-ion Biological Reactors – Photograph by Alastair R Agutter

One of the main contributing reasons for these results is the presence of healthy thriving plants, as they are also filtering the water. Then the regulated flow rate through the bacterial culture in the filtration systems are at a speed that allows the micro-organisms of the bacterial culture sufficient time in the chambers of the Polyatomic-ion Biological Reactors to breakdown the waste matter efficiently.

Sometimes this is why when you have what I describe as a violent filter of any form the water can be cloudy in an aquarium. However, other factors can include from over feeding a culture of micro-organisms and white worms in the aquarium itself that leads to fish sometimes rubbing themselves against objects and not necessarily a sign of gill flukes as is normally indicated. Learning to read the conditions comes overtime from experience and having a sensitive nose is often a very good thing for an aquarist, for it enables them to quickly identify any toxin build up in the water such as Ammonia, as this will also cause fish to rub themselves against objects as chemicals such as Ammonia, causes fish to itch as these chemical and toxins in the water inflame and attacks delicate skin tissues namely gill areas.

POWER OR GRAVITY FED EXTERNAL SUMP OR RESERVOIR BIOLOGICAL FILTRATION

In the commercial world of tropical fish keeping, sump or reservoir biological filtration has now been in existence for a good number of decades. For when it comes to breeding vast numbers of tropical fish in captivity, a siphon pipe and a bucket will no longer suffice. However in saying that, in the early days of commercial fish breeding and especially surrounding sensitive species such as Discus (symphysodon) the siphon pipe and bucket was still in use and this was the main method used by Carol Friswold, Mack Galbreath and Jack Wattley to mention some who come to mind in the early days.

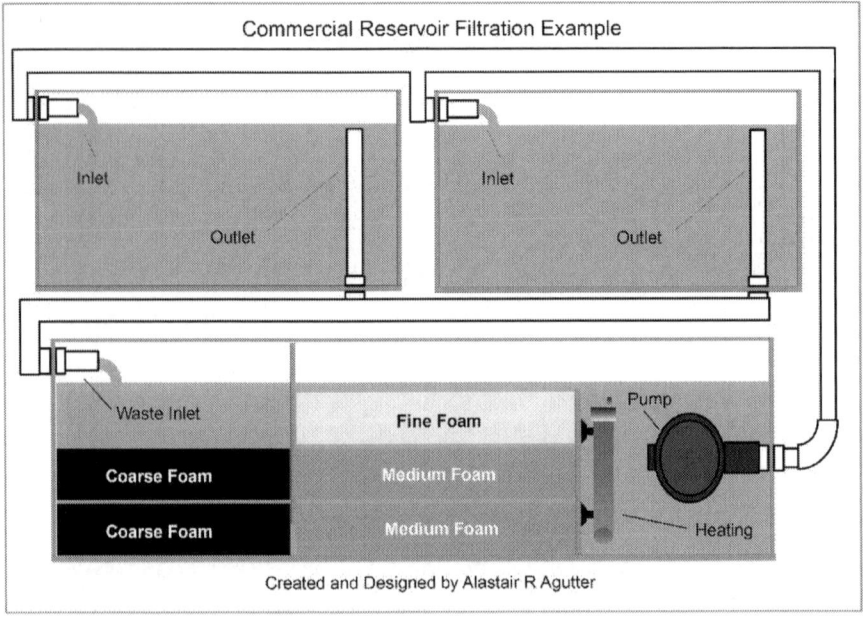

A diagram example of a Commercial Sump and Reservoir Filtration System for the supply of multiple breeding aquariums – Illustration Diagram Created by Alastair R Agutter

What commercial breeders done, was to set up very large reservoir tanks containing thousands of gallons of water and designing a partition system, where they could place foam and other preferred materials to create a biological filtration system in the reservoir.

Then they would heat this reservoir and then run pipes from the reservoir to the head of each aquarium. They would also have holes specially drilled in the aquariums at the bottom to attach pipes, and these were joined up and meandered their way back to the reservoir, where the water from the tanks would then be filtered in the reservoir and re-cycled again by the water being pumped out from the reservoir to the aquariums, again using the feeder, or header pipes. The outlet pipes would not be at floor level in the aquariums. To ensure in the event of failure and for water to always be present in the aquariums, the waste pipe in the aquarium was of a considerable height and as the aquarium filled with the fresh water from the header pipes, the over flow would run off into the outlet waste pipe.

I hope the following diagram provides an idea on how reservoir and sump filtration systems look and work. Here we show just two aquariums as an example and where both aquariums are connected up to the reservoir.

If you have ever been to a large commercial reservoir, you will very often see a tower, almost like a flight tower at an airport. In the centre of such a tower, very often will be found a huge funnel aperture leading down into a hole, where water overflows from the reservoir and is carried to a processing water treatment plant (filters), before the water reaches the domestic home user.

Now this method of water filtration at this stage is sump and reservoir and not trickle filtration. The process and methods of trickle filtration is slightly different to sump and reservoir systems and will be covered next along with some background.

TRICKLE FILTRATION SYSTEMS

Aquarium filtration over the decades has been at the centre of many a discussion in the Aquatic World as mentioned earlier and none more so than with dedicated Aquarists of the Discus (symphysodon) fraternity.

Back in the 1980's for me personally, it was a subject area of great interest and frustration at times, as I battled with the last bastion of tropical fish keeping, and that was to successfully breed in captivity Discus, "The King of the Tropical Fish Aquarium," so we could ensure the species survival.

For at the time in the 1980's, the constant reports of a reckless program of deforestation in South America was without doubt completely out of control and threatening Discus and many other majestic species of the Wild in the Great River Amazon and adjoining Rivers and Tributaries in South America, and so if we could successfully breed these beautiful creatures in captivity, all would not be lost if extinction to the region became a tragic reality, and at the time and still now it is a real threat.

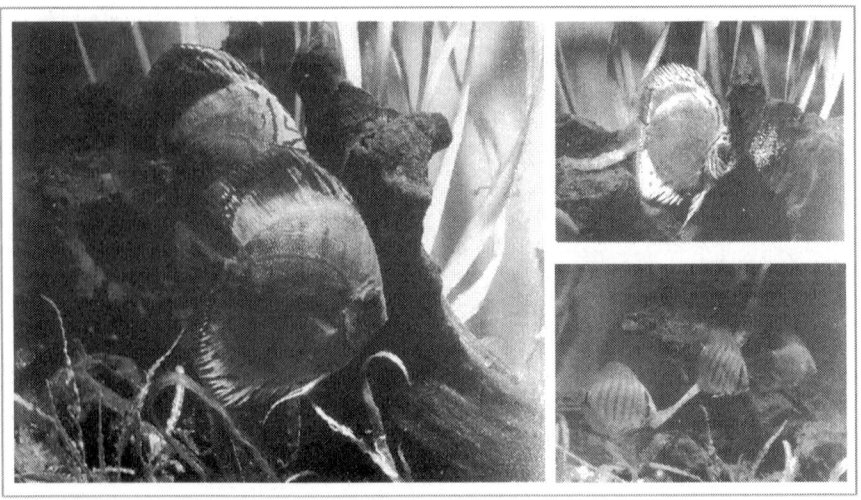

Timeless Moments back in the 1980's with Author's Discus Breeding in a Naturally Planted Aquarium with a newly invented Filtration System. Pic 1/. Parents Pic 2/. Parent Guarding Eggs Pic 3/. 8 week old Juveniles – Photograph by Alastair R Agutter

The above photographs were taken featuring one of my Discus Naturally Planted Aquariums back in the 1980's. In the picture you can see one of my descendant pairs from wild bred species spawning and with fertile eggs. This was achieved at the time by the development of a filtration system I invented after studying the Wild and the water exchange rates.

I managed to establish across the Wild on average in Rivers, Streams, Estuaries and other Natural Waterways, the average exchange rate for water per hour in the wild was 10 times. In old money terms as I say, this meant that the aquarium in the above picture that held 120 gallons of water would have to filter 1200 gallons of water an hour. Or in modern day litre (4.54609) terms, this meant 5,455.30 litres of water was to be filtered every hour.

Now I like to think even as I near my 60's in a couple of years-time, I describe myself as a modern day man and like to think all chaps, especially the guys younger than myself are now familiar with a domestic appliance known as a washing machine and familiar with its cycles and functions.

So the scenario presented to me regarding water exchange in a confined area of a few cubic feet of an aquarium posed a significant problem, unless the tropical fish inhabitants in question were familiar with, and enjoyed the turbulent rough and tumble of washing machine cycles. For to pump so much water through 13 to 22 mm aquarium pipes would equate to hell for any fish inhabitants, let alone the more sedate and serene species such as Discus and Angel Fish.

Around the time of this problem presented to me regarding filtration, a well-respected manufacturer named "Hagen" had developed a device known as a "Powerhead" and I began to see many of these devices attached to under gravel filter uplifts and not to very good effect.

The powerhead itself as a device to transport water in volume was a stroke of genius. But a new form of filtration had to be developed to compliment such a piece of kit.

At the time another great debate surrounded deionized water, a subject I will discuss in more detail in the water conditions section of the book later to dispel the myths surrounding this subject and how it is not practical when engaged in any serious breeding program. In short, deionization is the removal of metal trace elements in the water and it was a big deal years ago as it is today, regarding the belief of successfully breeding certain difficult species of tropical fish.

The following picture below shows a photo (sorry for the quality) of my original drawing back in the 1980's of the "Power Vain Filtration System" that I invented and developed.

The filtration system was designed to be able to deliver a transfer rate of 1200 gallons (5,455.30 litres) of water an hour and was the beginning of a new age in Tropical and Saltwater Marine Fish Keeping, known as "Trickle Filtration" for the dedicated Aquarist and Tropical Fish Hobbyist.

Unlike external sump and reservoir filtration systems that are often level or below the aquarium or a bank of aquariums, dependent upon the operations in question. The trickle filters medium for filtering the water was above the aquarium and where water poured and trickled down over a number of mediums to filter the water and then trickled back into the aquarium, dispersing the water in such a way where it was not turbulent to the fish inhabitants in the aquarium.

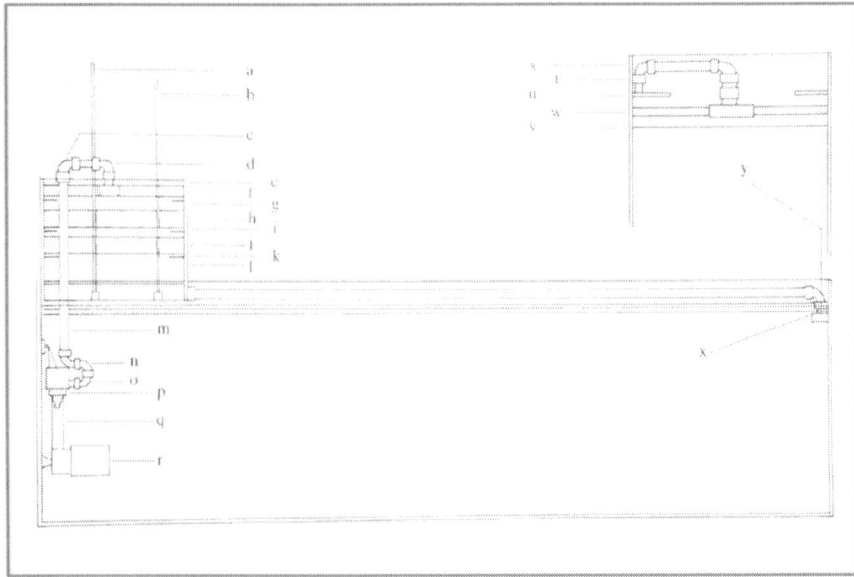

Timeless Moments a Photograph of the Original Drawing of the Power Vain Filtration System back in the 1980's and the birth of Trickle Filters – Photograph by Alastair R Agutter

The diagram above is not very clear, and since developing this trickle filter system back in the 1980's, I have since developed a number of new super trickle filter system designs to help today's aquarist. For I believe if using sterile aquarium conditions, naturally planted aquariums, or any theme of aquarium for that matter. The trickle filtration system is by far the most superior for efficiency and the most technically advanced with the option of introducing a deionization chamber to lower the general hardness of water, regarding metal trace elements and particles if desired.

The following diagrams show a new trickle filter system design that can be hidden and housed to the side of an aquarium. The design also allows you to hide both the pump and heater thermostat in the filtration system chambers. With this design you can also set-up further plant life to further help in the filtration of the aquarium further reducing general hardness of the water.

Below the diagram shows the new trickle filter system and its working features and components. The next illustration shows the system with the cabinet trimmings.

As you can see in the above diagram and illustration how you can house the heater thermostat and the pump in a chamber department of the filter system. This method also helps to ensure the aquarium water is heated thoroughly and therefore preventing any cold pockets of water in the aquarium that can happen.

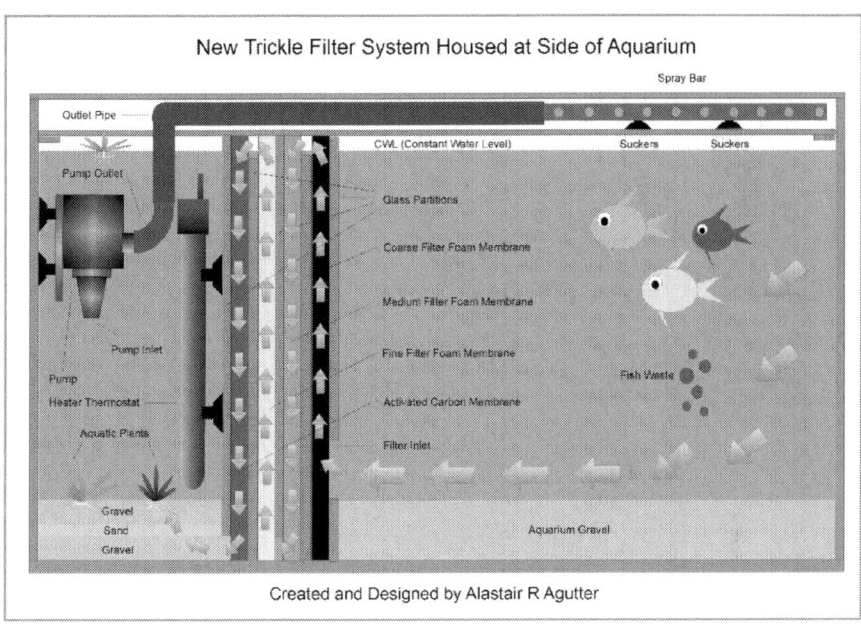

The New Trickle Filter System designed and developed by the Author showing the working parts and components without cover – Illustration Created by Alastair R Agutter

The intake of the filter across the width of the aquarium provides a gentle even intake of water and a gentle flow across the aquarium's substrate surface and therefore provides opportunity in a planted aquarium for aquatic plants to collect essential nitrates and metal trace elements.

The trickle filter outlet delivers a gentle stream of water onto the surface. By having the spray bar above the water's surface, this allows for the generation of oxygen to the aquarium from the water descending from the spray bar, when the spray bar is placed in such a position in the aquarium.

The following diagram provides us with a slight idea of appearance and how the workings of a filtration system can be covered, leaving a clear aquarium area and free of any electrical appliance or pump devices.

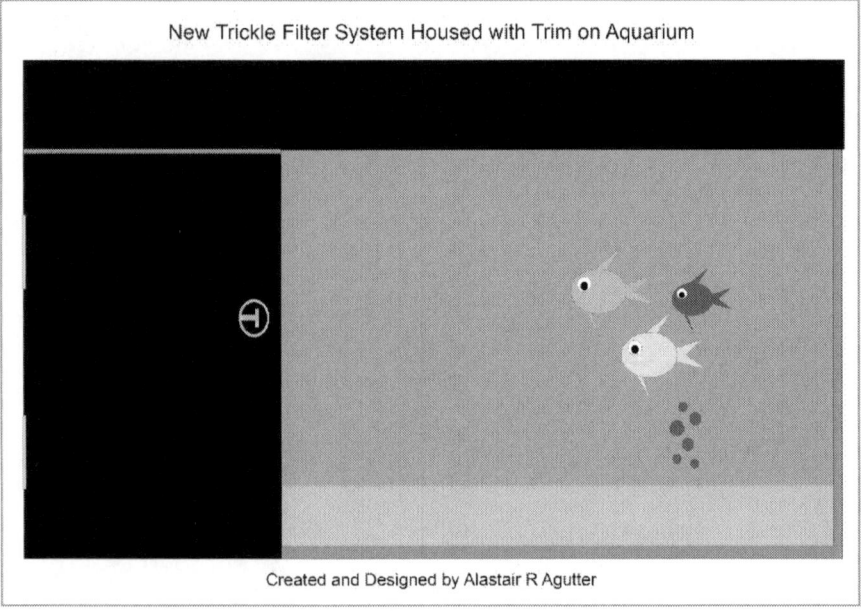

The New Trickle Filter System designed and developed by the Author showing the Trim finish to provide an idea how the Aquarium looks – Illustration Created by Alastair R Agutter

I mentioned earlier the general hardness (DH or GH) of water regarding metal trace elements. Deionization is a process covered more in the next chapter, but it is essentially a method to remove mineral and metal trace elements from the water. This process is achieved with silica and fine membranes and where the water is forced through specially designed canisters. Species such as Discus, Angel, Hatchet, Neon and Cardinal Tetras to mention a few are native to certain regions of South America where there is very little mineral and metal trace elements and in very acid water conditions. So if you are seeking a reduction of the general hardness of your water, with the presence of sand in the substrate of a filter chamber and plants present, this will help to remove mineral and metal trace elements overtime, as water continually passes through the substrate containing the sand (silica), as seen in the detailed diagram of the trickle filtration system. Such a substrate in the trickle filtration system will also help remove unwanted gases and chemical toxins, including methane and carbon dioxide.

The scale-ability of an aquarium, so it appears stunning and pleasing to the eye, can easily be achieved by determining the size of filtration system chamber that needs to be created. To help you here on a personal note, I would consider working in a 1 to 5 or 1 to 6 ratio. So if I wanted to have a long stunning aquarium, say in a lounge, along a wall. I would plum as just one example for an aquarium that was say 7 foot 6 inches in length and make my filtration system 18 inches long. So I would have a clear aquarium view of 6 foot and an 18 inch cabinet to the side.

So there is optimal efficiency for delivering crystal clear water, I would seek an exchange rate of water per hour to be to the power of one. So if I had a 120 gallon aquarium for example approximately 500 litres I would want a pump with a 500 liter per hour capacity. This would deliver a complete filtered exchange of water every hour.

The objective is to have an optimal exchange of filtered water, but with the least current flow, as this can be stressful to most fish, especially more serene species. A too higher flow of water in an aquarium will also inhibit growth of fish, for their energy is being used to swim in the current created, rather than from their eating, growing larger and healthier from the energy intake of food.

This now leads us on nicely onto aquarium water conditions in the book found in the very next chapter.

CHAPTER EIGHT
Aquarium Water Conditions

As we seek to care and look after Marine Life entities, water is without doubt the primary element for sustaining life, and a water quality consistency to ensure a stable marine environment is obviously critical for healthy thriving fish.

Some of the Author's Teenage Discus –You know when water conditions are right as survival mode is replaced with bickering over food and territory – Photograph by Alastair R Agutter

The more we study Wild Life that grace our Earth, the less apparent will be the arrogance of man, as we continue the path of enlightenment (knowledge), to further understand our fellow creatures that have existed for millions of years, and evolved just as much as we, and some far wiser, I might add!

Sometimes I do cringe and despair, when I hear folk through no fault of their own in a tropical fish shop say "I'll have one of them, one of them and two of them" for example. We can all be guilty at some time in the journey of learning in our lives to look at Marine life fish species, just as "fish," but they are all truly magnificent creatures and far more than just fish, for found within every specie is intelligence and a long legacy of evolution since the beginning of time to back this up!

It may be hard to believe, but fish will come to love you, just as you love them, and there will come a day if you study your new family members long enough, you will finally see little signs of them wanting to connect with you. Being able to connect with Wild Life species are priceless moments in ones lives and memories that will last an eternity.

The beginning of all life on Earth became possible with the presence of Carbon Dioxide in our atmosphere measuring 275 parts per million. Sadly, from Corporate Industrialization today (2016), the Carbon Dioxide content in our atmosphere now measures over 400 ppm and rising. As a result of such dramatic changes to our atmosphere, this is having a dangerous impact on all life forms. In fact, we have lost in the past 50 years, nearly one third of plant, animal, bird and insect life species. The impact now to our own health from climate change as human beings, is now becoming more apparent, as we see greater breathing health problems, the rise in Cancers and other Neurological degenerative diseases, such as Parkinson's, Alzheimer's, as a result of air pollution, thus in turn depriving the brain of pollutant free oxygen for cell regeneration.

By considering these factors above, we can see the increasing health problems and implications leading to illness, brought about by our environment. The same is relevant when we consider the water conditions and environment we need to create for our fish and plants, for the greatest threat to fish I have learned over the years regarding diseases and health is the water quality environment.

The danger when setting up any new aquarium by an Aquarist is when there are signs of stress, or health issues to fish. Then very often poor advice is attained from the local tropical fish retail assistant, this then leads to the recommendation of a commercial product or products, resulting in heaps of chemicals being deposited in the aquarium water. This action is very often a certain tragic guarantee of death to the fish inhabitants, as they try to battle with biological changes, chemicals and toxins in the water.

Again I may be accused of being old school, but let's step back and ask ourselves, what did we do before tropical fish keeping commercial chemical products were in existence and used.

Well fortunately being an Aquarist spanning 50 years next year in 2017, I am in a position to tell you what we done in the way of water before the mass introduction of chemicals and quick fixes, all of which worked and still does today.

To be able to determine the type of water quality that we need for our Aquarium is for us to first familiarize ourselves with the "pH" range. The two letters "pH" form a universally recognized symbol standard internationally relating to a table series concerning alkaline to acid adjustments, namely water. The symbol of "PH" derived in the 20th century from Germany, where "P" represented the term "Potenz" or "Power" and the "H" represents "Hydrogen" (H) from the periodic table of symbols and of course H2O being water.

The following diagram I have created, shows the "pH" Table and the Logarithm Scale. The table shows the range from Acid to Alkaline and between these ranges, can be found Neutral, and this means and measures a standard we describe as pure water.

Now with regards to the pH range of water quality today, we are fortunate that many, if not most tropical fish found in retail shops, or from Aquarist members of a society are tank bred.

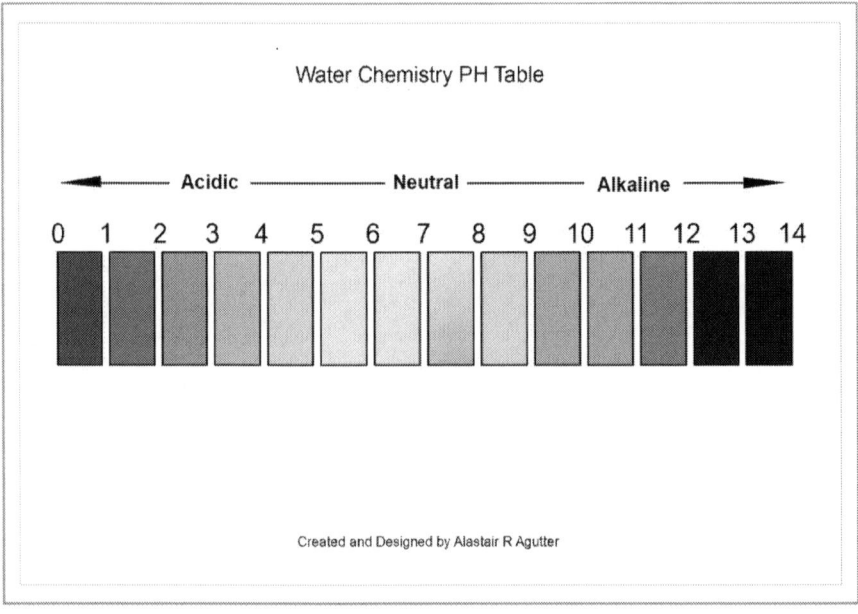

Water Chemistry pH Table Range detailing Acid to Alkaline – Illustration by Alastair R Agutter

Now if we take most advanced Western Societies, their Water Utility Authorities have today sophisticated water purification processes.

Water treatment works today remove in the purification process organic, nonorganic, viruses, algae, bacteria, protozoa, natural organic matter, inorganic suspended matter such as clay and silt to mention just some elements. Others include inorganic coagulants such as Aluminium Sulphate, Irons, Salts and Chlorides etc.

These processes of removing these unwanted elements take place as they go through various water treatment works stages and consist of both sedimentation and flocculation filtration systems and methods. Sometimes sediment processes are assisted by the use of aquatic plants that form part of the purification process, and this is a particularly effective and popular process in the Netherlands, and for the record, the Dutch are one of the World's leading Tropical Fish Breeders.

Certain salts and chemicals are added towards the end of the water treatment process before water reaches the consumer household, or the business user, and this relates to the retaining of fresh water, with the addition of chlorine and also salts, or calcium's, to adjust the pH, to meet a set standard, that normally ranges between 6.8 to 7.6 ph.

If we consider a commercial tropical fish environment, the one most critical element these establishments require is a consistent supply of quality water for breeding tropical fish.

For many years when trying to breed Discus (symphysodon) in captivity the one main element of consideration was finding the perfect water quality. I think on reflection I was not the only dedicated aquarist to try and create a water quality that Wild Discus (symphysodon) were accustomed too in the wild, to achieve the ultimate goal of breeding these majestic species in captivity.

However, I found from the retaining of rain water and carrying out various processes of deionization and chemical alterations to my water, to meet water conditions found in the wild, was virtually an impossible task. For I found I never had enough of this specially prepared water when it came to water changes that were critical to remove any unwanted food and waste that could cause very quickly an ammonia build up in the water leading to toxin poisoning to the Discus (symphysodon).

The Heckel Discus was a particular challenge for the water conditions in the Wild where they most inhabited was very acid and lacking many mineral trace elements resulting in a very low general hardness (DH).

The mistake I was making was trying to make my water replicate the Wild. However, when having a Eureka moment one evening, I realized the key was to acclimatize my Heckel, Axelrodi, Haraldi and Aequifasciata Tefe Discus to my local water. So then I would have an unlimited supply of water on tap to coin a phrase, to be able to carry out as many water changes that were required. To put this problem into perspective, I had aquariums ranging from 25 to 120 gallon aquariums for my Discus program and all requiring water changes on a daily basis averaging between 20 to 50%. So you can imagine the amount of water I required ranging anything from between 2 to 4000 gallons of water a week.

By applying these changes to the program, my Discus fish only took around two weeks to fully adjust to my local tap water and after this change, I was flying as they say!

The more water changes I carried out in the following weeks and months, the more food my Discus fish ate, bringing these beautiful species into full physical health.

The behaviour and body language of the fish also changed. I was receiving a positive greeting from my fish every morning, as I carried out water changes and interrupted by my Discus refusing to move, as I siphoned the aquariums with a clear message form my fish of "we want feeding" by flicking their fins and moving to the front and top of the aquarium.

Today since breeding wild Discus in captivity some 25 plus years ago, my Discus and other tropical fish family members still behave the same way and even eat out of my hands, as seen in the following photographs.

So one of the very key secrets to keeping healthy, thriving tropical fish is to acclimatize your new inhabitants, to your local tap water supply ideally!

So how did we do things years ago regarding water, before the days of modern day commercial chemicals, for adjusting water and the combating of fish diseases?

Aquarium water in year's gone bye was created very often by using rainwater from strategically placed water butts around the home collecting natural rainwater from garage and greenhouse roofs. This natural rainwater was then topped up if required for the aquarium by using tap water.

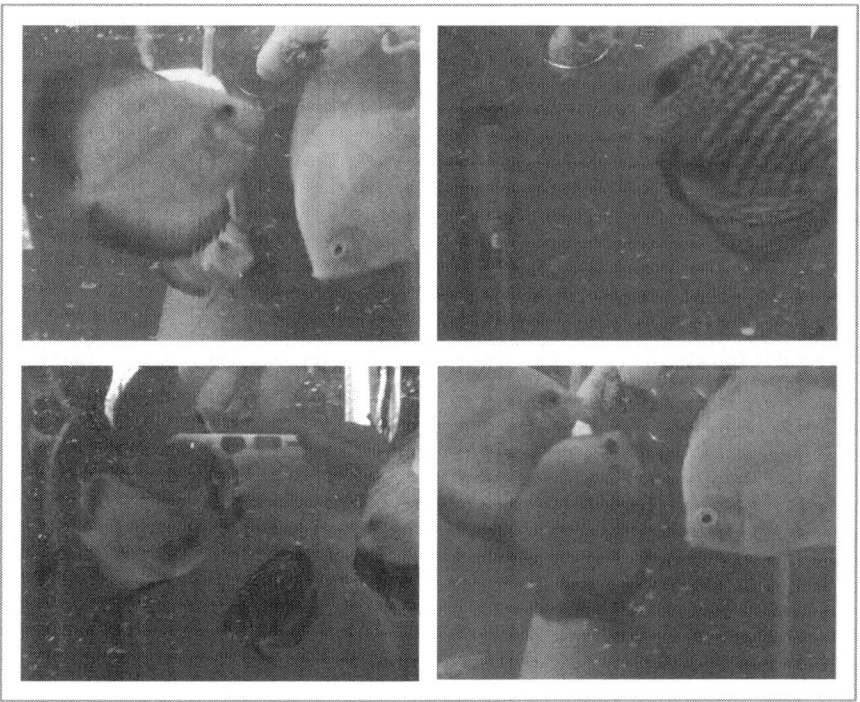

Author feeding Healthy Juvenile and Adult Discus by Hand and an example of the right Water Conditions, Love and Care of Healthy, Thriving Fishes – Photograph by Alastair R Agutter

Tap water in year's gone bye was far different than it is today. Water purification processes from local water utilities in earlier times were not so rigorous, as less potential pollutants existed in water. Tap water collection in those times to service consumer households and businesses came very often from a Country's Natural Water Table, Streams, Rivers and Natural Springs.

Rainwater collected from water butts year's gone bye, was also different and free of many climate change atmospheric pollutants that find their way into our rainwater today, such as Sulphur (SO_2) and Nitrogen Dioxides (NO_2) from vehicles and fossils fuels namely oil, diesel and petrol (gasoline).

Rainwater year's gone bye on average provided a water pH reading of between 6.7 to 7.0 ph. And the General Hardness (DH) of rainwater collected in water butts was between 5.0 to 8.0 DH.

Regarding tap water in year's gone bye, very often water treatment in any form consisted of the addition of small amounts of copper sulphates and salts. The

Calcium salts added as a form of water treatment sterilization to water would rise the pH level only slightly and the copper sulphate added to the tap water in small amounts, is very much a frequent mineral and chemical found in tropical fish foods and medicines, and quiet frequently found in the Wild on rock formations, where mineral deposits are present from erosion and very often Iron (Fe) or Copper (Cu).

Even though this water was used year's gone bye, there is still a period for establishing a natural biological culture in the water and this process begins with the breakdown of matter such as fish waste and aquatic plant vegetation debris such as dead leaves etc. However, the natural rainwater stored in water butts, did have the unquestionable presence of life in existence and very often in the form of mosquito larvae and so this ensured the water being placed in the aquarium from a water butt for example, already had an active natural bacterial culture in existence. In such a scenario, it was just a question of this bacteria culture establishing itself after several days in the aquarium, after the water butt rainwater had been added to the fish tank and more importantly, the bacteria culture finding its way to the filtration system devised or used.

Now, today's tap water goes through as mentioned earlier a far more rigorous process of purification. Now at this point, if you are eating a sandwich, tea, breakfast or dinner, I suggest you put it down and decide to eat later. A great deal of water used today for households and business establishments we know as tap water, has been recycled, including sewage waste.

Utility Tap Water today goes through a number of very sophisticated processes, before this water can become tap drinking water again. Whereas, in year's gone bye, sewage waste water was very often and sadly transported through Victorian drainage systems, that eventually found their way to coastal regions and expelled into Estuaries and large River systems.

Still today, if you visit your local seaside resort, you could very easily see these structures when the tide ebbs out. They look like little piers, or walkways going out into the mud, known as sewer outfalls.

Today, in our modern society, we use every form of water resource possible. Water treatment processes today, include a great many more chemicals and advanced sterilizers, such as UV (Ultra Violet). These water treatment processes, completely remove any life form or organism from the water, and this is further ensured by the use and presence of chlorine in our water.

Water Hardness DH Table

PPM CaCo3	DH	Conditioning
20 40 60	1.12 2.25 3.37	Soft
80 100	4.49 5.61	Moderately Soft
140 180	7.87 10.11	Ideal
220 260	12.36 14.61	Hard
300	16.85	Very Hard

Created and Designed by Alastair R Agutter

Diagram showing the Water General Hardness (DH) Table – Illustration by Alastair R Agutter

So unlike years ago with regards to tap water, when many natural elements and organisms were still present in our drinking water, today's tap water is mostly free of any life forms, including bacterial cultures that help to breakdown matter.

So today, when starting a new aquarium system from tap water, we have to create our very own bacterial biological culture from scratch, unlike in the past, when we could use rainwater as an accelerator to get things moving faster.

As then in year's gone bye and today, the reasons why fish become ill when setting up a new aquarium, is caused from stress as mentioned earlier, and this is as a result of the aquarium water going through a process of change, as the aquarium establishes a natural biological bacteria culture of water in the fish tank. Now, you may read articles or material in books, that state it takes on average some 3 to 6 months to establish aquarium water in a fish tank, before you can introduce tropical fish inhabitants, but alas this is not true or accurate.

The actual average period of time for establishing a safe biological culture in an aquarium is in fact 28 days. In this period of 28 days, there are significant changes to the water in the aquarium regarding the establishment of a biologically active aquarium water environment.

One thing I have learnt over the years regarding the biological bacterial processes in an aquarium and in the wild, is that this subject is not as straight forward as believed, with regards to whether a biological bacterial culture exists, or doesn't.

Now to help explain the establishment of a biological bacterial process in the aquarium, you will see the following table below, and a table that you would never have seen before in any aquatic publication, or book, as it has been created and developed by yours sincerely, to help understand the very many varying changes regarding biological bacterial cultures.

Biological Bacteria Volume Mass Diagram			
Fish Units	**Temperature**	**BBVM's**	**Filter Flow Rate**
5	78	40 BBVM	10 Gallons
5	84	55 BBVM	10 Gallons
10	78	80 BBVM	15 Gallons
10	84	110 BBVM	15 Gallons
15	78	120 BBVM	20 Gallons
15	84	165 BBVM	20 Gallons
20	78	160 BBVM	25 Gallons
20	84	220 BBVM	25 Gallons
Per Unit	Fahrenheit	Per Million	Gallons
Created and Designed by Alastair R Agutter			

Diagram showing Biological Bacteria Volume Mass Table – Illustration by Alastair R Agutter

Bacterial cultures populate at different rates per hour. The diagram above can be seen where an aquarium temperature at 78 degrees Fahrenheit will populate biological bacteria at a rate of 8 million per hour for every unit of fish present. At a temperature of 84 degrees Fahrenheit, the bacterial culture population rate increases to 11 million per hour for every unit of fish present in an aquarium.

Therefore with the presence of 5 tropical fish in an aquarium and at a temperature of 78 degrees Fahrenheit, the population rate of bacteria per hour is 40 million BBVM's.

The biological bacteria populates based on the number of fish species and their waste mostly, and so if there is a significant reduction of fish in the aquarium at any one time, there needs to be adjustments to counteract any negatives and the most commonly known problem is a bacterial explosion.

When setting up an aquarium for the first time, the number and type of new fish species inhabitants needs to be seriously considered. The first 28 days of establishing an aquarium as mentioned earlier is critical and so the addition of fish needs to be gradual and in small numbers. The new inhabitants also need to be of certain species types that are resilient to such environments.

So what are we confronted with when setting up a new aquarium and how does a bacterial biological process work in an aquarium?

To understand how we arrive at the biological processes to break down matter in an aquarium is to first look at the Nitrogen Cycle with regards to the protagonists and players surrounding this subject. The common three elements deriving from the presence of fish waste, un-eaten food, aquatic plant degradation and decomposing organic matter that create toxins are Ammonia, Nitrite and Nitrate.

Ammonia in an aquarium is highly toxic and can lead to the killing of tropical fish species. Biological bacterial processes oxidize this ammonia into a slightly less harmful toxin known as Nitrites. The next process in the Nitrogen Cycle is when Nitrites are then oxidized, and formed into the much less toxin known as Nitrates. In a Naturally Planted Aquarium these Nitrates are then picked up and collected by Aquatic Plants as a food fertilizer and then lastly, the aquatic plants digest these chemicals, converting them to sugars (food) and then the waste by-product by the plant is then converted to oxygen and released into the aquarium.

Aquariums as we know are confined areas where we keep our new family inhabitants. Our tropical fish then from the processes of eating create waste (excreta), generating toxins that are then broken down from the bacteria cycle as discussed. A biological bacteria process is not only isolated to a filtration system, in fact this bacteria process is found throughout the aquarium, but a filtration system provides an environment to produce a larger bacteria culture by the set-up formed with reference to the medium material (foam) provided and present.

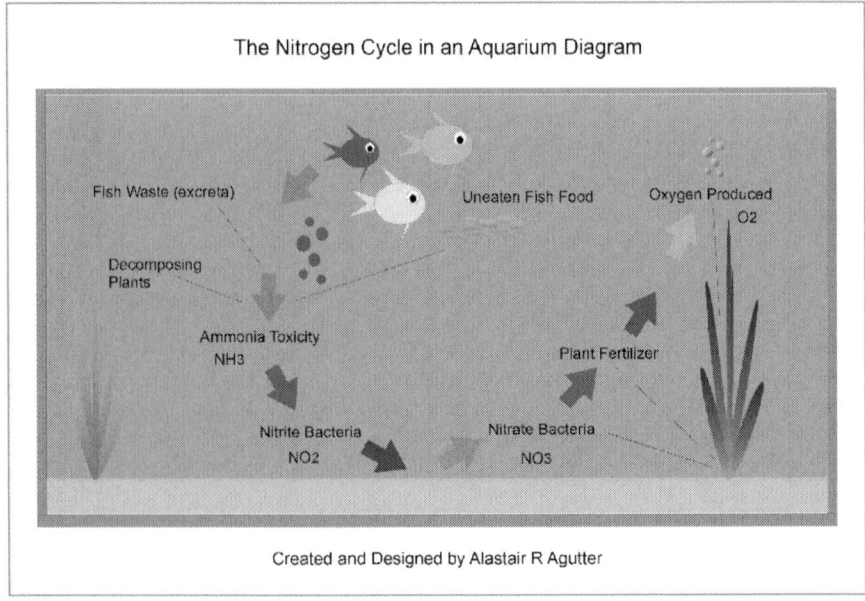

Diagram showing The Nitrogen Cycle in an Aquarium – Illustration by Alastair R Agutter

Even when an aquariums biological bacterial filtration system is working in a confined area, regular water changes is the secret and key to healthy thriving tropical fish. Regular water changes also stimulates existing water, adding greater amounts of oxygen into the aquarium and the small amounts of chlorine from the tap water, serves as an antiseptic to ensure your fish remain free of basic fundamental diseases.

Regular water changes will be discussed in more detail in the chapter section of aquarium maintenance and care. So it is now time to give advice on the best practices, regarding the setting up of the aquarium with new water.

From the discussions thus far in this section of the book, I hope you are in concert with commercial breeders and me, with regards to using your local tap water for an unlimited supply.

Next we then have to determine the pH of your local tap water. This can be easily achieved by acquiring online, or from your local tropical fish retailer a pH test kit. This will allow you to run pH tests on your tap water to determine the water's PH and the instructions provided with these products are very straight forward.

Two of the most popular PH Test Kits to buy are; the Litmus type PH Test Kits, or the Digital Testers as seen in the photograph above and now these days such digital testers are at an affordable price for all aquarists.

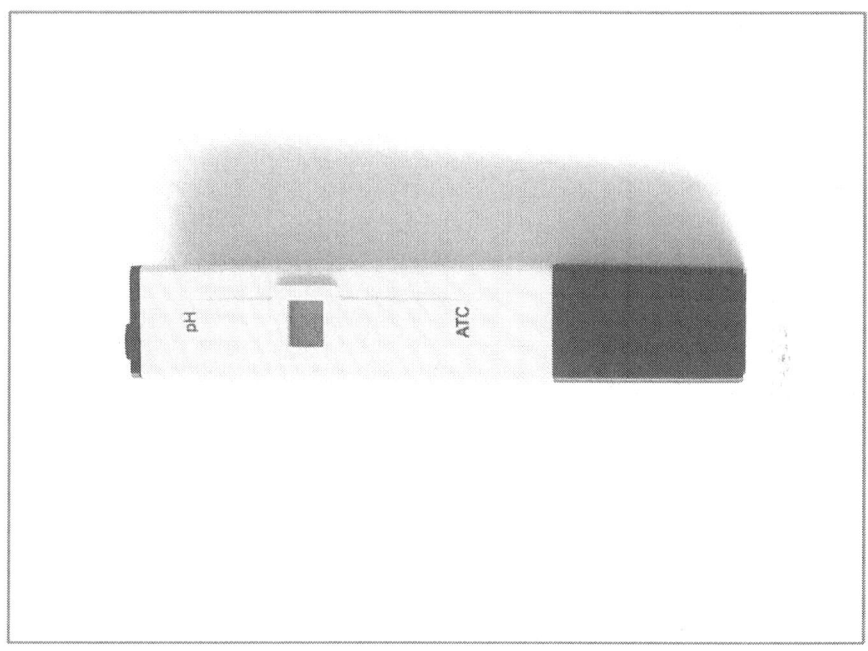

A Well-Priced Digital PH Tester for Aquarists – Photograph by Alastair R Agutter

So what range are we ideally looking for regarding your local tap water?

The PH range that I call the "Goldey-Locks Range" is when the pH is between 6.0 to 8.0 ph. This range is described in the industry as neutral and the safe zone.

My own local tap water pH range is normally between 7.4 to 7.6 PH, and this water is enjoyed by all my tropical fish family members, including my adult pairs who are renowned for being difficult to breed in captivity, these being my Angel and Discus Fish who all regularly spawn.

The acclimatization of your new tropical fish to these water conditions is best achieved when endeavouring to acquire your new tropical fish inhabitants locally, for there is every chance the same water from the same water utility is being used for your local tropical fish retail shop or garden pet centre.

Before we go through the procedures and process for the 28 day cycle to establish aquarium water in your fish tank, if your local PH tests produce results for your tap water where they do not meet the range mentioned above of 6.0 to 8.0, which is highly unlikely, that we call the safe zone. Do not worry, as we can make adjustments naturally to the water hardness or acidity, if the biological filtration systems planned to be used are canister, trickle, sump or reservoir.

It will only be on extremely rare occasions that the water PH range is outside of 6.0 to 8.0 ph. If however that is the case, to raise the PH level of your aquarium water is too soft acid, you can place in with your filter medium granules of chalk rock. If the water by chance is too hard, then you can add to your filter medium aquarium peat that will bring down the hardness of the water as the filter system continues to recycle the water.

Today from technology there are computerized aquarium systems that use gases and chemicals to make these adjustments to PH, DH and even Biological Toxicity. But as I have warned earlier, the secret to being a good tropical fish hobbyist is risk aversion and routine consistency.

All dedicated aquarists are aware and know what is going on with regards to their aquarium(s) in relation to water chemistry, feeding and occasional disease issues. Part of the enjoyment in tropical fish keeping, is to experience the grass root aspects of the pastime. Nothing gives me personally, greater pleasure and long standing fond memories of the aquarist meets at a local clubs, where ideas were exchanged and shared.

The reason I and many other long standing aquarists are anti-chemicals is for good reason, and I will explain why!

Certain chemicals especially sulphates, can leave long lasting problems to your tropical fish. Very often tropical fish when young and treated for fundamental diseases, caused from poor fish husbandry in tropical fish establishments where chemicals are used, can leave young tropical fish with internal organ issues throughout the rest of their lives where there has been damage done to hearts, kidneys and livers.

One particular very important condition, from the use of chemicals, is where the sexual reproduction organs have been permanently damaged and so then the tropical fish species in question are rendered sterile and unable to reproduce, as a result of chemical treatments in earlier months and years.

As mentioned earlier in the book and repeated again here, most fish diseases are brought about by stress and this relates to water quality and conditions (poor fish husbandry). In the disease section of the book will be found proven cures without the use of commercial chemicals to many of the most common fish diseases.

Tropical fish can be very resilient at times and this comes down to the mental frame of mind of the species in question, a subject area I will discuss later in the book regarding fish behaviour. But another one of the biggest causes of death to fish and related to stress, even losing the will to live!

So from the outset water quality is paramount and we need to ensure we have a safe and reliable supply of water in abundance for good fish husbandry and in the safe zone regarding the PH.

Now earlier in this chapter, there is a diagram that I created regarding the General Hardness Water Table and this relates to coagulants, minerals and toxins in the water.

For nearly five decades, I have obviously studied water quality to the end degree and encompassed within this topic, the General Hardness of water. Certain tropical fish species, specific to certain regions of the World have what is best described as unique measurements of PH and DH (General Hardness). Some tributaries and rivers branching off of the Great River Amazon, produce pockets of water with very low Acid PH levels and also very Low General Hardness water measurements.

However, due to the very vastness of the Great River Amazon, these same tropical fish species found in these extreme conditions of low Acidic PH levels and Low General Hardness water conditions can also be found in many other parts of the Great River Amazon and adjoining Rivers. From such findings, this demonstrates the adaptability of the same said tropical fish species. General Hardness can appear to be relevant at times regarding certain species of tropical fish when reproducing. It is believed by the creation of a lower general hardness of water, this will help and aid in the retaining of fish eggs when laid, reducing the risk of fungus deterioration. However, from the facts presented above regarding the same tropical fish species found in different regions and with very extreme and contrasting water quality variations regarding PH and DH (general hardness). It is clear that these same fish species have been able to produce off-spring successfully and therefore demonstrates acclimatization adaptability.

All creatures including ourselves require a wide and varied range of minerals for survival. Some of the most common being Iron, Potassium and Zinc for example. In fact Iron is found in significant quantities to many parts of the Great River Amazon, in some regions the Iron mineral presence is so significant, that these regions substrate and silt areas are in fact of a rich brown and red colouration.

Speaking from personal experience regarding difficult species to breed in captivity such as Discus, Angel and Tetra Fish I have been blessed to experience great success in breeding such species with water retaining a considerable general hardness.

I have often believed over the years based on experience, that some of the material I have read through the decades, can very often appear to be a red herring with reference to acquiring sound advice on the topic area of successfully breeding numerous species of tropical fish in captivity, in relation to the general hardness of the water.

The reason why I say that I believe sometimes reading material of this subject can sometimes seem to be a red herring regarding the general hardness of water. This is because those who seem to write about the subject to an almost obsessive extent, tend to set a president importance for general hardness as a topic before water, food and routine, that I have found to be the key ingredients for successfully breeding tropical fish species in captivity.

General Hardness regarding mineral content in water is of far less concern and importance compared to subject area of toxicity in water, that is of primary concern and importance, covered earlier in this chapter and the filtration chapter.

So this leads me onto the frequent subject of Deionization surrounding the General Hardness (DH) of water.

Deionized water in effect is battery water!

The process for creating deionized water is by using a series of tubes filled with silica and very fine membranes. The silicone-gel crystals in effect collect and trap the mineral atoms and particles. The tap water or rainwater is passed very slowly through these cylinders and at the end of this process the deionized water descends into a receptacle such as a bucket, or barrel, that is often made from a nylon material.

This process regarding the deionization of water can work for a short period of time. However, from moisture in such systems can give rise to bacterial cultures that will interact and feed on the collected mineral and particle atoms.

To produce enough deionized water for any breeding program even for a small operation by an individual aquarist is a virtual impossibility. Let me explain!

Taking just one of my Discus breeding Aquariums of 27 gallons as just one example, I carry out on a daily basis, a water change of at least 5 to 10 gallons of water. If we take the most conservative number of 5 gallons regarding the above numbers, this means in the course of just one week, I replace over 35 gallons of water in just this one breeding aquarium. If I have ten breeding aquariums running excluding rearing tanks for fry, this equates to 350 gallons (1,589 Litres approx.) of water every week.

So as you can see from the facts presented above, even as an Amateur breeder, let alone a Commercial breeder of tropical fish, it is clear that the general hardness of water is not a critical consideration.

However, the pH with regards to the scale of acidity through to alkalinity does present a serious consideration. A far too harder water, as just one example surrounding the PH of water, can affect the skin tissue of certain fish species, as can a water quality that is acidic if particular species are sensitive. Some evolved species such as Discus, produce milt on the body of their skin, this milt is full of antibodies for the young fry to feed upon when born and having the wrong PH quality of water in these circumstances can be fatal.

PH levels in water, also determines the biological bacterial culture process. We have already mentioned the notable changes in bacteria cultures regarding varied water temperatures. A good example regarding hardness and acidity, is where a lower PH that is acid, will cause a biological bacterial process to be slower to populate, as opposed to if the water quality has a PH in the neutral or safe zone where biological bacterial culture populations will be higher and faster.

What is very rarely discussed in any depth surrounding this subject of water quality related to PH and DH (degrees of hardness) is the topic area of electromagnetic sensors, waves and gravity. Most fish have highly evolved sense organs. Also tropical fish species we have come to love and know are defined as daylight fish species and have colour vision that is just as good humans. Tropical fish also have chemoreceptors for their highly tuned senses of sight, taste and smell. Whilst fish do have ears, their hearing is more determined by vibration and water condition changes (currents) in the environment that are a tuned to the lateral line. Therefore the presence of minerals and trace elements in water with reference to DH (degrees of hardness) and PH are both linked to fish sensors, especially electromagnetic sensors. All such sensors, be it taste, hearing, smell or sight, are all related to energy frequencies (hertz) and water being a conductor of energy, means these receptors in fish are highly sensitive and evolved. So you can see even from this brief discussion, a fish should no longer be looked upon as just a fish!

All creatures including ourselves are influenced by electromagnetic energies. As a simple example being, is where many folk suffer from headaches before a storm. This is caused when there is more moisture in the atmosphere attracting more electromagnetic energy and resulting in a heavier air pressure triggering our sensors.

In fish these electroreceptors are highly tuned and can detect electric fields and currents, some species many miles away. It is one of the reasons why I recommend deploying heater devices, such as heater thermostats if possible, ideally in the filtration system, so they are not directly in contact with the tropical fish.

The presence of excess metal in water can also cause fish to react, where they will experience electro-charges from the water environment and can sometimes become disorientated in relation to a fishes navigation that is achieved by object recognition and sight, coupled to the inner ear, where the sensors are able to map out and subconsciously store the data, so they are able to negotiate every plant and object in an aquarium.

So the idea that a Goldfish species only has memory recognition of just 6 seconds is a myth, for Gold fish are evolved species and a member of the tooth carp family.

In the chapter of fish behaviour, heating and lighting, we will discuss these areas in greater detail, as all living creatures generate electromagnetic fields and this is worth mentioning now, as these energies do bear relevance when we discuss water quality in the form of PH and DH (degrees of hardness or general hardness) particularly.

Again the above gives us good reason why we need to consider risk aversion in tropical fish keeping. For all technologies we introduce into an environment, especially computerized and electrical has consequence. The cardinal rule and covenant surrounding Natural Law in relation to the two key subject areas for all that exists, these being Natural Branching and Quantum Mechanics, is to "Evolve and Refine," and certainly not to over complicate, a negative habit that the human race continues to pursue and therefore trying to defy this universal law and framework throughout the Cosmos.

THE 28 DAY WATER CONDITIONING CYCLE

This is the 28 day water conditioning cycle, using localized tap water to create a thriving biologically active aquarium environment for tropical fish inhabitants and accompanied with diagrams.

Now some may say you do not need to do this and chemicals are available to buy for this procedure. But as I have stated before, there is consequence from poor advice and this method is proven and works if aquarists adhere to the instructions set out.

DAY ONE

First test the PH of your tap water, to ensure the water is in the safe zone. Ensure your aquarium is safely located in the correct position, your filter system and heating devices are correctly set-up. The desired substrate is placed in the aquarium ready to receive local tap water. Use a small dish and gently place it on the substrate surface, so the water from your hose can gently descend down onto the saucer, or dish's surface area, so the water is not disturbing the substrate. Make sure the other end of your hose is connected to both the hot and cold taps by using a splitter and so the water filling up the aquarium is regulated, to ensure the water to the touch is lukewarm.

At this time of the process of filling up your aquarium with water, no electrical appliance should be switched on, neither the heater thermostat(s) or the aquarium filter(s) or pumps.

As a word of caution and for health and safety reasons, please ensure any **electrical plug** or connection surrounding electricity is fitted with **"3 amp fuses"** only.

Continue to ensure the water filling up the aquarium is lukewarm and also ensure the hose pipe is clipped, or secured safely, so the hose does not fall down or out of the aquarium onto your floor.

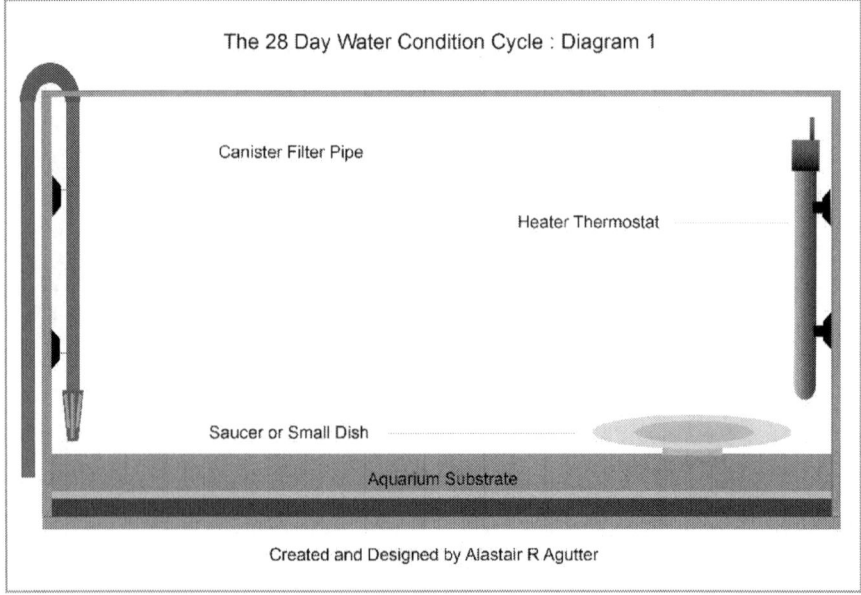

Day One: Aquarium Safely Placed in Position to fill with Tap Water and no electrical appliances connected at this stage and all plugs fitted with 3 Amp Fuses – Diagram by Alastair R Agutter

Continue to fill the aquarium up to around ¾ full as seen in the next diagram to allow for the easy management of placing and positioning your plants and ornament objects into the aquarium.

On heavy objects such as rocks, or slate for example, it is best to place these items in the aquarium before you fill the fish tank with water, in the event of dropping such heavy items that could cause the aquarium base to break.

Once the aquarium is ¾ filled with water as in the diagram below, then you can begin to plant out your aquarium with aquatic plants and ornaments.

By filling the aquarium with water only ¾ full, this allows for object water displacement and is easier to manage if you decide to make changes as you go, regarding the look of the underwater scene being created.

Once your aquatic plants and ornaments have been successfully placed in the aquarium and you are happy with the underwater scene created.

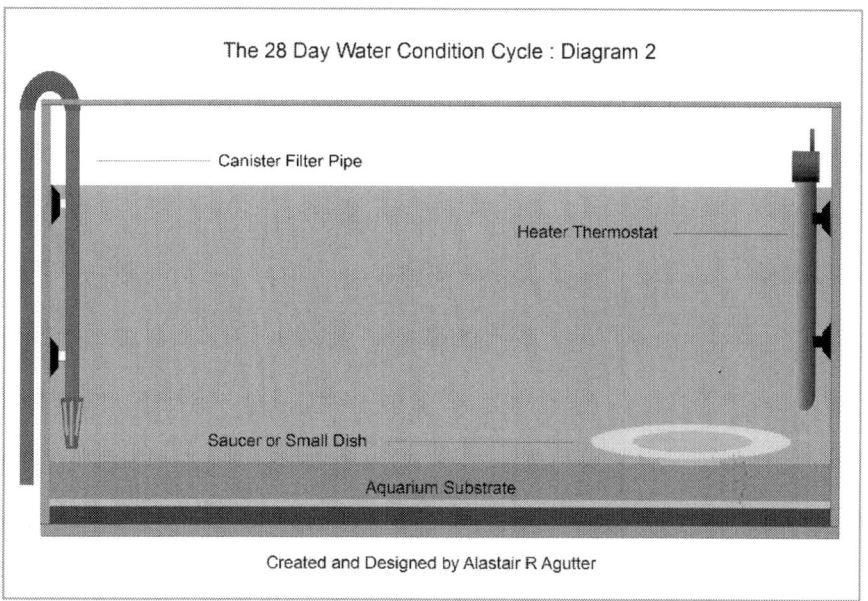

Day One: Aquarium is filled to ¾ full of water and ready to be planted out with aquatic plants and the addition of ornaments and bogwoods for example – Diagram by Alastair R Agutter

Then you can switch on your filter(s), pump(s) and heater thermostat(s). The heater thermostat(s) would have already been set regarding the desired temperature, before placing them in the aquarium and switching on. This is covered in more detail in the heater thermostat chapter of the book and advice on the most suitable devices for your needs.

Designer aquariums ready-made will come fitted with sliding glass condensation trays to keep condensation from making contact with any lighting electricals and to prevent evaporation. If your aquarium does not have condensation trays, they can be easily obtained for a few pounds or dollars from your local tropical fish retailer or garden pet centre.

Next attach and fit the lid of your aquarium housing your lighting and then switch on, making absolutely sure there are no electrical cables or wires exposed that could make contact with the aquarium water. Always ensure any electrical appliances for the aquarium are correctly installed and use cable ties for any tidying up of loose wires and cables.

Any chlorine in the water will be removed as the water descends down onto the dish or plate when filling the aquarium and also from the switching on of the aquarium filtration system. Any small amounts of chlorine remaining in the aquarium water at this time, is safe to fish and plant life working as an antiseptic.

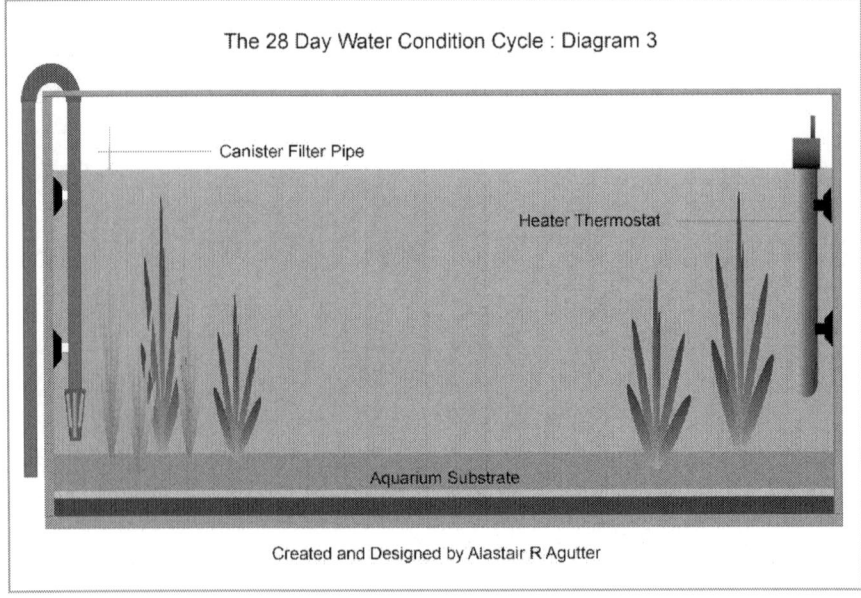

Day One: Diagram of the Aquarium being planted out with aquatic plants and ornaments such as bogwoods for example before any electricity is switched on – Diagram by Alastair R Agutter

Never **"switch-off"** your aquarium filtration system, any temporary halt in filtration can have a significant and negative effect, causing the water to cloud and toxins to build up namely Ammonia. Always leave the filter on and running.

Lighting will be covered in greater detail in the lighting chapter, but the rule of thumb for healthy thriving aquatic plants, is to ensure sunlight/aquarium lighting to be at least 10 to 12 hours a day.

Never **"switch-off"** your heater thermostat(s) only at times of aquarium maintenance to prevent any form of electrocution in the event of a device breaking or failing.

Once all your plants and ornaments are in place, you can then top up the aquarium with the remaining tap water to the desired level.

DAY TWO

After the first 24 hours, carry out a water change of 20% in the aquarium. This can be achieved, by using a bucket and siphon pipe. In the following set of photographs, it shows the siphon pipe I have made, which consists of a piece of garden hose, attached to a piece of plastic plumbing pipe, both of which can be obtained from your local DIY, or Builder Centre Store. I also use a builder's bucket that is very sturdy and holds on average around 5 gallons of water.

When I am siphoning water from any of my aquariums, I use a stall near the aquarium to place the bucket upon, but ensuring that the bucket's height is below the aquarium. This enables me to get a good gravitational draw down of the water, once I have sucked on the pipe initially and began the siphon process.

The two following photographs show the bucket and siphon pipe I use on the stall, also the siphon pipe in one of my Discus rearing aquariums. The fish are not troubled by the siphon pipe, in fact when cleaning an aquarium, I find these youngsters following me around with the pipe, as small amounts of un-eaten food swirls up in the aquarium water.

Pictures showing Author's Bucket and Siphon Pipe – Photographs by Alastair R Agutter

As seen in the photographs above, I use a piece of white pipe connected to the hose, as it gives me rigidity with the siphon pipe. This enables me to be more accurate when removing any fish feces and uneaten food or debris in an aquarium.

This process is more paramount when maintaining sterile aquariums that have no substrate. In a naturally planted aquarium, most of this waste is converted into plant fertilizer as mentioned earlier in the book's chapter on plants and so the removal of such waste is not so important. However, the regular water changes always are.

The diagram below shows day two where we have carried out a water change of 20% and replaced this water with fresh tap water again, that has been mixed to a lukewarm temperature as we have done before.

This is a time to just check and make sure that all filtration, heating and lighting systems are working properly.

This is also a time to ensure the aquarium's water is at the desired temperature for the aquarium theme and fish you have chosen.

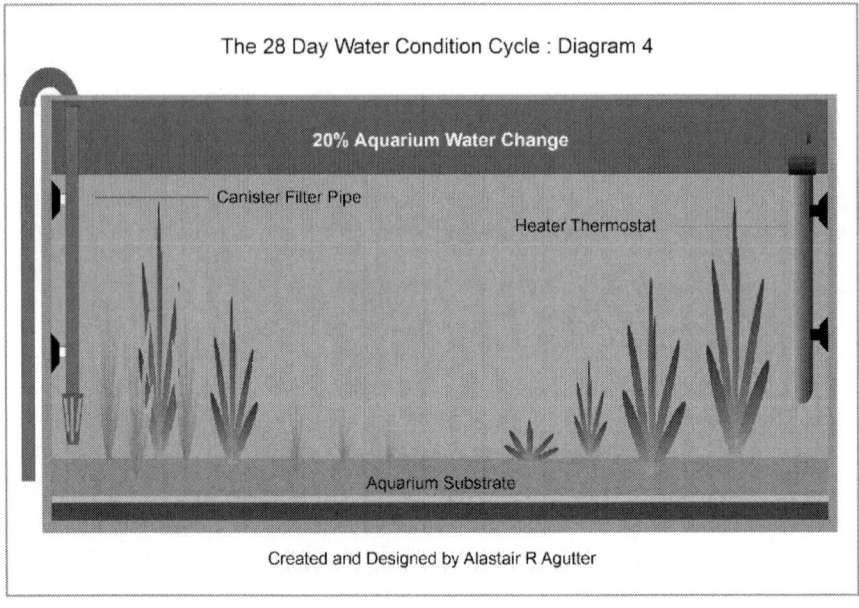

Day Two: Diagram showing a 20 percent water change in the Aquarium using tap water as before and a time to check equipment – Diagram by Alastair R Agutter

Now at this stage most Aquarists decide to acquire a Thermometer, so they can regularly read and check on the aquarium water temperature and this is very important and a commendable idea.

Today, we are again very much spoilt for choice regarding the many varying designs of thermometers on the market, but they are all I might add very well priced.

Personally speaking, I use two types of thermometers and here's why. As age continues to catch up on me, my eyesight today is not as good as it was in years gone-bye and so for a quick glance at my aquariums to ensure all is well and Aquarium temperatures are safe, I use the sticky type thermometers, and for a more accurate reading, I use the traditional mercury filled glass thermometers, supported with an aquarium sucker as seen in the photographs below.

Two very Popular Stick-on and Glass Thermometers, so Aquarists are able to read and check on the Aquarium's water temperature – Photographs by Alastair R Agutter

It is worth remembering however, that the stick-on type thermometers are not as accurate as traditional mercury filled glass thermometers. If the atmosphere outside of the aquarium in a family room for example is normally cold, this will be reflected in the temperature reading seen on the sticky type thermometer, counteracting to a degree the actual temperature in the aquarium. Another incident is if the aquarium glass is 10mm or thicker, again the aquarium temperature reading will not be as accurate.

Other thermometers available today are digital devices that can be suction clamped to the aquarium glass providing a visual digital reading of the temperature.

DAY THREE

On day three carry out another 20 percent water change making sure the water being replaced back into the aquarium is lukewarm to assist in the stability of the fish tanks temperature and to prevent the heater thermostat device(s) having to work unnecessarily hard if the water is too cold.

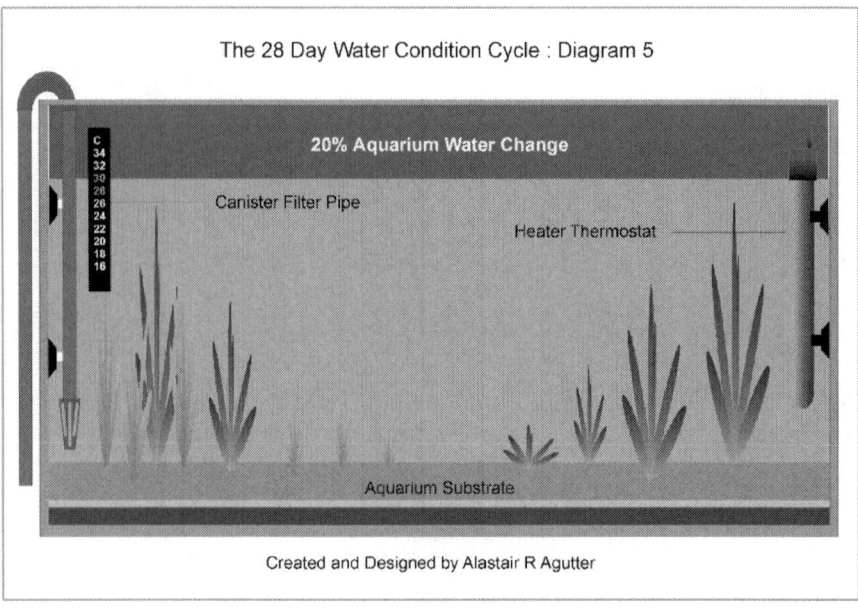

Day Three: Another 20 percent Water change and replaced with fresh lukewarm tap water again. Check all devices again to ensure all are functioning properly – Diagram by Alastair R Agutter

Again carryout a route check on devices to make sure all is working well and examine the clarity of your water. At this stage any clouding of the water over the past 24 to 48 hours should have gone.

Now we need to start establishing a biological bacterial culture in the aquarium and filtration system. This can only really be achieved with the introduction of a small number of tropical fish.

The number of small tropical fish I would introduce initially would be around 3 if I were to set up a naturally planted community aquarium. These would be 1 male and 2 female guppies, as these fish are vigorous eaters and very resilient to a wide range of temperatures and conditions. Guppies will also be compatible with other tropical fish in a community aquarium.

Another species you could consider are White Cloud Mountain Minnows or members of the Danio family, such as Zebra or Pearl Danios.

When obtaining your tropical fish, try to purchase these locally, as the water supply will invariably be the same as your own. Check to see and make sure the tropical fish are active in the retailer's aquarium with fins fanned and splayed out when swimming and when turning. Check and make sure the fish's eyes are clear and not cloudy.

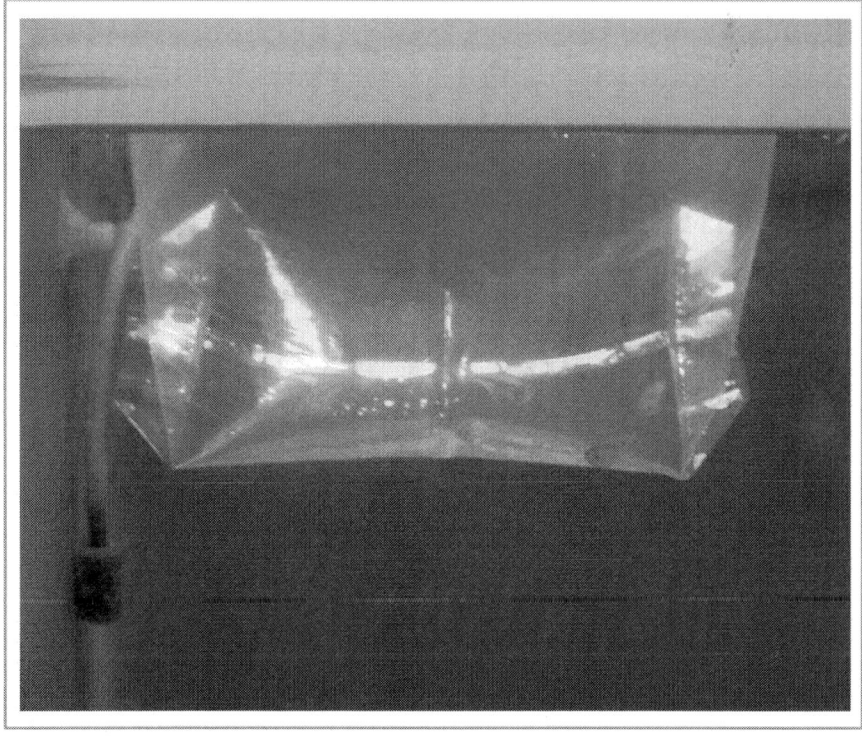

Day Three: Floating Tropical Fish in a bag in the Aquarium for around 15 minutes to allow for temperature adjustment and then adding some Aquarium water to the bag and floating for a further after 15 mins to allow for PH & DH adjustment – Photograph by Alastair R Agutter

Upon the arrival with your bag of tropical fish, simply lift the lid of your aquarium, remove or slide across one of the condensation trays and first float the bag with your tropical fish in the aquarium for around 15 minutes. This will ensure the temperature of the water in the bag adjusts to the temperature of the aquarium water.

After 15 to 20 minutes, open the top of the bag with your new arrivals and gently add some of the aquarium water into the bag and then just wedge the bag end by hanging it over the aquarium side, so the bag does not sink down into the aquarium. This process allows for the aquarium water in the bag to adjust with the aquarium water and therefore any variation in PH or DH (degrees of hardness) is greatly reduced. Leave the fish in the bag for a further 15 minutes and then very gently lower the bag into the aquarium water holding one end, so your new tropical fish can gently swim out. There is no need to switch off aquarium lights, to the contrary, tropical fish will prefer to see what is going on and with the aquarium lights being on, this helps the tropical fish to quickly begin to map out the aquarium terrain and adjust to the new environment using their electromagnetic recognition.

DAY FOUR

On day four, make this the first time you feed your new tropical fish in the aquarium and with just a very small pinch of tropical fish flake food. The eating and digesting of this food, which is then passed as waste (excreta), will start to help along the biological bacterial process that had been underway now for three days, when water first entered the aquarium.

After feeding your tropical fish for the very first time in the morning of day four, towards the end of the day, again carryout another 20% water change. The small amount of chlorine in the water will not harm the fish, but help inhibit and retard the ammonia and nitrite build up in the aquarium, which at this time is only slight.

DAY FIVE

At this stage of the water conditioning process there will begin to be a slight build-up of ammonia and nitrite in the water. The smell of ammonia should be familiar to you, as many hair dyes, shampoos and conditioners often carry a fair degree of ammonia and has a distinct smell that will be recognizable if present in any large quantity.

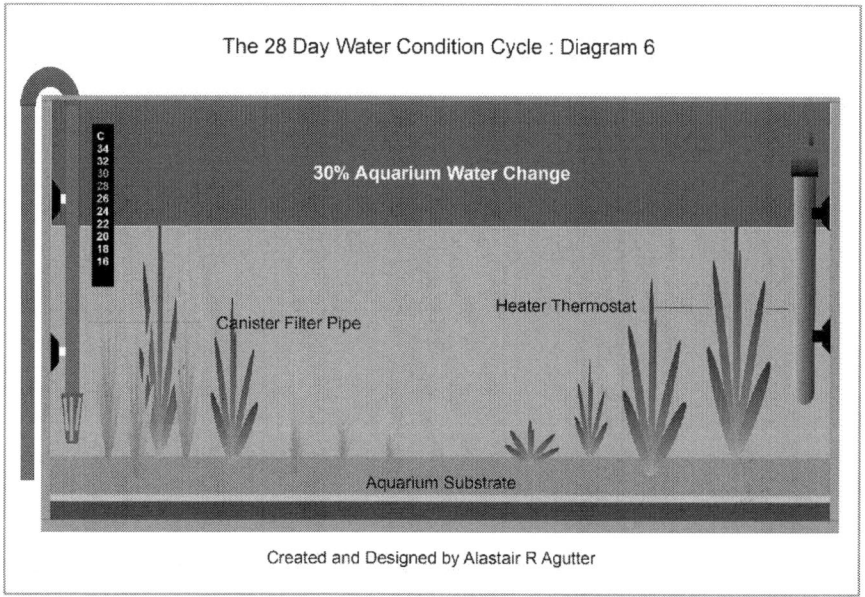

Day Five: Carryout another Water Change of 30% this time on Day Five to reduce the beginning of Ammonia and Nitrite Build-up in the Aquarium – Diagram by Alastair R Agutter

On day five, as the ammonia and nitrite begins to become more active and starts to populate, carryout a 30% water change. Again, using your hose to top up the aquarium with tap water, making sure the water entering the aquarium is lukewarm to the touch.

Feed the new inhabitant guppies again just a very small pinch of aquarium flake food. And carry out this process of feeding your guppies just once a day for the remaining 22 days. Your new fish inhabitants will not starve from only being fed once a day, as guppies are very resourceful and will happily swim up and down aquatic plants, collecting small particles of food and algae forming on the aquatic plants in your aquarium and such organisms as infusoria at this time that are invisible to the human eye.

DAY SIX

On day six just as before, feed your guppies once and carryout a 30% water change again, replacing the old aquarium siphoned water with new tap water. These water changes and instructions are critical and must be adhered too. Sorry ☹

Carryout routine checks again to make sure all electrical devices are working and also check your aquarium's water temperature.

DAY SEVEN

On day seven just as before, feed your guppies once and carryout a 30% water change again, this will alleviate the changes taking place biologically now regarding the ammonia and nitrite build-up.

DAY EIGHT

On day eight just as before, feed your guppies once and carryout a 30% water change again, this will alleviate the changes taking place biologically regarding ammonia and nitrite build-up that are now considerable.

This period between day eight, to day seventeen starts to see a more significant build-up of nitrite in the aquarium water and so the continuation of these water changes are very significant and I cannot emphasize enough how critical they are.

DAY NINE

On day nine just as before, feed your guppies once and carryout a 30% water change again, this will alleviate the changes taking place biologically regarding ammonia and nitrite build-up.

DAY TEN

On day ten just as before, feed your guppies once and carryout a 30% water change again, this will alleviate the changes taking place biologically regarding ammonia and nitrite build-up.

DAY ELEVEN

On day eleven just as before, feed your guppies once and carryout a 30% water change again, this will alleviate the changes taking place biologically regarding ammonia and nitrite build-up.

DAY TWELVE

On day twelve just as before, feed your guppies once and carryout a 30% water change again, this will alleviate the changes taking place biologically regarding ammonia and nitrite build-up.

DAY THIRTEEN

On day thirteen just as before, feed your guppies once and carryout a 30% water change again, this will alleviate the changes taking place biologically regarding ammonia and nitrite build-up.

DAY FOURTEEN

Now on day fourteen the Ammonia and Nitrite levels continue to build-up considerably and the continued 30% water changes at this stage is helping to combat this biological activity. So again, continue to carry out another 30% water change and feed your tropical fish once a day sparingly as before.

DAY FIFTEEN

On day fifteen again to combat Ammonia and Nitrite build-up, carryout another 30% water change and continue to feed your tropical fish once a day.

DAY SIXTEEN

On day sixteen the good news is you are on the home stretch with regards to establishing good quality aquarium water. The Nitrate at this stage is now beginning to populate to digest the Nitrite oxide in the water. Ammonia levels should also be under control if you have maintained a feeding regime of just feeding once a day very sparingly. Again carryout another 30% water change.

DAY SEVENTEEN

By day seventeen, this is a period where Ammonia is still present and the Nitrite levels are reaching a critical peak period in this 28 day cycle.

So today you need to carry-out a 50% water change and when doing so, make sure your Heater Thermostat is still submerged in the water. If the Heater Thermostat begins be exposed above water, switch-off the Heater Thermostat and remember to switch the device back on, once the 50% water change has been successfully carried out.

DAY EIGHTEEN

On day eighteen, again carryout a 50% water change, as this is a peak period of biological activity and where changes dramatically happen in the next 24 to 48 hours.

Again, remember to switch-off the Heater Thermostat if it becomes exposed out of the water. This is to protect the glass of the Heater Thermostat as they do become considerably hot and can crack if knocked or overheat from a fault.

Day eighteen is in fact the peak period for Nitrite and where dramatic changes take place in the next 24 hours.

DAY NINETEEN

Yesterday on day eighteen, was where the Nitrite levels reached a peak in the 28 day cycle. Now in the last 24 hours, Nitrate has now populated to a level to digest Nitrite oxides in the water biologically and therefore decreasing this harmful biological toxin element.

Carry out a 30% water change and again just feed your tropical fish once a day sparingly. Whilst Nitrate is now breaking down Ammonia and Nitrites in the aquarium water, it is important that we do not create a bacterial explosion from the presence of too much waste in comparison to fish and plant populations, as we want to ensure we create a balanced and safe biological eco-system.

DAY TWENTY

On day twenty Ammonia and Nitrite levels will continue to decrease, being countered by the water changes and the continued populating of Nitrate in the aquarium water.

Again carryout a 30% water change and again feed your tropical fish sparingly just once a day.

DAY TWENTY ONE

On day twenty one, Ammonia and Nitrite levels continue to drop biologically. Again, carryout a 30% water change and again feed your tropical fish sparingly just once a day.

At this time again, carryout a routine maintenance check on your aquarium equipment, to make sure all is well and all devices are functioning properly.

DAY TWENTY TWO

On day twenty two the aquarium water has now stabilized where Ammonia and Nitrite levels are being managed by the biological breakdown process with the presence of populating Nitrates.

Again, carryout a 30% water change in the aquarium and feed your tropical fish just once a day sparingly.

DAY TWENTY THREE

By day twenty three you are on the home stretch as the water continues to remain stable. Carryout just a 20% water change and now you can feed your tropical fish twice a day sparingly.

At no time in this process have the guppies starved, as they would have eaten dead vegetation on the plants as they adjust and acclimatize to the new conditions, just like any new plants introduced to a garden it normally takes a week or two for them to adjust before you see signs of new growth.

DAY TWENTY FOUR

On day twenty four there is no need to carry out a water change in your aquarium. Just continue to feed your tropical fish twice a day sparingly.

DAY TWENTY FIVE

On day twenty five carryout a 20% water change and continue to feed your tropical fish just twice a day. The Ammonia levels should remain low if you are still feeding your fish sparingly and the aquatic plants have become established in the aquarium.

DAY TWENTY SIX

On day twenty six the water is now safe and suitable to accommodate more tropical fish inhabitants and no water change is required on this day. Again tropical fish can be introduced in small numbers, so as to allow the biological system to populate in a controlled and gradual way to prevent a biological bacterial explosion if too many fish are introduced to the aquarium at any one time.

This may seem a contradiction advising of a gradual introduction of tropical fish, as opposed to what can be read, or advised at times, when setting up a new system and adding large numbers of tropical fish into a new aquarium environment any one time. But please be assured, the addition of too many fish at any one time, will cause a water chemistry and biological bacterial change and imbalance to the eco-system environment. In fact this is obvious, if we only look at our own everyday lives, where there has been a significant impact to an area when there has been a sudden population growth in a community that is condensed.

Again we are reminded of Natural Law, where all that we know is gradual and balanced, to "evolve and refine" preventing catastrophe to our environment.

DAY TWENTY SEVEN

On day twenty seven again carry out a small water change of 20% as this helps to introduce new water, minerals (plant food) and oxygen into the aquarium environment system.

Now the amount of aquarium fish one can house is obviously dependent upon the size of the aquarium and the filtration system created, or deployed and this will be explained and shortly follow in this chapter.

DAY TWENTY EIGHT

On day twenty eight the aquarium environment and water is completely stable and any ammonia, or nitrites present are being safely broken down with nitrates in the biological bacterial process in the aquarium and filtration system.

We will now discuss the number of tropical fish we can accommodate in aquariums, with the aid of a table I created and also a second table showing the filtration flow rates of water, as these figures and rates are different dependent upon the number of tropical fish inhabitants in an aquarium at any one time.

FISH NUMBER INHABITANTS IN AN AQUARIUM

The normal rule of thumb regarding the number of fish one can accommodate in an aquarium is 12 inches of fish per every cubic foot of water. However, this is very much hit and miss, for varying types of filtration systems can have a bearing on the number of tropical fish one can accommodate in an aquarium at any one time and also the type of species of fish.

Let me give you an example, you may have an Angel fish for example that is four inches in length, then if we make a comparison with say a red tail shark that is four inches in length. Even though the fish are of equal length, the volume mass of these fish are significantly different. In fact the Angel Fish body mass in most cases would equate to the Angel fish being two to three times larger in volume mass.

Water conditions and quality is based on a number of factors in a tropical fish aquarium. One being the filtration of the aquarium and the type of filtration deployed, also the number of tropical fish and aquatic plants.

As we know plants greatly aid the aquarium environment as providers and not consumers. However, through the aquarium environment process with the existence of aquatic plants, they do help and form part of the filtration process, by filtering out chemicals and trace elements from the water, converting these to carbohydrate sugars as food for the aquatic plants.

The size of fish and the amount of by-product waste (excreta) from the fish has also a bearing on water conditions and quality. Also the flow rate of the filtration process in the tropical fish aquarium and the right type of filtration in operation, to be able to deliver good quality crystal clear water has a significant bearing.

You can very often read stories from aquarists where they have a fully functioning filtration system but the water clarity in the terms of visibility is very poor (cloudy).

Now this can relate to a number of factors, one being a bacterial explosion, or the type of food being fed to the tropical fish in the aquarium, but very often the problem lays mostly regarding the water clarity is the flow rates of water though the filtration system, where the filter medium is unable to biologically breakdown this matter for having insufficient time.

This is caused by the water carrying the waste matter from fish and plants; including food that is passing through the filter system medium too fast, resulting in cloudy water and not crystal clear water conditions for an optimal standard aquarium environment.

Very often when the above happens from a too faster flow through the filtration system resulting in cloudy water fish will react in the aquarium by rubbing themselves against plants and objects. On these occasions it is very easy for the new aquarist to read or get the wrong advice where they are told such activity is caused from the presence of gill flukes. But this is not the case but a case of an excessive amount of bacteria distributed through the aquarium as a result of the filtration system not processing or functioning correctly. Regulated flow rates as you can see are of a primary importance.

Aquarium Sizes For Number of Fish Inhabitants Table			
Aquarium Size	Cubic Inches of Fish	Aquarium Size	Cubic Inches of Fish
18" x 12" x 12"	18 inches of fish	48" x 12" x 15"	60 inches of fish
24" x 12" x 15"	25 inches of fish	48" x 12" x 18"	72 inches of fish
24" x 12" x 18"	30 inches of fish	48" x 18" x 18"	108 inches of fish
24" x 24" x 24"	48 inches of fish	48" x 18" x 24"	144 inches of fish
30" x 12" x 15"	37 inches of fish	60" x 12" x 18"	75 inches of fish
30" x 12" x 18"	45 inches of fish	60" x 18" x 18"	135 inches of fish
36" x 12" x 15"	35 inches of fish	60" x 18" x 24"	180 inches of fish
36" x 12" x 18"	54 inches of fish	72" x 18" x 18"	162 inches of fish
36" x 18" x 18"	81 inches of fish	72" x 18" x 24"	216 inches of fish
Created and Designed by Alastair R Agutter			

The above table detailing the size of tropical fish aquariums and the recommended numbers surrounding the inches of tropical fish per tank – Table Diagram by Alastair R Agutter

As you can see from the above diagram table, it provides you with an accurate insight to the amount of tropical fish that can be comfortably placed into the respective sized aquariums.

Now I know aquariums come in all shapes and sizes, so the following mathematical formula enables you to establish how many fish you can actually put in your aquarium, if you cannot find the size above.

NUMBER OF FISH MATHEMATICAL FORMULA

To derive at the figure for establishing the number of inches of fish you can place in your aquarium is as follows. Multiply the Length of the Aquarium by the height of the Aquarium by the depth of the Aquarium. Then take this total figure and divide it by the cubic inches in a square cubic foot of water which is 1728. Then multiply that total figure by 12 and this will provide you with the number of inches of fish you can have in your aquarium.

Here is the following example:-

I have an Aquarium 72" x 24" x 24" and so the mathematical formula is as follows;-

72 x 24 x 24 = 41472 and then divide as follows 41472 divided by 1728 = 24, then multiply 24 x 12 = 288 and this figure is the number of fish inches.

1728 = 1 square cubic foot. 12

12 inches = the number of fish in inches per foot.

288 is the total number of inches of fish for an aquarium size of 72" x 24" x 24"

Now when you look at the above table, remember this is the length of fish inches per aquarium. So if we take the smallest aquarium of 18" x 12" 12" equaling 18 inches of fish. This means in effect if you choose to have guppies, platies or tetras in this aquarium and the fish are all around an inch in length, you can therefore safely keep 18 of these tropical fish. Another random example is say an aquarium of 48" x 12" x 18" a very popular size that can house 72 inches of fish.

If you want to keep cichlids, you could easily place 18 four inch cichlids in this 48" x 12" x 18" aquarium, or if the fish are 2 inch in length, you can house 36 tropical fish. If we looked at this size of aquarium (48" x 12" x 18") as a community fish tank for platies, guppies, swordtails, tetras and barbs, all around 1 inch in length, would mean you can comfortably house 72 fish in this size of aquarium.

FILTRATION FLOW RATES IN AN AQUARIUM

Now the next table diagram to follow is the flow rate of filtration in aquariums and number of fish. This will help you to determine the size of filter capacity you require for your aquarium.

This table diagram I have created for filtration flow rates are what I believe to be optimal, after many years of research and can be applied to all methods of filtration and I will explain how with some examples. Plus the mathematical formula if your aquarium size is not present.

Now the filter medium I have used to obtain the best results has been covered in the filtration chapter of the book. But as a slight refresher, here is the following relevant and important information. Subject to the trickle, sump, reservoir filter area or canister filters size. First, I have used course membrane foam, secondly medium membrane foam, thirdly fine membrane foam and finally, an activated charcoal or carbon membrane sheet. These sheets are very often available in tropical fish retail shops and pet or pond garden centres that specialize in cold water koi carp fish, as these filter foam membrane medium sheets are often used in large pond filtration systems. These foam sheets are very versatile and can be cut to any size to accommodate the filtration area that is to be used.

As mentioned earlier, below is the following optimal filter flow rates table diagram and hope this information really helps aquarists, as this subject is rarely covered and I think, I may be wrong, but I think this is the first time a table of this nature has been created with the calculated optimal flow rates deriving from my mathematical formula.

I will explain after the table diagram, how to use the mathematical formula just in the event your aquarium size is not on the flow rate table diagram to establish the filter flow rate for your aquarium.

I have found that the optimal filtration flow of water per cubic foot of water is 7.7 litres an hour. So to establish the optimal flow rate of filtration for your aquarium if it is not listed above is to follow the mathematical formula I have set out below.

Multiply the length x depth x height of your aquarium. Then divide this figure by 1728 and this will provide you with the cubic square feet of your aquarium. Then simply multiply that total figure by 7.7 and this will provide you with an accurate figure for the optimal flow rate per hour for your aquarium.

My First Aquarium Collectors Edition

Aquarium Sizes and Optimal Filter Flow Rates Table			
Aquarium Size	Filter Flow Rate	Aquarium Size	Filter Flow Rate
18" x 12" x 12"	11.55 Litres per hour	48" x 12" x 15"	38.50 Litres per hour
24" x 12" x 15"	19.25 Litres per hour	48" x 12" x 18"	46.20 Litres per hour
24" x 12" x 18"	23.10 Litres per hour	48" x 18" x 18"	69.30 Litres per hour
24" x 24" x 24"	61.60 Litres per hour	48" x 18" x 24"	92.40 Litres per hour
30" x 12" x 15"	24.02 Litres per hour	60" x 12" x 18"	57.75 Litres per hour
30" x 12" x 18"	28.87 Litres per hour	60" x 18" x 18"	86.62 Litres per hour
36" x 12" x 15"	28.87 Litres per hour	60" x 18" x 24"	115.50 Litres per hour
36" x 12" x 18"	34.65 Litres per hour	72" x 18" x 18"	103.95 Litres per hour
36" x 18" x 18"	51.97 Litres per hour	72" x 18" x 24"	138.60 Litres per hour

Created and Designed by Alastair R Agutter

The above table detailing the size of tropical fish aquariums and the optimal filtration flow rates per hour – Table Diagram by Alastair R Agutter

Here is the following example:-

Let's say we have an aquarium of an usual size, this being 66 inches long, 15 inches deep and 22 inches high (66" x 15" x 22").

First I multiply 66 x 15 x 22 = 21780

Then we divide 21780 by 1728, this equals 12.60 and this figure is the square cubic feet of water for this aquarium.

Then simply multiply 12.60 x 7.7 = 97.02

97.02 litres is the aquarium flow rate per hour for the above aquarium.

Now today aquarium air pumps, canister filters and power head pumps come in varying sizes and indicate their capacity of filtration, or transfer of water in litres per hour, on the device packaging and instructions.

The external packaging, advertising the litre size of the pumps or canister filters, then enables you to buy the correct size of product for your aquarium's filtration needs.

Now some may say you need far more powerful pumps for a greater filtration flow rate. But this is not so, for a flow rate that is too fast and powerful, may draw the water too quickly through the filter medium and therefore not allowing sufficient time for the biological bacteria culture in the filtration system to break down the matter, and as a result, causing the aquarium to be cloudy.

Water quality is paramount obviously and one of the biggest problems regarding the health of fish is from poor water quality, as a result of a lack of water changes and incorrect filtration flow rates.

Regarding a normal naturally planted community aquarium, a regular water change of around 20% once a week will prevent many diseases to your tropical fish.

The retention and maintaining of good quality water in your aquarium is greatly assisted and achieved when you feed your tropical fish sparingly with small amounts, but on a regular basis often coined "little and often" to prevent toxicity in the water in the form of Ammonia build-up.

If you decide to operate a sterile aquarium theme with ornate pots to keep more unusual exotic tropical fish such as Discus (symphysodon), well then water changes will need to be on a more regular basis, say two to three times a week, dependent upon the amount of fish waste (feces) and uneaten food. This will ensure the water quality remains high and reduces toxin levels in the form of Ammonia.

Fish and plant population variants can have an effect on your aquarium's water conditions and always worth remembering. If you have 10 fish in an aquarium and increase this number dramatically to say 20 tropical fish, this will alter the biological parity and water conditions.

To ensure these fluctuations do not have a detrimental effect on your aquarium environment from the significant increase of tropical fish, the best advice is to carry out for a 5 day period 20% water changes each day. This will help in the adjustments required regarding the biological culture population in the aquarium to adjust, preventing a biological bacterial explosion in relation to the following toxins and oxides; ammonia, nitrites and nitrates.

If you are only adding one of two tropical fish to the aquarium, this will not have a dramatic effect on the fish tanks biological environment as the increased numbers are gradual and the biological culture will populate gradually and accordingly to compensate the new number of inhabitants.

With the frequent water changes as mentioned here and throughout this chapter, by using localized tap water that your fish have now become acclimatized too, serves as a tonic for the fish and the small amounts of chlorine serves also as an antiseptic to reduce or prevent unwelcomed diseases.

Over my many years of tropical fish keeping, I have found regular water changes has prevented disease and greatly helped the growth of tropical fish in addition to them remaining healthy and vibrant.

In the disease chapter of the book we will discuss how water changes serve to cure and help many common conditions tropical fish can incur.

In the products chapter I will cover Deionizers, UV Sterilization and also Reverse Osmosis all areas often considered in tropical fish keeping surrounding water quality. But I have no intention of confusing you regarding these gadgets here.

The above methods I have explained in this chapter surrounding water quality are techniques I continue to use myself and been rewarded by having large, healthy, thriving, happy tropical fish over decades and also successfully breeding the most difficult tropical fish species in the world.

CHAPTER NINE

Heating and Thermostats

Over the years heaters, thermostats and heater thermostats have changed, but in many respects, only slightly that I best describe as taking a leaf out of Natural Law and Quantum Mechanics, by "evolving and refining" these magnificent creations over a balanced period of time.

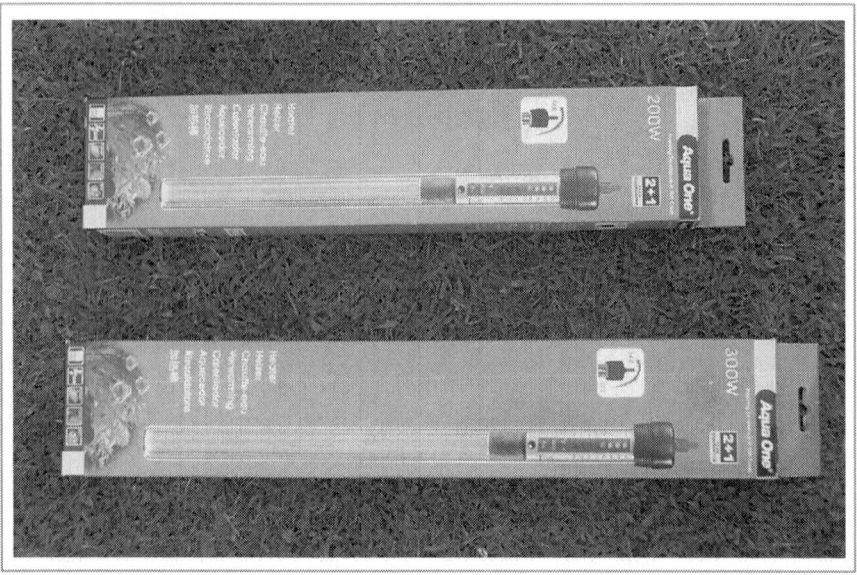

Two Aqua One Heater Thermostats with the wattage displayed on the products packaging to prevent any confusion when purchasing – Photograph by Alastair R Agutter

Prior to electrical heaters and thermostats, aquariums were either heated in say a Fish House by using Oil, or Paraffin heaters. In the Home, aquarium heating methods were achieved, by the use of slate bottom angle iron fish tanks, where Lighting, Gas, or Oil heating was used, where the devices were placed below the aquarium and as a result, directing the heat from the heating device to the underneath of the aquarium slate base to heat the water.

With the very many different sizes of heating devices available today, I have created the following table to help with the decision making, when acquiring these heating device items from your local tropical fish retailer, or an online supplier using the World Wide Web via the Internet.

The table below shows the recommended number of heating devices and wattage required for a wide range of different aquarium sizes in the table as a useful guide.

Heater Thermostats Wattage and Aquarium Sizes Table			
Aquarium Size	Heater Thermostats	Aquarium Size	Heater Thermostats
18" x 12" x 12"	1 x 100 watt	48" x 12" x 15"	2 x 100 watt
24" x 12" x 15"	1 x 150 watt	48" x 12" x 18"	2 x 150 watt
24" x 12" x 18"	1 x 150 watt	48" x 18" x 18"	2 x 200 watt
24" x 24" x 24"	1 x 300 watt	48" x 18" x 24"	2 x 200 watt
30" x 12" x 15"	1 x 150 watt	60" x 12" x 18"	2 x 200 watt
30" x 12" x 18"	1 x 200 watt	60" x 18" x 18"	2 x 200 watt
36" x 12" x 15"	1 x 200 watt	60" x 18" x 24"	2 x 300 watt
36" x 12" x 18"	1 x 200 watt	72" x 18" x 18"	2 x 300 watt
36" x 18" x 18"	1 x 300 watt	72" x 18" x 24"	2 x 300 watt

Created and Designed by Alastair R Agutter

Heater Thermostats Wattage and Aquarium Sizes to establish the ideal heating device(s) required for the Aquarists Fish Tank – Diagram and Illustration Created by Alastair R Agutter

Today's Aquarium heating devices in the form of Heater Thermostats especially as mentioned earlier have evolved and been refined over the years where adjustment of temperatures are able to be made far easier and the internal elements that make up the heating device are far more robust.

There are a number of different heating model devices available today and these are as follows and some devices mentioned earlier in the book briefly. The most popular heating devices and prices will now be highlighted and covered as follows; 1/. Heater Thermostats 2/. Heater and External Thermostats 3/. Flexible Cable Heaters and External Thermostats

HEATER THERMOSTATS

Heater Thermostats today are probably the most popular form of heating device for a tropical fish aquarium. On a personal note for reliability, accuracy and economic reasons, I use Heater Thermostats for all my aquariums.

Heater Thermostat in one of the Author's Naturally Planted Aquarium showing the adjustment knob at the top of the device to regulate the temperature - Photograph by Alastair R Agutter

Heater Thermostat's as seen in the picture above, is a combined unit in a cylindrical glass object that looks similar to a test tube found in a laboratory.

These heater thermostat devices today, are far easier to adjust to regulate the temperature by adjusting the narrow knob on the top of the device, that can be turned in a clock wise, or anti-clock wise motion, to set the required temperature on the heater thermostat.

These heater thermostats purchased today in most cases come with two clips and rubber suckers to safely position the heater thermostat in the aquarium.

These heater thermostats should come with a plug already fitted and with a 3 amp fuse. Please check and make sure when you have purchased a heater thermostat that the plug does have installed a 3 amp fuse. For recently I purchased three heater thermostats for my Daughter and myself, and found the plugs on these heater thermostats, had 13 amp fuses fitted, instead of 3 amp fuses.

Heater thermostats can be easily hidden or disguised in a naturally planted aquarium. However, if you are running a sump or reservoir powered or trickle filtration system, I would recommend placing the heater thermostat in the water area space inside the filter chamber, as shown in the filtration chapter. This will ensure the water in the aquarium is of a consistent temperature throughout.

In specialized aquariums for breeding, where the water flow rates can be very slight, you can easily get dead pockets of water in the aquarium. The following picture is one of my Discus Aquariums, and where it shows the heater thermostat upright and one of my polyatomic-ion biological reactors has the aperture expelling oxygen and water angled towards the heater thermostat, so a steady slow flow of water can be attained around the aquarium, removing the risk of dead pockets.

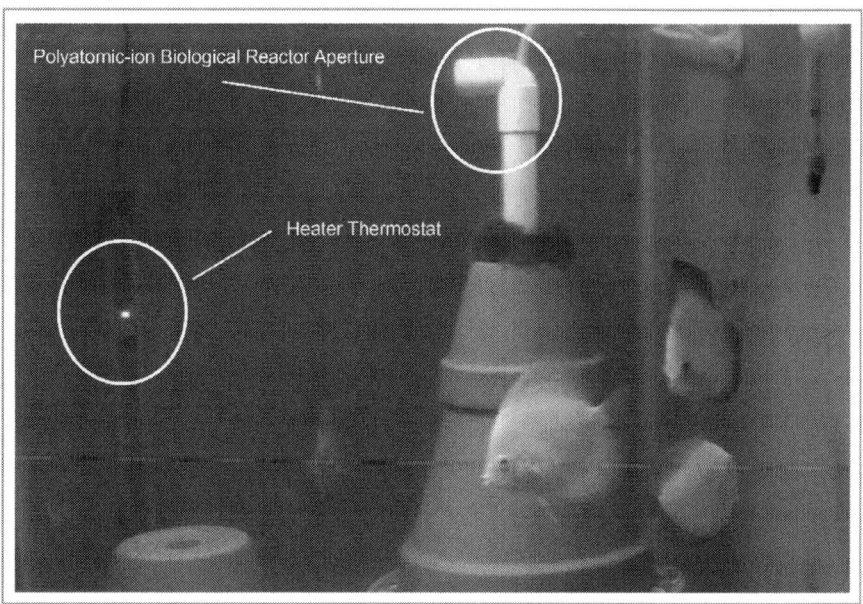

The Picture above shows the filtration aperture angled towards the heater thermostat to ensure there is a gentle circulation of warm water in the aquarium - Photograph by Alastair R Agutter

In the picture above, you can see the heater thermostat in an upright position in the aquarium and this is the normal desired position, as recommended by the product manufacturer.

Maintenance to these heater thermostats is very easy and straight forward, simply every month or so, un-plug the heater thermostat and allow to cool for a short while, then with a kitchen towel, or clean sponge that is chemically free, gently wipe the heater thermostat. This will remove any algae or bacterial build-up that could cause the heater thermostat to over-heat or malfunction in some form.

If you decide to have a bare bottom sterile aquarium and decide to use a heater thermostat. One idea to help protect the heater thermostat in the event of the device being knocked and possibly descending to the bottom of the aquarium, with the risk of cracking, or breaking to the base of the glass, is to use a tip that a good friend and fellow aquarist Eberhard Schultze suggested, that is to put a small blob of clear silicone sealer on the bottom end of the heater thermostat glass. This will cushion the heater thermostat glass in the event of the device being dropped or knocked.

HEATER AND EXTERNAL THERMOSTATS

The very first Aquarium that I owned, purchased for me by my Father as a Birthday present back in 1967, came with an external thermostat and a separate aquarium glass heater.

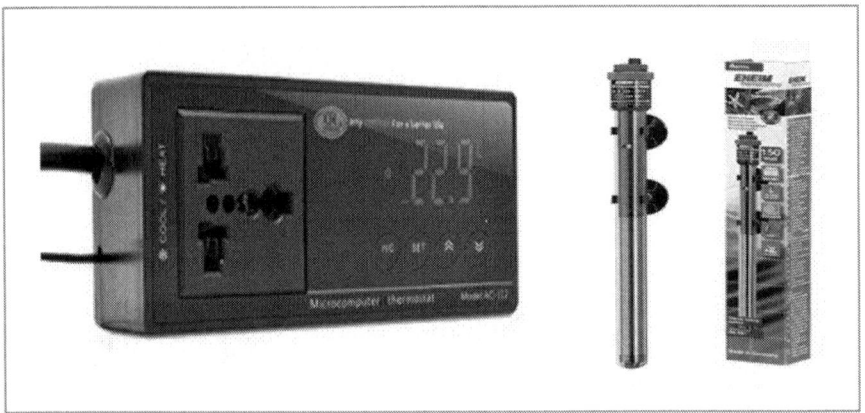

Picture above to the left shows a modern day External Thermostat by Anself incorporating microcomputer technology today. Also pictured Eheim Heaters - Compiled by Alastair R Agutter

The External Thermostat was made in those days from a Bakelite material and where the casing of the external thermostat was finished in a marbled chocolate brown colouration.

The device could be clipped onto the outside of the aquarium. On the thermostat itself, was a dial that you could manually adjust to regulate the water temperature in Fahrenheit.

Today as you can see from the picture above showing an external thermostat, these device types have come a very long way since 1967 when I began this time honoured pastime. These devices as seen in the picture above manufactured by Anself, uses LED and Microcomputer Technology, to try and deliver an accurate temperature for today's Aquarists.

FLEXIBLE CABLE HEATERS AND EXTERNAL THERMOSTATS

Flexible cable heaters are laid in the aquarium substrate and then again connected to an external thermostat as seen in the picture earlier.

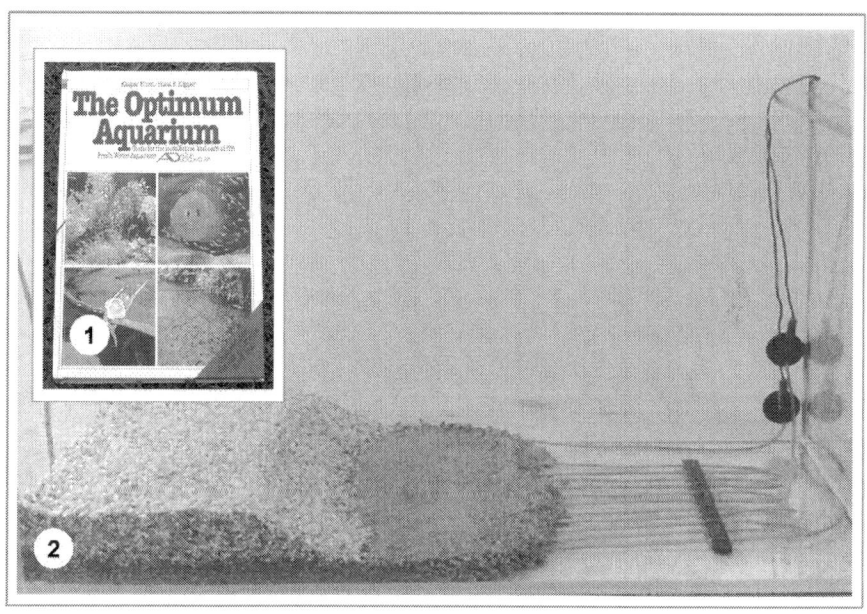

1/ Picture above shows the Optimum Aquarium Book written by Kasper Horst and Horst E. Kipper
2/. Picture shows the under gravel heating element piping that can be laid and covered with substrate
– Photographs Taken and Compiled by Alastair R Agutter

This heating method can be expensive and there can be set-backs that concern me when using such a heating method. For example, if any of the elements fail at any one time, particularly in a naturally planted aquarium, you will have to take out the faulty heater element, thus causing massive disruption to the substrate and plants, resulting in the need to start again in the aquarium.

I always believe in giving credit where credit is due, and the first time I ever saw and read about this method of heating was from a book I purchased written by Kasper Horst and Horst E. Kipper titled "The Optimum Aquarium" back in the 1980's that was in fairness years ahead of its time, as a tropical fish keeping publication in 1986. The photographs above, I have taken from my original copy of the book. If you are fortunate enough to obtain a copy of this publication, I would suggest and urge you to do so, as the book will be a valuable addition to your Aquarist Library.

When it comes to heaters of any form for your aquarium, please always be diligent regarding water and electricity. Always make sure any heater, or aquatic electrical device is only ever fitted with 3 Amp fuses. Thank You!

LOCATION AND POSITIONING OF HEATERS

As mentioned briefly earlier in this chapter, in an ideal scenario regarding the practicality of use and positioning, I would place a heater thermostat in the chamber area of the trickle, sump or reservoir filtration system. So then, the water being filtered through and being expelled into the aquarium is always of the desired consistent water temperature, thus eliminating aquarium water cold spots.

In the 1960's, 1970's and 1980's through to a good part of the 1990's, the positioning of a heater thermostat in an aquarium tended to be at the back of the aquarium, positioned in the middle and disguised with rocks, bogwood or plants etc.

Or if the aquarium was particularly large say 72" x 18" x 18" and required two heater thermostats, these were in most cases placed towards the back and at each end of the aquarium, again disguised with bogwood and plants etc.

Heater thermostats can in truth be located in any part of the aquarium if they are to be disguised to fall in line with your planed underwater world design.

Always read however, the instructions from the product manufacturer, for some heater thermostats whilst designed very similarly today, may require more specific positioning to ensure the heater's thermostat engages and disengages efficiently and does not become stuck that can cause overheating.

CHAPTER TEN
The Aquarium Lighting Methods

When I first took up tropical fish keeping back in the 1960's, aquariums very often had aquarium hoods, and these were quit considerable in height placed upon the top of the aquarium and housed within the aquarium hood the lighting system, that mainly consisted of one, or two, conventional household electricity bulbs and with a wattage varying between 40 to 100 watts.

Above are two pictures from part of the Author's Fish House, 1dt picture showing his energy saving lights and the 2nd picture showing when the cabinet doors are closed showing healthy thriving plants and tropical fish – Photographs taken and Compiled by Alastair R Agutter

A few years later regarding lighting systems for aquariums, we started to see fluorescent tubes being used, this came about with the emergence of a new age in aquarium design, starting with all glass aquariums joined by clear silicone sealer developed by the Space Industry and Science Community.

These new aquariums no longer required the heavy angle iron construction of fish tanks from the past, where the glass was sealed into the angle iron frames using putty.

Soon these all glass aquariums began to be finished in fine trim around the tops of these new style of fish tanks and then fluorescent tubes came to the fore, using slim-line chokes, housed in the top, or at the back of these aquariums. The aquarium hoods were then soon replaced with two pieces of laminated timbers or plastics that were hinged or slid. The top heavy looking and bulky aquarium hoods of the past were now no more.

Colour of the fish and plants became all important for these new aquarium designs and the aquarium lighting system, saw the emergence of Grolux Lighting that produced a softer purple blue light that brought out the colours of the fish and plants. Grolux however, was not known as a "White Light" that is required for plants, but standard fluorescent light tubes did offer white light. Eventually the format of lighting consisted of two lights, one being a White Light for the plants growth and the second, a Grolux Light to bring out the fish and plant colours.

This format of lighting remained the same in many respects through the 1970's, 1980's and 1990's with one or two exceptions in luxury custom design aquariums.

In the mid 1980's, we began to explore the use of Halogen Lighting, with spot lights suspended, hanging from the ceiling and positioned just above these new super aquarium designs using 10 to 13 mm plate glass in the construction and with timers on the lighting systems, to achieve with mercury vapour halogen lighting a sunrise and sunset effect from using such elements that take a while to heat up and cool down.

As we turned and welcomed in the new millennium, where we saw the emergence of even more new concepts of lighting and with a focus on green energy saving.

From the development of more sophisticated glass and polycarbonate lens configurations that could magnify and intensify photons, LED (Light-emitting Diode) Lighting became one of the new innovations in lighting and was very impressive, with regards to the energy conservation aspects and the intensity of light generated from such small units.

Today with the constant concerns rightly about Climate Change, even in the domestic home and at work, we are using more conservation lighting methods to conserve energy. Whereby we are replacing the old standard light bulbs with new light energy saving bulbs today and these are the same type that I use in my fish house. With white light, it encourages plant growth, and by using dark backgrounds as like my aquariums, this helps to bring out the magnificent colours of the tropical fish.

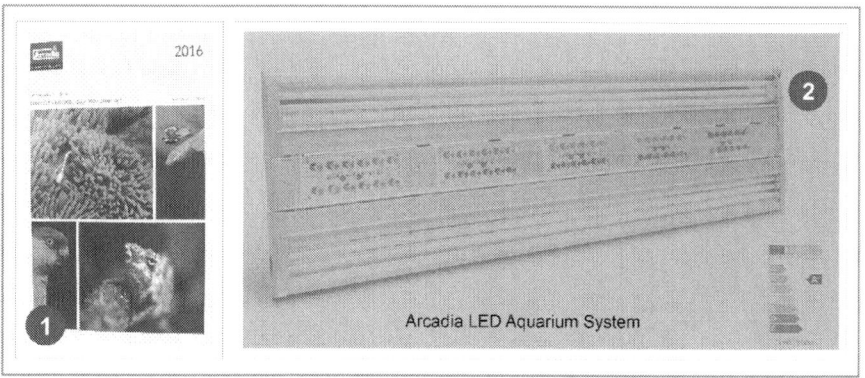

Two pictures above, the 1st picture showing the Arcadia Catalogue for 2016 and the 2nd picture showing a modern day Arcadia LED (Lighting-emitting Diode) Lighting System Unit – Photographs taken and Compiled by Alastair R Agutter

Today regarding lighting systems for the aquarium, they can range considerably in price. We can also be more flamboyant and creative, regarding the many lighting systems available to use.

In the coming years, I hope we see more aquarists adopting suspended lighting, to set-off stunning aquarium displays of colourful magical underwater worlds created.

THE IMPORTANCE OF AQUARIUM LIGHTING

So let us now consider the importance of lighting in an aquarium.

Again in this chapter of the book and regarding this section covering lighting, I have developed and created a lighting table accompanied with aquarium sizes and light wattage for growing healthy thriving plants.

Lighting is not only important to plants, but also very important for your tropical fish, for even marine species need sunlight to help develop vertebrate (tropical fish) bone and cartilaginous (catfish, rays and sharks) structures.

Light is also important for most if not all tropical fish species brain development and recognition in relation to navigational mapping out especially, and the environment in relation to gravitational and electromagnetic sensors, lateral line and swim bladder mechanisms, the latter primarily concerning water pressure.

Later in the book on the topic and subject of fish behaviour, we will go into far more detail including, the generalized anatomical form of fish, to accustom you with these areas, so as to help you be able to relate to fish characteristics and behavioural patterns, all of which are relevant and important to know as an aquarist, as we discuss species. In other words, learning and knowing the signs!

Fish species are like us and require a varying number of key essential vitamins for bone development and growth, two of these being, vitamin B, vitamin C and vitamin D. So sunlight plays a significant part for healthy thriving fish. So we need to establish how much sunlight do fish species actually require?

As we know ourselves, sunlight is governed by seasonal cycles, where certain times a year, daylight periods can be far shorter and at other times much longer.

These seasonal cycles and changes with regards to the weather affect air and water pressure conditions, also electromagnetic varying intensities. All of these factors have to be considered and appreciated, to be able to understand why so often Aquarists are perplexed when evenly using lighting over a consistent period throughout a year, still sees varying changes in plant and fish growth activity.

In Autumn periods for example and moving into Winter months, tropical fish will appear to have a greater appetite, becoming far more vigorous eaters and start to put on a noticeable amounts of weight. Even though the artificial light amount is consistent throughout the day, weeks, months and years in an aquarium environment, fish and plants more than instinctively know of these seasonal changes, as this has been part of their evolutionary cycle for millions of years. Tropical Fish and Aquatic Plants are also processing other important factors in the form of humidity and atmospherics, in relation to air and water pressure changes through to electromagnetic and gravitational energies.

Other characteristics in fish like us humans again, is fish do sleep and some more than others. Some fish species are also early risers and early to bed, to coin a phrase.

So light does have a significant importance in an aquarium environment and is highly relevant regarding tropical fish and coupled to many related factors including breeding.

Fish like routine and so for lighting to come on at specific times, serves towards eliminating anxieties that fish species do get and have. One of the biggest killers to all tropical fish is stress and anxiety that can lead to many other disorders, and so all the time we can take away events that can and do cause stress, is a good thing for all tropical fish inhabitants.

So firstly, I would suggest Aquarists acquire a timer for the aquarium light system. As this will provide a regular time for when the lights to the aquarium go on and go off.

The next consideration is the length of time the lighting needs to be on, to ensure healthy thriving tropical fish and aquatic plants.

I have found from my experience over the years and now getting onto five decades in 2017 of tropical fish keeping, that a period of light between 10 to 12 hours, is an optimal length of light time in a tropical fish aquarium. In fact, many commercial breeders of aquatic plants advise and recommend to their customers, that they need to leave their aquarium lighting on for at least 10 hours a day, and so this figure by commercial breeders of aquatic plants, falls in line with my experiments and findings over the years, concerning the subject of lighting for tropical fish and plants.

Again as always, there is a balance to all that we know, so then as a word of advice and caution, when aquarium lighting is on for a too longer period, or the lighting wattage is too high, this can encourage too much algae growth. This can lead to aquatic plants in the aquarium and on the walls of the aquarium glass itself, becoming smothered in algae, caused from excessive lighting periods, leading to vigorous algae growth.

Below as promised is the Table for lighting wattage and aquarium sizes, based on the fact that we have determined the optimal lighting period is 10 to 12 hours every day.

I cannot emphasise enough the importance of routine, regarding lighting, water changes and feeding. As these valid points with reference to routine (fish husbandry) has proved to be the key secret and factor to successfully breeding tropical fish species in captivity.

In the following table below, it shows and helps the aquarist by providing the aquarium sizes and the recommended wattage figure next to every different aquarium size.

This will help aquarists determine the appropriate power lighting system requirements. This method and way is easier, as it allows you the aquarist to make your own choice and preference regarding styles and lights, but at the same time, having a guide so you know the magic figures so you can meet optimal lighting conditions.

Lighting Wattage and Aquarium Sizes Table			
Aquarium Size	Lighting Wattage	Aquarium Size	Lighting Wattage
18" x 12" x 12"	100 watts	48" x 12" x 15"	300 watts
24" x 12" x 15"	100 watts	48" x 12" x 18"	300 watts
24" x 12" x 18"	100 watts	48" x 18" x 18"	300 watts
24" x 24" x 24"	200 watts	48" x 18" x 24"	300 watts
30" x 12" x 15"	150 watts	60" x 12" x 18"	350 watts
30" x 12" x 18"	150 watts	60" x 18" x 18"	350 watts
36" x 12" x 15"	200 watts	60" x 18" x 24"	350 watts
36" x 12" x 18"	200 watts	72" x 18" x 18"	400 watts
36" x 18" x 18"	200 watts	72" x 18" x 24"	400 watts

Created and Designed by Alastair R Agutter

Above: The Lighting Wattage and Aquarium Sizes Table and based on the Lighting period being 10 to 12 hours a day – Photographs taken and Compiled by Alastair R Agutter

Always remember when installing any lighting in the lid of an aquarium, or a project involving a fish house, please take extra care over the electrics to ensure all electrical fittings and connections are completely safe. If you are unsure about the installation of your electrics, please seek professional help and ensure the trade professional is a qualified Electrician.

The following picture shows the type of energy saving bulbs I use as white light for my aquariums and fish house. These bulbs I use are made by Philips and come with a 12 years guarantee for starters.

Next, these energy saving bulbs are what they are and so a bulb producing a 100 watts of white light in energy consumption terms equates to just 20 watts. A 60 watt energy saving bulb equates to just 11 watts of energy consumption.

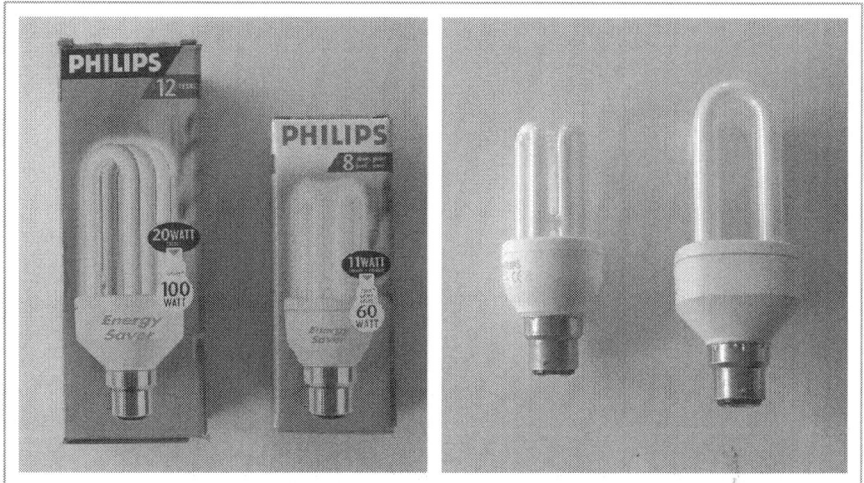

Photograph of Energy Saving Bulbs that the Author uses for his Tropical Fish Aquariums delivering White Light for Plants – Photographs taken and Compiled by Alastair R Agutter

So by using 2 x 100 watt energy saving light bulbs is the equivalent of just using 1 x 40 watt conventional light bulb.

So by using energy saving light bulbs, the energy costs are greatly reduced.

Now I know some of my readers are very affluent, where energy prices and costs to some folk is of no object financially, but my passionate pleas and requests to encourage more aquarists and folk to use more energy saving products, is for the very grave and serious threat of climate change.

CHAPTER ELEVEN

Fish Species Behaviour

I know as a new, or existing Aquarist, "fish are not just fish" but living species and beautiful miracles of evolution.

One of the Authors' breeding pair of Gold Angel Fish, operating and coordinating a cleaning regime before spawning on leaves and pots – Photograph by Alastair R Agutter

Very often, I hear the standing joke surrounding Goldfish, members of the tooth carp family, where some folk laugh about the species attention span of around 9 seconds. Well, I have some news and a surprise for those folk, for the average Human's attention span today has now gone from 30 seconds down to around 12 seconds and getting lower.

Attention span is far different to memory!

Attention span in many respects is more related to processing speed and ability. A fish's reaction and attention span is far less as a result of predators and threats in the wild. Fish do not have the time to weigh up their options like "is this shark going to eat me or not" and the reason why a human's attention span is dropping, is down to being re-wired as a result of smart technology and human advances?

One thing I have learned over the years is how humbled I continue to become, as I learn more surrounding our world that we know and a planet that is home for many millions of Wild Life species who all function within the covenant and rules of Natural Law, a subject area encompassing Natural Branching and Quantum Mechanics. For it is evident to me, the more informed we become, we are then presented with the task of needing to learn and understand so much more.

One of the great debates today in the Science Community is consciousness, the realization of life, living, being a live, and this subject area is now being expanded out to countless millions of Wild Life species world-wide and one very popular case example and project today being with Dolphins, where they recognize themselves in mirrors.

Now these projects and tests being carried out, I think are based on our naïve arrogance of understanding with regards to our fellow Wild Life. For whilst we have the power of speech in a vocal form, there is in fact another universal language of communication that is relevant to all life form species on the planet including ourselves. And this is emotion encompassed with electromagnetic gravity and wave (energy) frequencies.

You see every life form carries electromagnetic energy, we see this in our everyday lives but very rarely take any notice, a dog barking at you for example, hairs standing up on the back of your neck, headaches before a storm, these are all signatures of these energies being present in ourselves and all other species.

You see we give off these energies every day in our lives and some fellow humans can pick up on these energy frequencies more often, especially close couples and family pets. These electrical energy emotions can be seen and experienced by others when you are down for example, feeling a little upset, or depressed, such emotions and energies are not kept only to yourself.

Being able to acknowledge the presence of these energy forces, we can then begin to understand how it is possible to connect with other life forms, not through speech but through energy to realize our full potential as Human Beings. I sincerely hope, by finding the best in humanity, eventually we will all come to exercise the greatest and utmost respect for all other life form species here on Earth as we further evolve and understand.

My First Aquarium Collectors Edition

To further expand our knowledge of Marine Life concerning fish species, we need to familiarize ourselves with fish anatomy, and so I have created a number of diagrams, to help Aquarists come up to speed concerning this subject area, as we go through this chapter exploring fish behaviour and characteristics.

In this chapter there are also other illustrations and photographs to support the information provided to try and give a visual image of events, as I endeavour to try and articulate certain behavioral patterns, including communication between fellow fish species and even fish communication to the Aquarist that can very often be missed.

As we discuss the subject in detail, very frequently there will be reference to certain fish species limbs, namely fins and therefore it is worthwhile and helpful to the Aquarist if they are familiar with the fish species anatomy.

Later in the book especially surrounding disease subjects, there will very often be a reference to certain parts of the fish species anatomy, so as to help relay this information for successful diagnosis here is the following diagram.

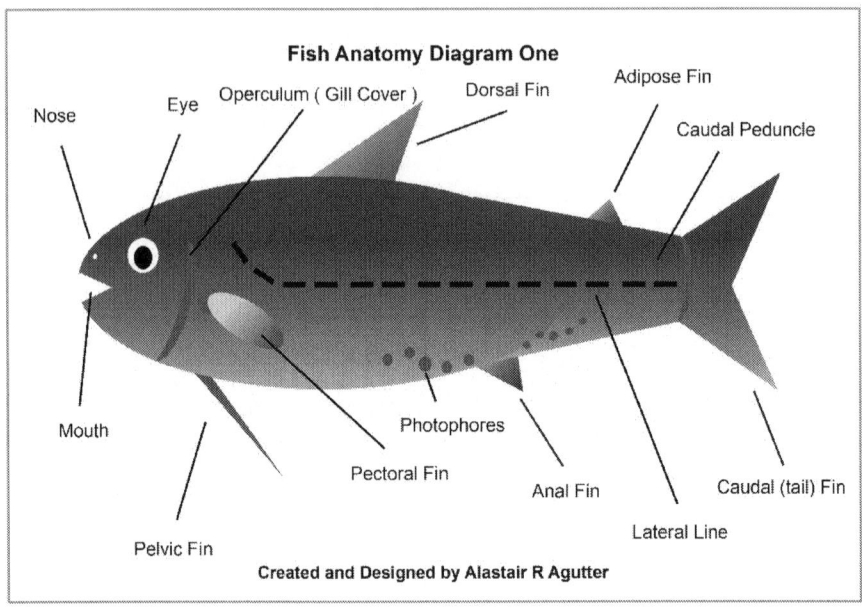

Diagram One of Fish Anatomy showing external features and limbs of fish species for Aquarists to familiarize themselves with – Diagram Created by Alastair R Agutter

The first diagram above shows a fish's anatomy covering the external features and limbs of fish species.

You will quickly concur as an aquarist, not all vertebrate fish species share the same body makeup. The adipose fin for example is not always present in all species of fish for example.

The next fish anatomy diagram and illustration provides us with the basic internal organs and structure of fish to help familiarize Aquarists.

Most fish species are vertebrates (spine and bone skeletal frames) and in the 1970's it was recorded that there were over 33,000 different species. However, there is another body make-up structure of fish called Cartilaginous, and in the 1970's, it was recorded that there were over 550 species. These species of fish have a cartilage (soft bone type) structure and members of such species include sharks, rays and a good number of catfish species.

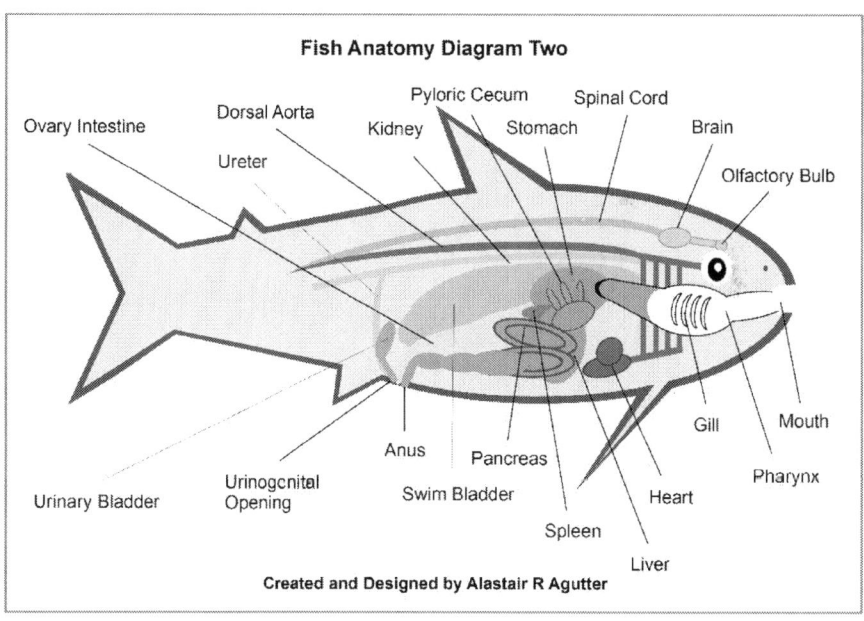

Diagram Two of Fish Anatomy showing the common internal organs of fish species for Aquarists to familiarize themselves with – Diagram Created by Alastair R Agutter

One apparent point to remember with regards to fish species anatomy, many do have scales but not all. Sharks for example have an abrasive skin tissue, literally like sand paper and it is still actually used as a sand medium for smoothing timbers by native fisherman where the skins are hung to dry.

One thing we can appreciate and agree on is the vast diversity of fish species from Coldwater, Saltwater to Tropical Fish Marine Species.

However, when we consider Charles Darwin's work we can find similarities in all species on Earth from Fish, Animal, Bird and Insect Life etc. where all creatures have limbs and similarly related internal organs. These similarities and characteristics also extends to varying intelligence levels by the acknowledgement that all species have brain capacity and communication skills, to enable reproduction and to execute normal Natural Law life cycles.

The more we study marine life, the more fascinating it becomes and especially surrounding tropical fish, as there are many ways in which fish communicate between each other and even ourselves, but we are very often guilty of missing the signs.

So I truly hope the information found in this chapter is very valuable advice and provides ground breaking insight.

With regards to marine fish species behaviour, the first rule of thumb is survival, and for fish to survive, we have to provide fish the right water conditions and environment when tropical fish species inhabit aquariums.

Once the water is of the right quality, fish will begin to show their natural instinctive characteristics, showing an appetite for food and exploring their new environment.

Very soon after several days or weeks depending on the acclimatization transition to the Aquarists aquarium, fish species will start to exercise a pecking order among their own species and others.

Some of this behaviour may relate to territoriality, especially if the fish species in question are cichlids.

Contrary to any myths or beliefs, all fish species have a pecking order and when establishing or marking out new territory, these can be moments and times of anxiety for the Aquarist, as fish begin to fight and ward-off interlopers once territory is gained or established.

In extreme circumstances these territorial battles can sometimes come at a considerable price, with the health deterioration of a fish and where they stop eating, or worse still death, as a result of persistent attacks.

Pecking orders are what they are, and throughout a shoal, or group of fish, there will be a pecking order right the way down to the last fish species in the shoal, group, or aquarium.

Very often this activity can be misinterpreted by a new aquarist, where they may believe that one of their new inhabitant acquisitions is just in plain and simple terms a bully in the aquarium environment.

In such instances of misinterpretation, I have seen these fish species who appear to be the aquarium bully isolated to another aquarium, or in extreme circumstances, returned to the retailer from where the fish species was purchased. However, this does not resolve the problem, but only causes all remaining fish inhabitants in the aquarium to start the process of fighting again in the fish tank to establish a new pecking order.

In the Aquarist's aquarium there will always be a dominant member of a pecking order in specific fish species groups and across fish species. From young species to adult fish, pecking order battles will be fought out.

From Platies, Guppies, Barbs, Tetras to Angel Fish and Discus there is always a pecking order in an aquarium environment just as there is in the Seas, Rivers, Streams and Tributaries of the Wild.

These pecking order battles after a period of time will settle down and rise up occasionally, as certain fish species members of the aquarium environment reach sexual reproduction age, as fish species start to find a suitable mates and pair-off.

Electromagnetic waves, gravity and energies play a significant part in pecking orders when establishing a hierarchy in an aquarium, as is the case in the Wild. This can be particularly noticeable in fish positioning and fin movement in addition to electromagnetic energy thought patterns transmitted between the fish species. Some of this behaviour with regards to thought patterns can be seen when a fish species moves off and away from another fish species that we interpret as instinctively knowing.

The pecking order battles consist of electromagnetic energies (thought patterns), actual pecking, nipping, nudging, fin displays, jaw locking, pushing and ramming.

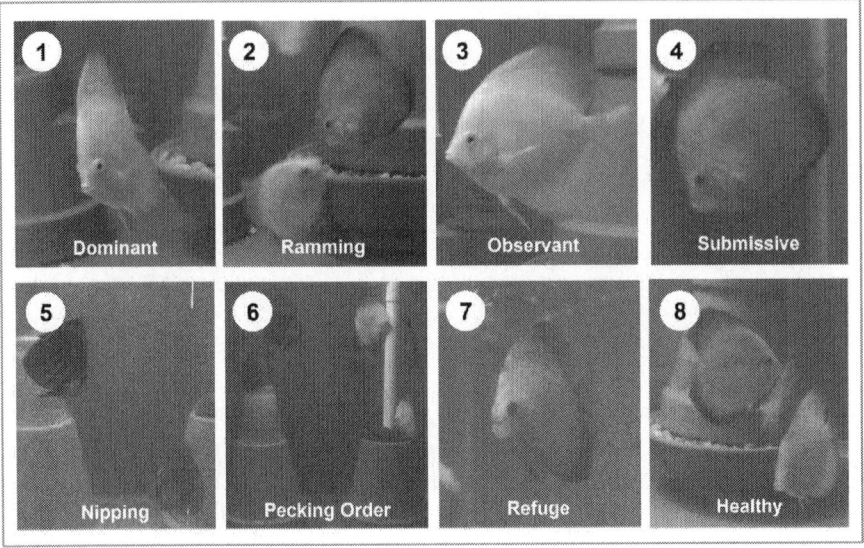

Above are some pictures of common fish behavioural characteristics and highlighting these to provide a visual as we discuss the topic in this chapter – Photographs by Alastair R Agutter

PUSHING AND RAMMING

The latter in the list above is the most effective and brutal of events, as fish dart towards each other at great speed, aiming to hit their opponent in the swim bladder or stomach region. Such aggressive activity winds a fish on the receiving end and can cause internal problems when the swim bladder is affected for short or long periods of time.

The victim fish when hurt can often seek refuge towards the top and in a corner of the aquarium, or even swim in a strange manner going round in circles repeatedly, with the occasional shaking of the head, as the fish tries to breath normally again.

JAW LOCKING

Interlocking with a jaw fight, is where the fish species push and pull at each other, to establish the strongest between the two fighting fish species. Such activity regarding the testing of wills and strength can go on for several hours, days and weeks until there is a conclusive outcome between the two parties involved.

FISH NIPPING

Nipping is a very common characteristic and behaviour pattern of fish, where the fish gives the odd nip to another fish species member of the aquarium, very often seen at feeding times, when another fish tries to take food from another.

FISH PECKING

Pecking is where sometimes a fish species will carry-out a series of nips to the tail of a fish and will pursue the victim for a short distance. This can also include more destructive behaviour towards another fish species where the pectoral fins are attacked to immobilize the fish. This I have witnessed first-hand with Angel Fish (*Pterophylium scalare*) especially.

FISH NUDGING

This behaviour of nudging can be seen more often with adult fish species, where they choose not to exert their power as adults, but just give a nudge to another fish to say, "hey, go away, give me some space" or at times in mating, where a female may nudge the male, reminding him to carry-out his cleaning duties, as they prepare to spawn.

FIN DISPLAYS

The behaviour of fish regarding fin display and movement is a whole new language in itself. Very often when a fish has fins displayed fully and just sitting in the water watching and observing is a sign of contentment.

When a fish have fins clamped (closed together) and towards the surface of the water this is a sign of displeasure and seeking a degree of sanctuary away from other members of the aquarium community. Very often this behaviour is seen in livebearers, where a female species especially are seeking some peace and quiet from the continued advances of an amorous male species.

The wave effect across a dorsal fin caused by fish species, such as Discus (*symphysodon*) that can look like a Mexican wave, is the sign of the fish species wanting to make it known of their presence and seeking acknowledgement. This can often be seen with fish species where a relationship already exists between two fish, or where a potential pairing relationship is being formed.

The rapid shaking of a fish's head from side to side and the flicking of the fins at the same time, is also another sign of seeking acknowledgement and attention. This is very often seen with cichlids, especially Angel and Discus Fish species towards the Aquarist in a great many cases, when fish want feeding. The fish are in fact motioning to the Aquarist when they start flicking their fins and head from side to side. At such times also the fish will carry out very short swim movements, on average half the length of the fish in a forward motion directly looking towards the top of the aquarium or at the Aquarist. In such instances the fish in question will literally move up at an angle towards the top of the aquarium saying "hey, feed me" and this behaviour can be seen across a whole host of fish species if carefully studied.

Pectoral and Pelvic fins are also frequently used in communication between fish species. Very often pelvic fins on cichlids such as Discus and Angel fish have the ability to flick their pelvic fins as they pass each other as a form of acknowledgment often seen in breeding pairs or where a relationship has been established with other aquarium tanks mates.

The flicking of the pelvic fins can also be seen when engaging in a fight with another fish species member. On these occasions the pelvic fins are flicked in a forward and back motion towards the oncoming protagonist to ward them off.

At mating times, some species use the pelvic fins for the stimulation of their male or female companion.

SEXING SPECIES

Sexing of fish species such as Cichlids can also be determined by the shape of the pelvic fins. Male cichlid species pelvic fins are very often more pointed, whereas the female's pelvic fins when meeting the pelvic fin tissues that form part of the pelvic fin are more curved.

As a new Aquarist, when it comes to sexing cichlid species, most indications regarding the sex of a species can be determined by a number of factors and in most cases, these being size of fish, the dorsal fin, anal fin, tail and pelvic fins.

Regarding cichlids and sexing them as a fish species, most males can often be smaller than the female, the males fins are often more pointed and trailing, this related to the following in question; Dorsal, Anal, Pelvic and Tail Fins.

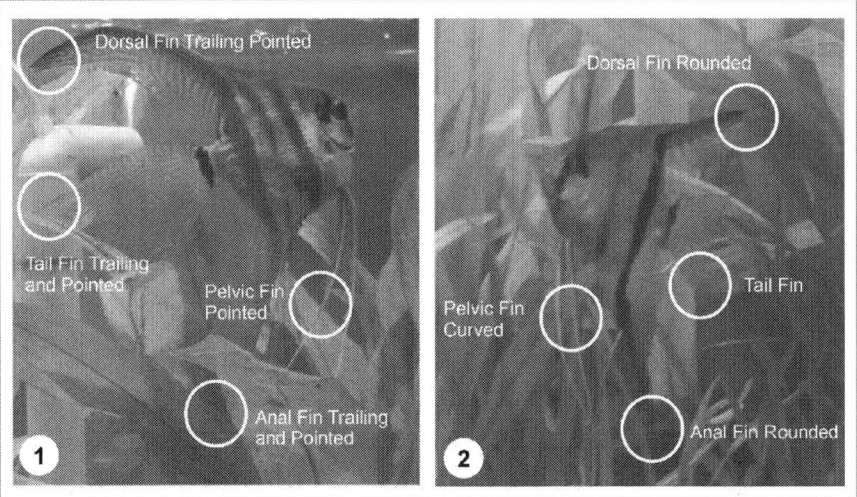

Picture 1 a Male Angel Fish highlighting his fin characteristics and Picture 2 shows a Female Angel Fish highlighting her fin characteristics – Photographs by Alastair R Agutter

In the above pictures I hope they show the subtle and distinct signs of sexual difference between the male and female of these species with regards to their fin anatomy configuration.

The female regarding this breeding pair, is also larger in size and is far heavier set in her body build.

Angel and Discus Fish (Cichlidae Family) are not the easiest of cichlid species to sex. Such awareness can only come in most cases over time by studying the species. Today regarding the same said species, they can vary considerably in shape as a result of breeding in captivity, where certain characteristics are accentuated in the selective breeding process, down through one generation of fish to another, namely colouration and ornate fins.

The sexual organs of egg laying fish species is 1/. The Ovipositor is the sexual organ of females and this protrudes from the body when egg laying and can look like a short blunt tube seen near the female's anus. 2/. The male sexual organ is pointed and tube (papilla) like, releasing sperm to fertilize the eggs.

In some instances with regards to sexing fish species, colouration can play a part in addition to fin shape. You only have to look at the difference between male and female guppies (Poeciliidae Family). The female guppy is much larger in size to her male counterpart, yet the male has greater colouration and very often exotic fanning tail fins.

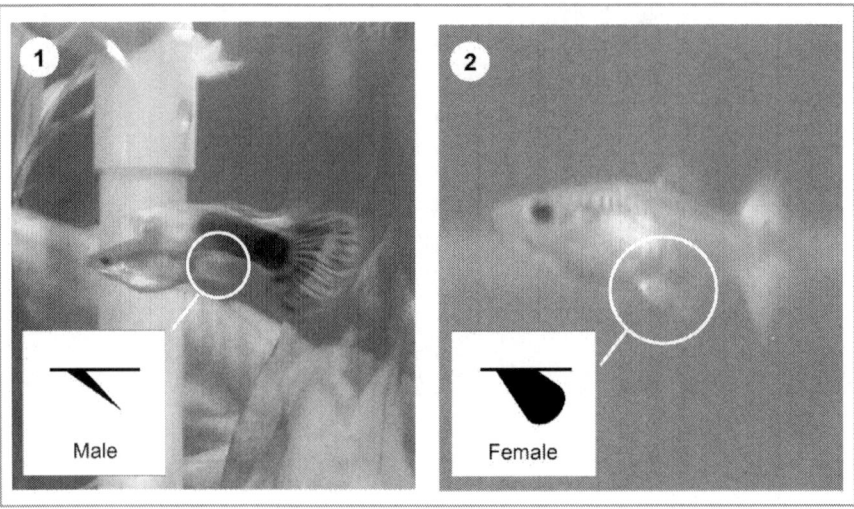

Picture 1 shows the Male Guppy and Sexual Point Anal Fin and Picture 2 shows the Female Guppy Fanned Sexual Anal Fin – Photographs and Drawings by Alastair R Agutter

The above two pictures shows both of the sexual reproductive fin orientation of male and female guppies with their unmistakable distinguishing differences.

Other similar species of livebearers such as Swordtails are far easier to sex, for the male does have a pointed tail, whereas the female of the species does not.

Most species of Barb's (Cyprinidae Family) when it comes to sexing is very difficult, it is very often the case, that females of this species genera family are larger in size and not so colourful.

Most species of Tetra's (Characins Family) are similar to Barb's, where the female of the species, tends to be the larger of the two, but slightly less colourful. However, as egg scatterers, very often in many female Tetra species such as Neon's and Cardinals can be found on the anal fins white flecks of colour and this indicates to me, to be a distinct navigational sign for males, so they are able to easily follow and fertilize the female's eggs when she is scattering her eggs in dark brackish water regions such as the Great River Amazon and adjoining Rivers and Tributaries.

The more you study these remarkable features and differences, the more things start to make sense when trying to understand the magnificent diversity of the Wild and in this instance particularly Marine Life.

In the next part of this chapter we now move onto other sexual related behavioural patterns in fish, where the end game and aim is to reproduce (create life).

Even soon after birth fish begin a pecking order as they seek out food and this behaviour continues throughout their life. Survival for all our Wild Life today has far greater relevance and more meaning throughout all species as like never before, as food resources continue to become less abundant from Climate Change caused from Corporate Industrialization and negligent State Governments destroying our Planet.

In captivity such behaviour patterns and drive by fry and young fish species for food should not really exist, as food is, or should be supplied in abundance and equally scattered around the aquarium when rearing the fry.

But such traits do exist in fry and young fish, for it is the case that these activities are genetically and instinctively passed down through the ages.

Within this melting pot of fish behaviour and characteristics from fry to adulthood are many facets. The belief that the strongest and fittest is the key, in reality is nothing more than a simplified myth of understanding. For in most cases, the most dominant fish species from any brood very rarely grow up to become the best parents.

More evolved fish species such as Angel and Discus fish when finding a partner, mate for life in most instances. However, a very dominant member in a community is not always so loyal and can very often seek to disrupt or hi-jack proceedings when a compatible pair are spawning. Extremely dominant fish in these circumstances I believe are a necessary evil to coin the phrase in the grand scheme of Mother Nature, for such an entity and presence encourages the devoted spawning pair to be closer in their bond towards each other and more protective towards their brood regarding this interloper and other fish species that threaten.

It is without doubt regarding all species on the Planet and throughout the Cosmos, that Mother Nature in relation to the covenant of Natural Law deals a hand that only ever totals 100%. So in other words, any form of evolution through Natural Branching and Quantum Mechanics whilst having the ability to evolve and refine, including work arounds, always has to work within the bounds of this mathematical formula and equation of 100%.

Good examples of the above is when a fish species becomes particularly large, the downside is very often the fish is either thinner in build or less colourful. Another example is fish species for example can be smaller in size from the same brood, but more colourful than many of their Brothers and Sisters. Another example is a member of the brood may become extremely powerful and large, but the downside is the member of the brood in question is a useless parent and always eats the eggs of his or her off-spring or neglect them full stop!

However, where the covenant of Natural Law only ever comes under threat is the resource for life in the way of food and perhaps this is why such a strong driving mechanism of eating exists within the gene code of all Wild Life species. Now I say all "Wild Life" species for good reason, for Human Beings should have by now evolved sufficiently beyond this primitive behaviour and be only driven by intelligence and learning that is the primary purpose and focus.

When Natural Law is threatened by a lack of food, it has dire consequences for individuals and groups of species. As one good example concerning Marine Life, was the continued catching of large Icelandic Cod over several decades to meet quotas and adhere to limit and size regulations, with the throwing back of the smaller species and a continued reduction in the food supply for these species, has led to where we are today (2016) where generations of Cod are now genetically much smaller as a result of poor diet and the breeding of only between the smaller members of the species.

So the dominance behaviour and characteristics in Marine Life is without doubt a deep genetic trait from birth through to adulthood and onto future generations at this time.

DOMINANT SIGNS

As mentioned above dominant behaviour in species will be found from fry stage through to adulthood. Within a matter of a few days and weeks young fry of any species will show signs of some members of the brood doing much better than others.

The appetite for food by all descendant fry of all Marine Fish species is an inherent gene code phenomenon, as discussed above. From experience, however good your fish husbandry skills are when rearing fry, you will always see a distinct differences in size of the brood members, especially after several weeks.

The following picture shows the rearing of some youngsters and where there is a distinct pecking order in play where from the dominance of some even with an abundance of food, as it reaches the bottom of the aquarium is guarded and eaten by the dominant members of the group as well as fighting off other group members trying to prevent them from reaching or eating the food.

Such events make you want to pull your hair out for sometimes you have to carry out water changes to prevent the water from spoiling or building up with too much Ammonia as a result of uneaten food.

Dominant behaviour in these instances, involve fish members hovering over the food with fins splayed out and a darkening in colour of the more dominant fish to ward-off others.

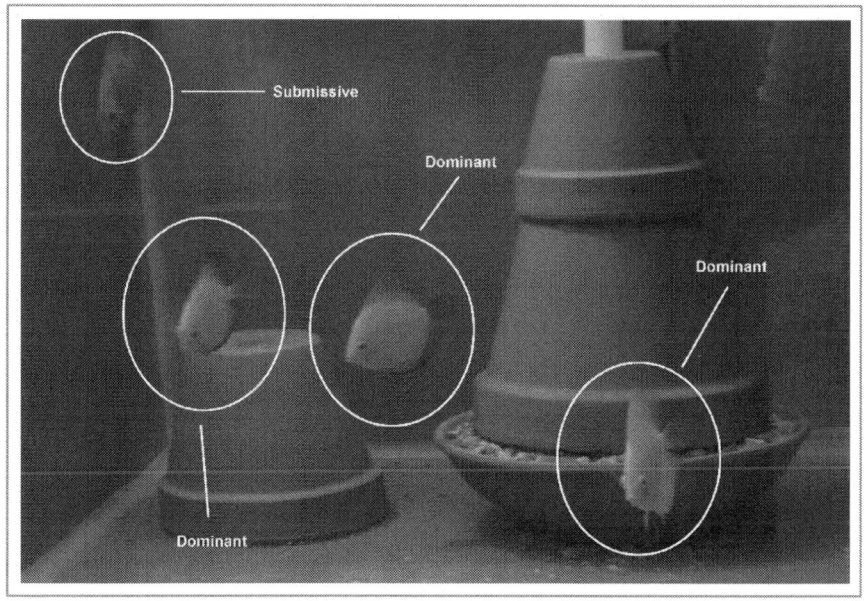

Picture above showing dominant activity in an aquarium where young Discus guard food and chase off other members in the fish tank – Photographs and Drawings by Alastair R Agutter

Other fish that near these dominant members will also see a darkening of the body and full fin displays, but also with a swishing of the fish's body from side to side. This causes a violent turbulence in the water and this is another form of communication and another fine example of how fin movements can send various waves of communication through the water and all attached with electromagnetic gravity, waves and energies.

Such an example of the above being; with the discovery by Marine Biologists when studying the reproductive migration cycles problems of the paddle fish from the Potomac and Missouri River, where from electromagnetic energies and currents from the high presence of metal runs in the water for the fish to by-pass dams etc. has prevented the fish from travelling up river to spawn.

SUBMISSIVE SIGNS

Fish when threatened will go into a submissive position and this is when the fish bow their heads and very often they back away when threatened. The picture above shows in the top left corner a Discus in a submissive mode, where the victim Discus has been driven away from the food by the other more dominant members in the aquarium.

However, there are other times when evolved cichlid species such as Discus especially will bow their head and this is when passing a mate, where they will subtly bow, almost giving acknowledgement and reverence to their fellow loved one.

FISH LIFE EXISTENCE

Whether at times of dominance or submissive periods by fish, the biggest and most dangerous threat to losing tropical fish member is where the fish loses the will to live. That's right!

One thing I want you to know as an Aquarist, when keeping tropical fish you are never a failure if fish die!

There can be a whole host of reasons for why fish die, yet very often an Aquarist will blame them self, thinking they have done something wrong, but this is not the case, if the golden rules are applied and followed, these being; acclimatization, regular feeding and regular water changes.

Fortunately, as an Aquarist now reaching my fiftieth year, I can share with you my knowledge and experience of tropical fish keeping. Very often fish can simply lose the will to live from bullying, can have complications in child birth (livebearers), can die of liver and kidney disease, heart disease from poor diet, die from stress caused from mental illness, die from genetic deformities, die from attack by another member in the aquarium, die from airborne and marine viruses, yes fish can catch colds.

But lastly and most often, simply die from old age and so in the next chapter, I will provide in the selection of popular tropical fish, also advise on the average age of fish species.

ELECTROMAGNETIC TRANSMISSION AND OBSERVATION

This may well be the very first time you have read from a tropical fish book the subject of Electromagnetic Energies in the form of Transmission, Gravity and Waves. Also observation and recognition by fish species.

This is not an excerpt or an extract from a Sci-fi Movie when I say we are not alone, or are we the centre of the Universe as some will have you believe, that is a fact. If it were the case that Earth (home) was the centre of the Universe, she would be around 13 billion plus years old and not around 4.5 billion years old.

All species on our planet consist of a brain (intelligence), limbs and organs, even whilst they are different on land, in water or in the air, this is a fact!

It was only a few hundred years ago Humans believed the World to be flat, today I like to think we all now know better, but you never know.

As a species (humans) we have reached a fork in the road, where we can continue to advance the human story and journey by learning to be good shepherds to our planet and all life, or in reality face total destruction from Corporate Industrialization this being consumerism resulting in climate change, for the more we advance the window of error becomes forever smaller.

In our noble pastime and hobby of tropical fish keeping, where we share a passion for beautiful majestic species of Marine Life, I like to think we are now ready and big enough to move forward further in a very measured and balanced way regarding a subject area that we have come to know and respect as Natural Law.

When you really drill down and analyse in atomic particle matter form the elements, we soon realize, all that we know is connected, be it our land, seas and skies. All we see and know is constructed from particle matter in all its diversity that we are now only really beginning to learn and digest and where there is so much more yet to be known and discovered.

One thing we have learned with the use of modern day technology and especially WiFi devices such as smart phones, is the power of radiation in the form of subatomic particle photons in frequency ranges.

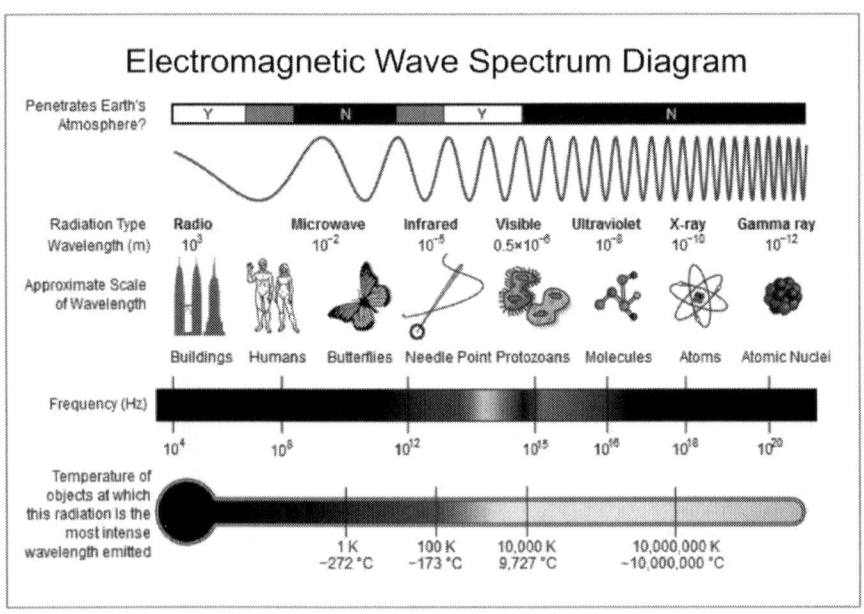

Above diagram shows the Electromagnetic Wave Spectrum to provide us with an insight to how wave lengths and frequencies work in conjunction with radiation – Diagram Courtesy of Nasa

Another thing we do know is, how water is a conductor to energy in many forms, and if you place a mobile device near a kettle, or a bowl of water for example, you will quickly be surprised to see how water immerses such energies and frequencies and where there is a noticeable change and difference in the receiving of signals and transmissions (reception).

We also know from fact that Whales and Dolphins (mammals), two of our close cousins use sonar, not just for navigation, but communication and planned collaborative strategies between groups and pods.

We also know as a fact, that Sharks are attracted to movement, caused by vibration and noise in the water. Sharks are cartilaginous species and regarded as one of the oldest and most advanced species on Earth and at the very top of the Marine Life food chain as a predator.

Below is a diagram of a Shark to familiarize Aquarists with the difference between fish species that are vertebrates and sharks, rays and many catfish that are cartilaginous species.

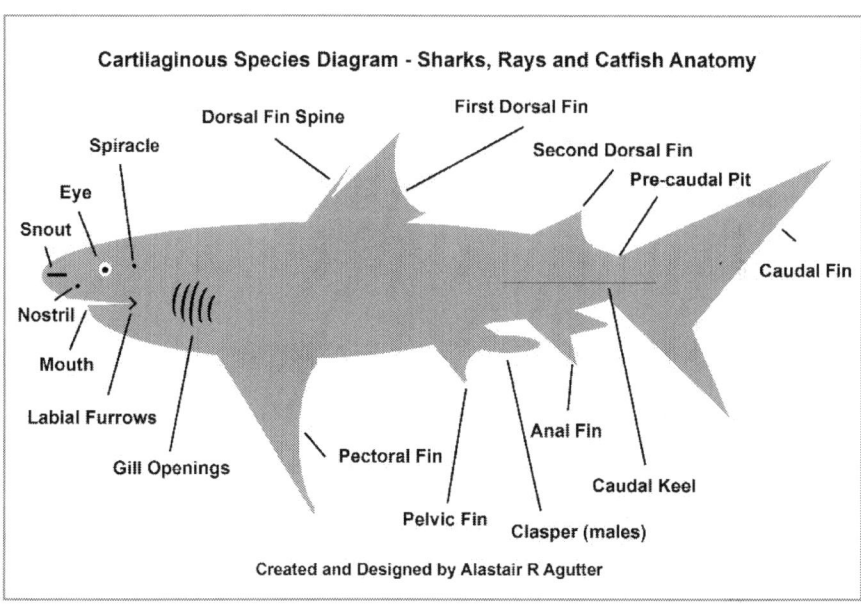

Diagram above showing the anatomy of most Cartilaginous Species that include Sharks, Rays and many Catfish – Diagram Illustration Created and Designed by Alastair R Agutter

Electromagnetic energies are used by countless species, in fact our humble Robin circumnavigates the Earth when migrating by Electromagnetic Gravity, this indicates variables in many forms and where I am not convinced that these are subtle frequencies, but more of the case that we have not wired ourselves today by our neuron emitters in the brain to read and understand.

Technology is showing from study that our memory and concentration periods are adapting and changing from the greater use of technology devices.

Have we ever had the ability to use electromagnetic frequencies and energies, I truly believe we use them all the time, but do not recognize our transmission of such data, or the receiving of it!

But I genuinely believe our fellow Wild Life species on Earth are able to pick up and read what we transmit in the form of Electromagnetic energies.

The more I study and understand this subject, the more it truly disturbs me to think human intention can be signaled and read, perhaps it is not a sixth sense that cattle know they are going to slaughter, but the ability to read our electromagnetic energy thought processes and patterns that emit a darker side.

I know it is not my imagination, but ten years ago from my studies, I never recall any of my tropical fish species after a short period of time in my company, becoming so aggressive towards their fellow species and others in an aquarium community. It is almost like my fish inhabitants are picking up my electromagnetic energies that are also storing and documenting my subconscious thoughts, where we are all currently storing some very sad stories and events in our troubled World.

There is a great deal we can learn from them, as they signal to me it's feeding time 1/. Golden Marbled Angel 2/. Rare White Discus part of the Author's Ark Project breeding program in the event of a major disaster in the Wild – Photographs by Alastair R Agutter

To some such claims may be crazy, but I think we need to seriously evaluate our importance in the grand scheme of things. Perhaps we are continually changing as a species to better ourselves, as we are the evolving species, the new kid on the block as they say and continuing to learn the story of co-existence with other fellow species of the World, all of whom have existed for millions of years before ourselves, who have "evolved" here on Earth.

Perhaps to the point where any process of change now regarding evolution by all other species, relates to countering our human activity and foot print that is having a devastating impact.

The more I study marine species as they study me, I now find myself more each day thinking of the Native American's, where every species were held in great respect and where there was a far better understanding than by us today.

Healthy thriving fish are without doubt from my studying and understanding, not only very trusting creatures once you have connected, but very social characters and this is why it is imperative to have an aquarium in a good position in the home and at a decent height, so the fish can see your activities, just as much as you see theirs.

I think the brutal aspects we see by Wild Life to a great degree, is as a result of the continued decline in food resources throughout our planet and the forever continued encroachment on their habitats.

The hope I hold in my heart for the future of all Wild Life and the Planet is from the Millennials and where just as one example recently, my young Daughter said "Dad you really love those fish don't you?" I acknowledged her by saying "I love all creatures," but remained silent in my words and thoughts, regarding our very own adult species, for their continued insane negligent behaviour so often demonstrated today in our world only fills me with great sadness and despair.

If you are a Millennial and care about our World at a time when the Bee is now being placed on the endangered extinction species list for Wild Life, towards the back of the book you will find details on "The Young Aquarists Ark Project" to help towards preserving our Marine Wild Life.

CHAPTER TWELVE
Aquarium Fish Species

In the 1970's when studying marine life, there were discovered over 33,500 species of vertebrate fish species and over 550 cartilaginous species. Today, I know these figures have dramatically changed in numerous directions, as more species have since been discovered and sadly others have since become extinct.

One of the Author's Naturally Planted Aquariums with a wide and varied selection of Community Aquaria Tropical Fish Species – Photograph by Alastair R Agutter

So in this chapter, I have decided to detail some of the most popular tropical fish species, accompanied with summary profiles. This will provide a good grounding for Aquarists to familiarize themselves with member family genera and regions that will then serve you well, as you further diversify your tropical fish keeping species collection.

The following colour plates will be accompanied with profiles as mentioned above on the following pages.

The information provided will be the common and full names of the fish species, the fish species genetic fish family, the regions from where the fish species reside in the wild, the suitability of the fish species whether they are suitable for a community aquarium or if they are an aggressive fish species, the average size attained by the fish species, the average temperature range for the fish species, the most suitable PH range of the fish species, the recommended diet I use for these fish species, the reproduction behaviour of the fish species and the average age span of the fish species.

I hope by taking a cross section of fish species from various genera families it will quickly familiarize you with what fish are suitable and compatible with each other. However, as we know from reading fish characteristics and behaviour in the previous chapter, nothing is ever set in stone with regards to dominant members of the aquarium and the trials and tribulations of pecking orders.

Regarding healthy thriving fish and their diets, this will be covered in detail later in the book. The reference to diet in these profiles serves as a guide for Aquarists.

The other factors covered with regards to water PH quality and temperatures etc. Have been written based on my experience over the years when successfully keeping all these fish species that are covered in this section of the book.

You may come across some slight differing reference material online or in other books regarding these profile facts, this is often the case as many Aquarists do have different methods and successful techniques.

My First Aquarium Collectors Edition

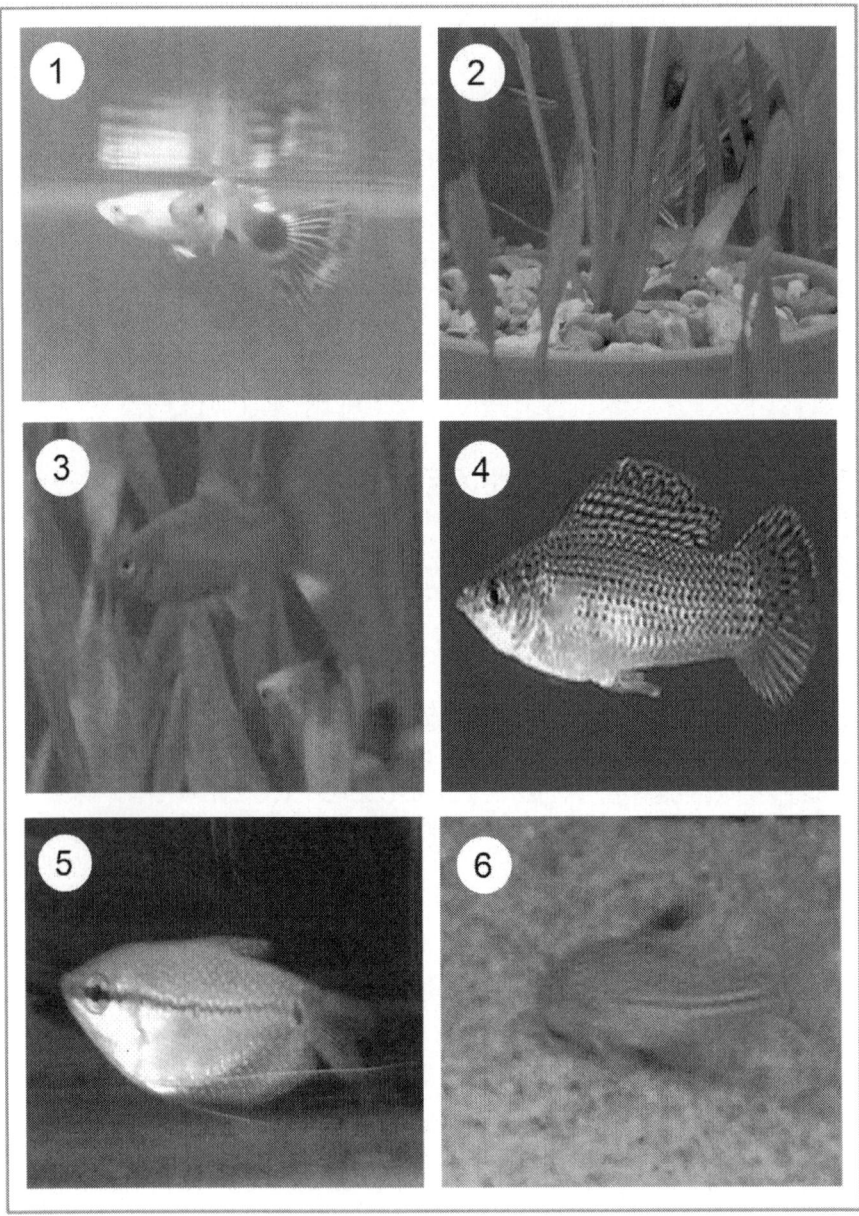

Plates Collection of Photographs and Artwork Compiled by Alastair R Agutter

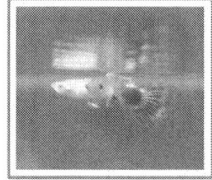
Photograph by Alastair R Agutter

1/. Name: Guppies

Species Name: *Poecilia reticulata*

Summary Description: Guppies over the decades in tropical fish keeping have been very much the star of the show. I should imagine at some time or another, every Aquarist has kept Guppies. They are an easy fish to keep and renowned prolific livebearer breeders discharging live fry on average several times a year. They have a very varied diet and always have a healthy appetite. Males are generally smaller in size compared to the females and the most colourful of the species.

Member Family Genera: Poeciliidae

Region(s): South America, Africa, Caribbean, Asia, North America and Europe

Disposition: Good Community Aquarium Fish

Average Adult Size: Males 1-1/2 inch, Females 2 to 2-1/2 inch

Average Temperature: 68 to 84 Fahrenheit

PH Range: 6.8 to 7.6 PH

Diet: Varied Diet Flake Foods

Reproduction: Livebearers

Lifespan: 2 years

Photograph by Alastair R Aguiler

2/. Name: Swordtails

Species Name: *Xiphophorus hellerii*

Summary Description: Swordtails are another popular livebearer tropical fish species and originally green in colour discovered by Johann Heckel in 1848 and remains still today a favourite with many Aquarists. One of the most popular colourations for many decades has been the orange coloured Swordtail as seen in the photograph above. Swordtails will produce off-spring several times a year similar to Platies and Guppies.

Member Family Genera: Poeciliidae

Region(s): North and Central America, Honduras and Mexico

Disposition: Suitable Community Aquarium Fish

Average Adult Size: 5 to 6.3 inches

Average Temperature: 72 to 84 Fahrenheit

PH Range: 6.8 to 7.6 PH

Diet: Varied Diet Flake Foods

Reproduction: Livebearer

Lifespan: 2 to 3 years

Photograph by Alastair R Agutter

3/. Name: Platies

Species Name: *Xiphophorus*

Summary Description: Platies are another very popular tropical fish species and very often found in community aquariums. Platies are again livebearers and produce on average between 30 to 50 young fry every 30 to 40 days. Platies can come in numerous colours and sizes today for the Aquarist and a very easy tropical fish to keep.

Member Family Genera: Poeciliidae

Region(s): Central America and Mexico

Disposition: Suitable Community Aquarium Fish

Average Adult Size: 2 to 2.8 inches

Average Temperature: 70 to 84 Fahrenheit

PH Range: 6.8 to 7.6 PH

Diet: Varied Diet Flake Foods

Reproduction: Livebearer

Lifespan: 2 to 3 years

Photograph by Alastair R Agutter

4/. Name: Sail Fin Molly

Species Name: Poecilia

Summary Description: Mollies are another favourite with the tropical fish hobbyist over many decades and in the wild can live in fresh and saltwater. The species Poecilia *latipunctata* and *sulphuraria* are now on the critical endangered list.

Fortunately Mollies are still readily available in captivity and can be obtained in various colours from most tropical fish retail outlets or Aquarist Clubs. Mollies are again a livebearer and produce off-spring several times during a year.

Member Family Genera: Poeciliidae

Region(s): Mexico, Central and South America

Disposition: Suitable Community Aquarium Fish

Average Adult Size: 4 to 6 inches

Average Temperature: 77 to 84 Fahrenheit

PH Range: 7.0 to 7.8 PH

Diet: Varied Diet Flake Foods

Reproduction: Livebearer

Lifespan: 2 to 3 years

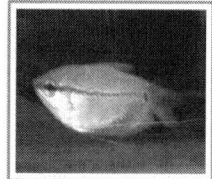

Photograph by Alastair R Agutter

5/. Name: Pearl Gourami

Species Name: *Trichopodus leerii*

Summary Description: The Pearl or Lace Gourami is another popular tropical fish for the community aquarium. The fish species are known as bubble nest builders where they create a unique nest from bubbles where the eggs are placed on the surface of the aquarium normally near floating plants such as wisteria. Males are normally slightly more colourful compared to the female and very often develop an orange tinge colouration. Gourami's very often live in brackish water and even known to be living in paddy fields. Gourami's as a species are Labyrinth fish and with the Labyrinth organ, it allows these fish species to breath in air from the surface of the water, to help oxygenate the blood stream.

Member Family Genera: Osphronemidae

Region(s): Thailand, Malaysia, Indonesian, Sumatra and Borneo

Disposition: Prefer Calm Community Aquarium Environments

Average Adult Size: 4 to 5 inches

Average Temperature: 74 to 84 Fahrenheit

PH Range: 6.8 to 7.6 PH

Diet: Varied Diet Flake Foods

Reproduction: Spawning Eggs, Bubble Nest Builders

Lifespan: 4 to 5 years

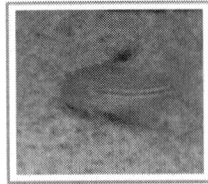

Photograph by Alastair R Agutter

6/. Name: Leopard Corydoras Catfish

Species Name: *Corydoras trilineatus*

Summary Description: The Leopard Corydoras Catfish or the Three Striped Corydoras catfish are excellent community aquarium catfish scavengers and very entertaining to watch, as they work their way along the bottom of the aquarium seeking out uneaten food.

If fed correctly they will grow to an adult size in a matter of weeks of around 2.5 inches in length. Other community aquarium members do not appear to be phased by their presence at all.

Member Family Genera: Callichthyidae

Region(s): Brazil, Peru and Columbia

Disposition: A Good Community Aquarium Scavenger

Average Adult Size: 2.5 inches

Average Temperature: 72 to 84 Fahrenheit

PH Range: 6.0 to 8.0 PH

Diet: Varied Diet, Flake Foods, Algae etc.

Reproduction: Egg Layer

Lifespan: 4 to 5 years

My First Aquarium Collectors Edition

Plates Collection of Photographs and Artwork Compiled by Alastair R Agutter

Photograph by Alastair R Agulter

7/. Name: Rummy-Nose Tetra

Species Name: *Hemigrammus rhodostomus*

Summary Description: In recent years the Rummy-Nose Tetra has become an ever increasing favourite tropical fish species with today's Aquarist.

A large number of these species in an aquarium can look stunning. Rummy-Nose Tetra's tend to always shoal and the bright red iridescent nose and silver body can be a sight to behold before a backdrop of a naturally planted fish tank. Rummy-Nose Tetra's are an easy fish species to keep, but a harder fish species to breed as they are egg scatterers.

Member Family Genera: Characin (Characidae).

Region(s): South America

Disposition: Excellent Community Aquarium Fish

Average Adult Size: 1.75 to 2.25 inches

Average Temperature: 76 to 84 Fahrenheit

PH Range: 6.8 to 7.8 PH

Diet: Varied Diet and Flake Foods

Reproduction: Egg Scatterers

Lifespan: 2 to 3 years

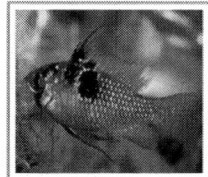

Photograph by Alastair R Agutter

8/. Name: Dwarf Ram Cichlid

Species Name: *Mikrogeophagus ramirezi*

Summary Description: The Dwarf Cichlid known as the Ram Cichlid is one of a few more peaceful species of this genera family. They are very brightly coloured species and can be very industrial and active at times.

Cichlids in most cases make good parents and at times of breeding can become very aggressive to other fish species. The Ramirez Cichlid is one of the very few however that can be enjoyed in a naturally planted community aquarium environment with other fish species. Cichlids are egg layers and very often use large broad plant leaves, rocks and slate materials to spawn on.

Member Family Genera: Cichlidae

Region(s): South America

Disposition: A Peaceful Community Cichlid

Average Adult Size: 3 to 4 inches

Average Temperature: 70 to 85 Fahrenheit

PH Range: 5.4 to 7.6 PH

Diet: Cichlid and Flake Foods

Reproduction: Egg Layers

Lifespan: 4 to 5 years

Photograph by Alastair R Agutter

9/. Name: Discus Fish

Species Name: *Symphysodon*

Summary Description: Discus Fish are known as "The King of the Aquarium" or "The King of Tropical Fish" and fully sized healthy Discus truly are a sight to behold. The above picture shows juvenile Discus species that are thankfully tank bred today and these particular colouration species are descendants of the famous Tefe Discus (symphysodon aequifasciata tefe) that had a stunning golden yellow body with red spots and blue turquoise transverse lines running through from the head of this beautiful fish species. Discus prefer to be kept on their own mainly, but small tropical fish species such as Neon's, Cardinal's and Rummy-nose tetra's in a naturally planted aquarium can work.

Member Family Genera: Cichlidae

Region(s): South America

Disposition: Highly Advanced Intelligent Cichlid Species

Average Adult Size: 6 to 9 inches

Average Temperature: 82 to 86 Fahrenheit.

PH Range: 6.0 to 8.0 PH

Diet: Beef Heart specially prepared foods and Bloodworms

Reproduction: Egg Layers

Lifespan: 5 to 10 years

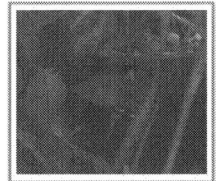

Photograph by Alastair R Agulter

10/. Name: Rosy Tetra

Species Name: *Hyphessobrycon rosaceus*

Summary Description: Rosy Tetra's are an ideal community aquarium fish species and are a very colourful attractive fish addition to any fish tank.

The Rosy Tetra's can and do shoal in numbers and serenely drift in and out of plants, causing little or no disturbance to other aquarium inhabitants. Rosy Tetra's like their other family genera members are egg scatterers in the reproduction cycle process.

Member Family Genera: Characidae

Region(s): South American Countries Guyana and Brazil

Disposition: Excellent Community Aquarium Member

Average Adult Size: 1.5 to 2 inches

Average Temperature: 78 to 85 Fahrenheit

PH Range: 6.4 to 7.8 PH

Diet: Varied Diet, Flake Foods

Reproduction: Egg Scatterers

Lifespan: 2 to 3 years

Photograph by Alastair R Agutter

11/. Name: Cardinal Tetra

Species Name: *Paracheirodon axelrodi*

Summary Description: Cardinal Tetra's named by discoverer Dr. Herbert Axelrod has complimented Aquarists Community Aquariums now for many decades. As a fish species they are easy to keep in a naturally planted aquarium and when in numbers shoaling, create a breathing taking effect. However like Neon Tetras and others as egg scatterers, have posed many a problem to the enthusiast breeder as they are particularly sensitive to water quality conditions regarding egg fertilization.

Member Family Genera: Characidae

Region(s): South America, mainly the Great River Amazon regions

Disposition: Excellent Community Aquarium Fish

Average Adult Size: 1.5 to 2 inches

Average Temperature: 76 to 86 Fahrenheit

PH Range: 5.8 to 7.8 PH

Diet: Varied Diet, Vegetation, Flake Foods

Reproduction: Egg Scatterers

Lifespan: 2 to 3 years

Photograph by Alastair R Agutter

12/. Name: Golden Gourami

Species Name: Trichogaster trichopterus

Summary Description: The Gold or Golden Gourami is a colourful sub species variation of the Three Spotted Gourami and often commonly known also as the Blue Gourami. The fish species is known as bubble nest builders and create these marvels (bubble nests) amongst floating leaves and plants on the water's surface.

These fish species can be compatible members in community aquariums and a very popular choice with many of today's Aquarists for their colour and aquarium activities, but sometimes very territorial when breeding.

Member Family Genera: Osphronemidae

Region(s): South East Asia

Disposition: Community Aquarium Compatible Fish

Average Adult Size: 3.5 to 5 inches.

Average Temperature: 76 to 84 Fahrenheit

PH Range: 6.0 to 8.0 PH

Diet: Varied Diet Flake Foods

Reproduction: Bubble Nest Builders

Lifespan: 3 to 5 years

My First Aquarium Collectors Edition

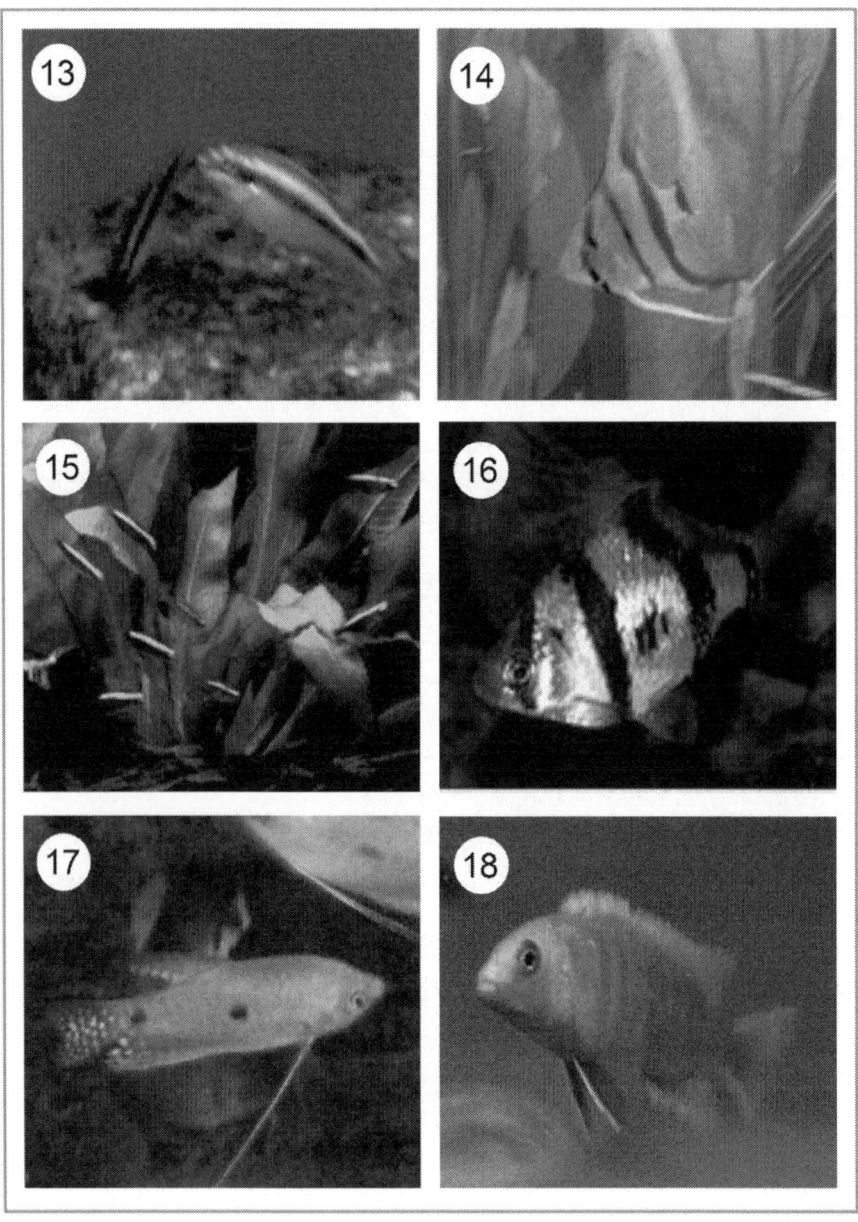

Plates Collection of Photographs and Artwork Compiled by Alastair R Agutter

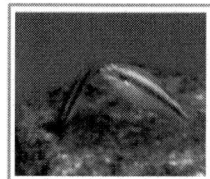

Photograph by Alastair R Agutter

13/. Name: Kribensis Cichlid

Species Name: *Pelvicachromis taeniatus*

Summary Description: Kribensis are dwarf cichlids and native to the regions of Cameroon and Nigeria in Africa. Kribensis inhabit mostly soft-water rivers throughout the above regions and can be a brightly coloured fish species, especially at breeding times displaying a cherry red belly colouration more predominantly on the female member of the species.

Kribensis in an aquarium environment are most suited to being with their own and very often Aquarists tend to put species such as Tiger Barbs with them.

Member Family Genera: Cichlidae

Region(s): Cameroon and Nigeria in Africa

Disposition: Shows Aggressive Behaviour Patterns

Average Adult Size: 2.5 to 3 inches

Average Temperature: 76 to 82 Fahrenheit

PH Range: 6.0 to 7.6 PH

Diet: Small Cichlid Pellets and Flake Foods

Reproduction: Egg Layers

Lifespan: 4 to 5 years

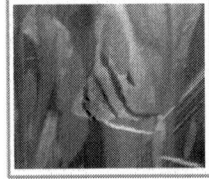

Photograph by Alastair R Agutter

14/. Name: Angel Fish

Species Name: *Pterophylium Scalare*

Summary Description: Angel fish are one of the more unusual looking tropical fish cichlid species who are native to South America, primarily the Great River Amazon.

They can be compatible in community aquariums, as long as they are in small numbers of only one or two. When in large numbers establishing a pecking order to pair off and breed, the fish can be extremely aggressive towards each other and species in the aquarium.

Member Family Genera: Cichlidae

Region(s): South America

Disposition: Compatible for Community Aquariums

Average Adult Size: 10 to 12 inches high including fins, 4 to 6 inches long

Average Temperature: 78 to 84 Fahrenheit

PH Range: 6.0 to 7.8 PH

Diet: Small Cichlid Pellets, Vegetation, Beef Heart and Flake Foods

Reproduction: Egg Layers

Lifespan: 5 to 10 years

Photograph by Alastair R Agutter

15/. Name: Neon Tetra

Species Name: *Paracheirodon innesi*

Summary Description: The Neon Tetra is one of the stars in the tropical fish keeping world and renowned for their translucent iridescent colours. I think when folk relate to tropical fish keeping, the Neon Tetra is the species that provides those lasting images and memories of our noble pastime. There is nothing more stunning than seeing a shoal of Neon Tetra's travelling past a sunken piece of bogwood in a magical underwater world in one's home. Neon Tetras are easy to keep in a community aquarium, but are known for being a difficult species to breed in captivity. However, the Dutch have now got the method of breeding these species in captivity down to a fine art.

Member Family Genera: Characidae

Region(s): Columbia, Peru and Brazil in South America

Disposition: Excellent Community Aquarium Fish

Average Adult Size: 1.2 to 1.5 inches

Average Temperature: 68 to 84 Fahrenheit

PH Range: 5.5 to 7.8 PH

Diet: Varied Diet, Vegetation and Flake Foods

Reproduction: Egg Scatterers

Lifespan: 2 to 3 years

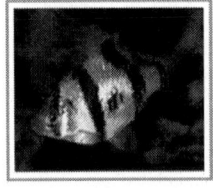

Photograph by Alastair R Agutter

16/. Name: Tiger Barb

Species Name: *Puntius tetrazona*

Summary Description: Tigers Barbs I think are another one of those fish species in tropical fish keeping that folk remember and relate too regarding the hobby. Tiger Barbs have a bright golden body with black vertical stripes and the fins of the species are of a bright red colouration. When in shoals, Tiger Barbs do look stunning in an aquarium. Tiger Barbs can be aggressive and very much a nipping fish towards others and so I would air caution when considering these for a community aquarium. Very often shoals of Tiger Barbs can be found in Aquarists aquariums who are also keeping smaller members of the cichlid family such as Kribensis, Blue Acara and Ramirez Dwarf Cichlids.

Member Family Genera: Cyprinidae

Region(s): Central and Eastern Asia

Disposition: Can be Aggressive, Nipping

Average Adult Size: 2 to 2.75 inches

Average Temperature: 76 to 82 Fahrenheit

PH Range: 6.0 to 8.0 PH

Diet: Varied Diet, Flake Foods

Reproduction: Egg Layers

Lifespan: 2 to 3 years

Photograph by Alastair R Agutter

17/. Name: Three Spotted Gourami

Species Name: *Trichopodus trichopterus*

Summary Description: The three spotted gourami is commonly known as the blue gourami, but today for aquarists there are many colour variations from breeding in captivity. The Golden Gourami is a fine example of this where there has been produced from constant selective breeding a Golden coloured variation for the Aquarist. Gourami species reproduce by creating a bubble nest on the surface of the water, supported by floating plants and leaves. Fry tend to become free swimming after 3 days and are initially fed on brine shrimp and infusoria (algae and micro-organisms).

Member Family Genera: Osphronemidae

Region(s): South East Asia

Disposition: Community Aquarium Compatible Fish

Average Adult Size: 3.5 to 5 inches.

Average Temperature: 76 to 84 Fahrenheit

PH Range: 6.0 to 8.0 PH

Diet: Varied Diet Flake Foods

Reproduction: Bubble Nest Builders

Lifespan: 3 to 5 years

Photograph by Alastair R Agutter

18/. Name: Mbuna Malawi Cichlid

Species Name: *Pseudotropheus Haplochromines*

Summary Description: Mbuna is the more accurate name of this Cichlid species given to them by natives of Africa and basically meaning "fish that live among rocks." These cichlid species are today still very much a morphology mystery to the Marine Biologist Community as more species are discovered by the day. Throughout the course of each year new species are being created as they morph and inter-breed between species. These Malawi Cichlids are highly aggressive and territorial. They breed by laying eggs and then incubating them in their mouths for protection against predators. They are NOT suitable for community aquariums.

Member Family Genera: Cichlidae

Region(s): Lake Malawi Africa

Disposition: Very Aggressive

Average Adult Size: 6 to 9 inches

Average Temperature: 77 to 84 Fahrenheit

PH Range: 7.5 to 8.4 PH

Diet: Cichlid Pellets, Vegetation Foods and Flake Food

Reproduction: Mouth-brooders

Lifespan: 4 to 7 years

My First Aquarium Collectors Edition

Plates Collection of Photographs and Artwork Compiled by Alastair R Agutter

Photograph by Alastair R Agutter

19/. Name: Clown Loach

Species Name: *Chromobotia macracanthus*

Summary Description: One of my most favourite fish has always been the Clown Loach even as a small boy. They are a fascinating species and very social towards each other, so eventually they will need to be kept in numbers. They are characters to watch in an aquarium rooting around by day and sleeping on leaves by the afternoon having a siesta. They can be sensitive to water conditions, so please make sure your fish tank is established before introducing them to a naturally planted community aquarium environment.

Member Family Genera: Botiidae

Region(s): Indonesia, Sumatra and Borneo

Disposition: Good Community Aquarium Member

Average Adult Size: 6 to 8 inches

Average Temperature: 77 to 86 Fahrenheit

PH Range: 5.0 to 8.0 PH

Diet: Varied Diet, Flake Foods, Worms, Infusoria in Substrates, Algae

Reproduction: Eggs Layers

Lifespan: 12 to 15 years plus

Photograph by Alastair R Agutter

20/. Name: Malawi Cichlid

Species Name: Male Malawi Mbuna Cichlid

Summary Description: I wanted to include yet another Malawi Cichlid of the same species to provide further insight to the shape and colour variations that are now materializing from morphing in the Wild and in captivity from selective breeding. Malawi Cichlids are always very active and have in most instances very bright canary blues and yellows in their colouration. So very often Aquarists can landscape an aquarium for these species where they almost look like marines to the untrained eye. They are popular, but alas no longer my cup of tea even after breeding them back in the 1970's.

Member Family Genera: Cichlidae

Region(s): Lake Malawi Africa

Disposition: Very Aggressive

Average Adult Size: 6 to 9 inches

Average Temperature: 77 to 84 Fahrenheit

PH Range: 7.5 to 8.4 PH

Diet: Cichlid Pellets, Vegetation Foods and Flake Food

Reproduction: Mouth-brooders

Lifespan: 4 to 7 years

Photograph by Alastair R Agutter

21/. Name: Gold Marbled Angel Fish

Species Name: *Pterophylium Altum and Pterophylium Scalare*

Summary Description: Today in tropical fish keeping from the dedication of many Club Aquarists and Amateur Breeders, a whole industry has evolved over the years from their endeavours, to bring out the very best in certain species, regarding size and colouration.

The Golden Marbled Angel Fish is a fine example of selective breeding over generations. The species original parents derived from cross breeding Pterophylium Altum and Pterophylium Scalare.

Member Family Genera: Cichlidae

Region(s): South America

Disposition: Compatible for Community Aquariums

Average Adult Size: 10 to 12 inches high including fins, 4 to 6 inches long

Average Temperature: 78 to 84 Fahrenheit

PH Range: 6.0 to 7.8 PH

Diet: Small Cichlid Pellets, Vegetation, Beef Heart and Flake Foods

Reproduction: Egg Layers

Lifespan: 5 to 10 years

Photograph by Alastair R Agutter

22/. Name: Firemouth Cichlid

Species Name: *Thorichthys meeki*

Summary Description: The Firemouth Cichlid is known to be an aggressive fish and especially at breeding times as an egg layer, depositing eggs normally on rocks or slate surfaces. The species will vigorously start cleaning the agreed spawning surface area a week or two before spawning and cleaning will continue throughout each day at intervals on a daily basis leading up to the big occasion.

The name Firemouth derives from the red and orange colouration around the mouth and gill areas. Males flare out their gills when protecting territory, being threatened or fighting over a mate.

Member Family Genera: Cichlidae

Region(s): Central and South America

Disposition: Very Aggressive Cichlid

Average Adult Size: 4 to 5 inches

Average Temperature: 75 to 86 Fahrenheit

PH Range: 6.5 to 8.0 PH

Diet: Varied Diet, Cichlid Pellets and Flake Foods

Reproduction: Egg Layers

Lifespan: 4 to 5 years

Photograph by Alastair R Agutter

23/. Name: Rosy Barb

Species Name: *Pethia conchonius*

Summary Description: The Rosy Barb is a colourful species and can grow to a considerable size and has a very healthy appetite to the point sometimes the fish species suffers from indigestion and hovers up towards the top of the aquarium facing down or moving around up and down the aquarium for short spells.

Rosy Barbs can often be a very peaceful fish and suitable for a community aquarium, even with smaller fish species. Occasionally the fish may nip, if threatened, or chased, by other aquarium inhabitants.

Member Family Genera: Cyprinidae

Region(s): Southern Asia, Bangladesh and Afghanistan

Disposition: Active Fish, Suitable in Community Aquarium in 1's and 2's

Average Adult Size: 5 to 6 inches

Average Temperature: 64 to 82 Fahrenheit

PH Range: 6.0 to 8.0 PH

Diet: Varied Diet, Vegetation and Flake Foods

Reproduction: Egg Layers

Lifespan: 4 to 5 years

Photograph by Alastair R Agutter

24/. Name: Red Fin Shark

Species Name: *Epalzeorhynchos frenatum*

Summary Description: The Red Fin Shark today has many names but I am sticking with the old and original name we aquarists have come to know over many decades of our noble pastime. The Red Fin Shark is a semi-aggressive fish and a ray finned fish and not cartilaginous like true sharks.

Red Fin Sharks or Rainbow Sharks as some call them, are essentially middle water and bottom cleaners, but also a great asset in a community aquarium for cleaning the algae from the leaves of plants and the aquarium glass.

Member Family Genera: Cyprinidae

Region(s): Mekong, Chao Phraya, Indochina Asia

Disposition: Semi-Aggressive

Average Adult Size: 6 inches

Average Temperature: 75 to 84 Fahrenheit

PH Range: 6.0 to 8.0 PH

Diet: Varied Diet, Algae, Vegetation and Flaked Foods

Reproduction: Egg Layers

Lifespan: 4 to 6 years

My First Aquarium Collectors Edition

Plates Collection of Photographs and Artwork Compiled by Alastair R Agutter

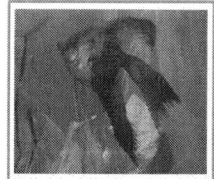

Photograph by Alastair R Agutter

25/. Name: Black Lace or Ghost Angel Fish

Species Name: *Pterophylium Altum*

Summary Description: The Black Lace or Ghost Angel Fish derived from the selective breeding of the Pterophylium Altum first discovered by Jacques Pellegrin in 1903 when in South America and is in fact the National Fish of Venezuela.

At one time the breeding of the Angel Fish in captivity was very challenging, but again thanks to Aquarist Club Members and Amateur Breeder enthusiasts, tropical fish hobbyists today, can enjoy a vast array of highly colourful tropical fish species.

Member Family Genera: Cichlidae

Region(s): Columbia, Venezuela, Brazil in South America

Disposition: Compatible for Community Aquariums

Average Adult Size: 12 to 15 inches high including fins, 4 to 6 inches long

Average Temperature: 78 to 84 Fahrenheit

PH Range: 6.0 to 7.8 PH

Diet: Small Cichlid Pellets, Vegetation, Beef Heart and Flake Foods

Reproduction: Egg Layers

Lifespan: 5 to 10 years

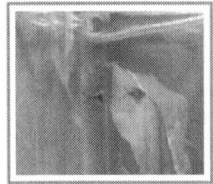

Photograph by Alastair R Agutter

26/. Name: Harlequin Rasbora

Species Name: *Trigonostigma heteromorpha*

Summary Description: The Harlequin is a delightful and colourful fish species to add to any community aquarium. A small unassuming species when in numbers can be a sight to behold when shoaling.

Harlequin Rasbora's live for up to 6 to 8 years, some considerable time and need to be kept some number in a naturally planted aquarium with live plants that the fish species use to lay eggs on the underside of the leaves.

Member Family Genera: Cyprinidae

Region(s): Malaysia, Singapore, Thailand and Sumatra

Disposition: Good Community Aquarium Fish

Average Adult Size: 2 inches

Average Temperature: 70 to 84 Fahrenheit

PH Range: 6.0 to 7.8 PH

Diet: Varied Diet, Vegetation and Flake Food

Reproduction: Egg Layer (underside of leaves)

Lifespan: 6 to 8 years

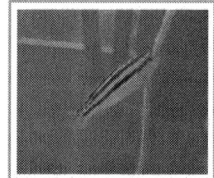

Photograph by Alastair R Agutter

27/. Name: The Malawi Auratus Cichlid

Species Name: *Melanochromis auratus*

Summary Description: This Malawi Lake cichlid in the native region and community is known as "The Golden Mbuna" and is one of the most aggressive tropical fish I have ever known. They are highly territorial and will even fight their own species to the death.

They also have very advanced evolutionary morphing ability, being able to change sex in the event of too many females, or too many males etc. Females are a bright vibrant yellow and black, whilst the males are normally black with blue iridescent stripes running horizontally through the body.

Member Family Genera: Cichlidae

Region(s): Lake Malawi Africa

Disposition: Very Aggressive Cichlid

Average Adult Size: 4.3 to 4.5 inches

Average Temperature: 77 to 84 Fahrenheit

PH Range: 7.5 to 8.4 PH

Diet: Cichlid Pellets, Vegetation Foods and Flake Food

Reproduction: Mouth-brooders

Lifespan: 4 to 7 years

Photograph by Alastair R Agutter

28/. Name: Bronze Corydoras Catfish

Species Name: *Corydoras aeneus*

Summary Description: The Bronze Corydoras Catfish is one of my very favourite scavengers and an ideal catfish for any community aquarium.

They have a great temperament and will busy away on the bottom of the aquarium cleaning it. Bronze Corydoras Catfish are good with other fish species and do not trouble them at all.

Corydoras are good scavengers and will always work hard for the Aquarist keeping the algae down and the aquarium clean.

Member Family Genera: Corydoras

Region(s): South America

Disposition: Good Community Fish

Average Adult Size: 2.5 to 2.75 inches

Average Temperature: 77 to 84 Fahrenheit

PH Range: 6.0 to 8.0 PH

Diet: Varied Diet and Flake Foods

Reproduction: Egg Layer Pouch

Lifespan: 5 to 8 years

Photograph by Alastair R Agutter

29/. Female Malawi Mbuna Cichlid

Species Name: *Pseudotropheus Haplochromines*

Summary Description: As you can see from the photograph above the Female Pseudotropheus Haplochromines can be of a different colour to the male. In this instance the female is a bright canary yellow, but just as territorial and aggressive as any male member of this species.

These Malawi Cichlids species as mentioned earlier in the book, are egg laying mouth-brooders. Once the eggs are laid and fertilized, the parents collect the eggs into their mouths and incubate the eggs. Once hatched and even free swimming, the parent's mouths will remain to be havens for the young fry.

Member Family Genera: Cichlidae

Region(s): Lake Malawi Africa

Disposition: Very Aggressive

Average Adult Size: 5 to 7 inches

Average Temperature: 77 to 84 Fahrenheit

PH Range: 7.5 to 8.4 PH

Diet: Cichlid Pellets, Vegetation Foods and Flake Food

Reproduction: Mouth-brooders

Lifespan: 4 to 7 years

Photograph by Alastair R Agutter

30/. Name: Elongate Mbuna Cichlid

Species Name: *Pseudotropheus elongatus*

Summary Description: The Pseudotropheus elongatus are still a very aggressive cichlid as a comparison to Pseudotropheus auratus and not suitable for a community aquarium, unless you plan to set up a Rift Lake Cichlid Aquarium, where you can then house a variety of these colourful species.

Malawi Cichlids are very industrial and constantly playing mind games with their fellow aquarium inhabitants where they seek to gain territory, food and mates.

Member Family Genera: Cichlidae

Region(s): Lake Malawi Africa

Disposition: Very Aggressive Cichlids

Average Adult Size: 3.5 to 4 inches

Average Temperature: 76 to 84 Fahrenheit

PH Range: 6.8 to 8.0 PH

Diet: Varied Diet, Small Cichlid Pellets, Vegetation and Fake Food

Reproduction: Mouth-brooders

Lifespan: 4 to 6 years

My First Aquarium Collectors Edition

CHAPTER THIRTEEN
Feeding Fish Species

The second most important aspect to tropical fish keeping after great aquarium water conditions is without doubt food.

Photograph above showing some high protein fresh fish food being made using one of the Author's Recipes – Photograph by Alastair R Agutter

The above photograph shows how as a tropical fish hobbyist and aquarist you can in fact make your own high protein tropical fish food and on the following pages as we discuss fish food are some recipes to try.

I became inspired to create my own fish food to compliment others we can all obtain from tropical fish shop retailers or online today, was when trying to breed Wild Discus (symphysodon) in captivity, for these poor souls being flown in from South America and arriving to me were terribly thin and run down, literally on death's door!

One thing we all learn as Aquarists as the years pass by on our continued journey of tropical fish keeping, is if we want to breed our fish successfully in captivity, we need to bring our tropical fish into a healthy breeding condition and this can only be achieved by providing the right food and conditions, so those very special magical days finally arrive, where your fish reward you for all your hard work and efforts by spawning.

Admittedly, some tropical fish species are prolific breeders, such as Guppies and Platies. But even with these fish species, by providing a balanced and healthy high protein fish food diet, this will see guppies and platies growing to a much larger size and producing far more off-spring.

Many ah Clubs Aquarist of old visiting another member, can always provide an experience and story surrounding fish food, water and breeding. Such dedication is like the Leek, or Marrow grower in prize gardening, and if you are lucky enough to be invited into their World, you become blown away from their vegetable growing results and in our case regarding their tropical fish keeping exploits and charges.

In the 1960's and 1970's, I was fortunate enough to experience some of those memorable golden moments when visiting other aquarists. Such special moments and fond memories in tropical fish keeping that will last and stay with me the rest of my life and for all eternity. The sight of Guppies and Platies in their tens of thousands, Neon and Cardinal Tetra's being bred successfully amongst horse hair in old slowly leaking and rusting angle iron aquariums, to Discus fish the size and diameter of dinner plates, are cherished moments that can never be forgot.

So let's take a detailed look at tropical fish foods, so you can too hopefully become successful like those memorable aquarists I have had the pleasure to know in the past!

Regarding tropical fish food there are essentially four general types and these are 1/. Flake Foods, 2/. Live Foods, 3/. Frozen Foods and 4/. Pellet and Freeze Dried Foods.

For today's aquarists, over the years the diversity and makes available in tropical fish foods has forever increased. Today's Tropical Fish Hobbyists and Aquarists are very much spoilt for choice and sometimes it can become a little confusing.

So I hope the way I have set out the details of fish foods in this chapter sheds some light on the subject and greatly helps.

My First Aquarium Collectors Edition

FLAKE FISH FOODS

Over the years, three of the main staple diet flake foods that can be readily obtained are King British, Aquarian and Tetra.

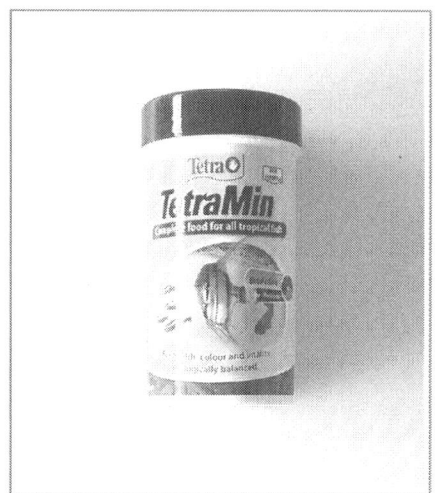 

Photographs above showing two of the most well-known flake foods on the market today TetraMin and King British Flake for aquarists – Photographs by Alastair R Agutter

In fact King British was the first food I ever fed to my tropical fish back in 1967, and so as you can see these firms have been around a good while.

However, over the decades from their commercial clout, the Tetra Group have lead the way as a market leader in fish food, and from personal experience, I still buy the product TetraMin today, as I alternate from time to time my flake foods, but there is a distinct difference with the ingredients from one flake food to another.

My own tropical fish seem to prefer King British. Why I cannot say, but they always seem to be far eager to eat this flake food, compared to others like Aquarian that I have tried and used on numerous occasions, to try and mix things up regarding a varied diet.

With regards to feeding my community aquarium fish, I tend to feed them two to three times a day, especially when the fish are at a juvenile stage of growth. When the fish are younger, I tend to feed my tropical fish around 4 to 5 times a day, to help build them up, grow faster and continue to have an eager appetite. When feeding at those times, I use small amounts of food. In other words, little and often!

Photographs above showing a more recent addition to flake foods a brand known as Vitalis and to the right a photograph showing King British Flake Food – Photographs by Alastair R Agutter

The normal rule of thumb and practice over the years and decades, has been to feed just enough food that will be consumed by your tropical fish within a 5 minute period. This is especially pertinent regarding smaller aquarium sizes, for the reason being with smaller Litre or Gallon capacity fish tanks, the water can spoil much easier than an aquarium of a much larger size with a greater volume of water. Little and often also encourages tropical fish to remain eager at feeding times.

Even if fish are more intelligent, evolved and sensitive like Discus (symphysodon), they should always be very keen to eat. In the next set of pictures below, one of the photographs shows some of my Discus just about reaching adult age and size of around 4 inches in diameter and just 12 months old, eagerly eating my own specially prepared food from my hands.

When fish have the right water conditions and the right high protein food, you will always have healthy thriving fish and ones that are not shy, or timid, if the aquariums have been set up in the right location and at the right height, as recommended in the Chapter of the book covering aquarium locations.

Photograph above the Author's Discus feeding out of his hands and the picture to the right showing a close-up of the specially prepared food he makes – Photographs by Alastair R Agutter

With the right healthy diet, you can get fish growing to maturity just as fast as in the wild, or even quicker. Taking Discus (symphysodon) as an example, they do not normally reach adult age until they are around 18 to 24 months old. But these Discus in the above picture, are reaching adult age and size in nearly half the time.

Another secret as mentioned earlier in the book is being able to connect with your tropical fish, where you then have their trust and this goes a very long way, especially surrounding Cichlids. For members of the cichlid family can live for many years, some Discus today since bred in captivity over 25 years ago, are now reaching up to 12, 14, 16 to 18 years in age.

FISH HEATH AND HYGIENE AT FEEDING TIMES

Now before any feeding is carried out, always remember to give your hands a very good wash with soap and water and then rinse your hands thoroughly with hot water, to ensure there is no soap residue left over on your hands. Then use a clean towel, or tissue (kitchen roll), to dry your hands.

I want you to try and imagine cooking for your loved ones, a delightful meal and then spraying it with aftershave, perfume, or deodorant and then expecting the food to be enthusiastically eaten.

One of the biggest toxicity problems and even killers to tropical fish is the gradual build-up of alcohol based toxins, such as perfumes and aftershaves in the aquarium water. This can be extended to aerosols (air fresheners).

Food given to your tropical fish without washing your hands also becomes tainted and unpalatable from perfumes and aftershaves, resulting in your fish losing their appetite.

Other serious problems that can also arise from not washing your hands, is the great risk of transmitting a virus to your aquarium via the food. This can very often happen during, or after suffering a cold, or flu bout for example, for fish species can catch viruses and do die from them!

The recent events in South America now spreading across the World by Mosquito, this being the Zika Virus, may not only be lethal to human's, but could also be fatal to many countless thousands of Marine and Animal life forms, where new off-spring could well be born with microcephaly disabilities.

At this time in 2016, the media headlines are only focusing on the disease surrounding human activity and this is currently pre-occupying the efforts of Medical Professionals, Zoologists and Marine Biologists world-wide, surrounding the transmission of Zika by Mosquito species.

In the 1980's many aquarists lost Discus (symphysodon) and other exotic tropical fish species from a long drought period, where there became poor water quality across many reservoirs in Europe, yet water from these reservoirs via treatment works was being delivered to the domestic tap water. Aquarists carrying out water changes to their tropical fish soon found that their fish had contracted a virus known as "respiratory distress syndrome," a horrible disease eventually affecting all tropical fish hobbyists aquariums in their homes or fish houses, as the said particular virus once present in water, was able to become airborne and could therefore be transmitted via atmosphere and especially condensation.

So washing your hands on a regular basis is always very important when wanting to keep healthy thriving tropical fish. Thank You!

FLAKE FISH FOOD FEEDING TIMES

As you begin your journey of tropical fish keeping, as an Aquarist, it would be prudent and safe to feed your fish twice a day for starters. This should be easy enough to do, regarding work or school commitments by feeding once in the morning before work or school, and then feeding once in the evening upon returning home from work or school.

The normal rule of thumb again is to feed one or two pinches of flake food every feeding time, if you have say between 10 to 30 tropical fish in a naturally planted community aquarium.

Flake foods are obviously mass produced today, with stringent specially prepared recipes by the producers, which include specific ingredients for healthy thriving tropical fish.

The ingredients in flake foods are varied and mixed, with essential ingredients that all fish need in their diet. However, in a community aquarium at feeding times, it can become noticeable that some of your tropical fish have a preference to some of the flake food and not the other.

The main ingredients used for most tropical fish flake foods are;

Composition: Fish derivatives, Cereal, Vegetable Protein Extracts, Yeast derivatives of Vegetable origin, Molluscs and Crustacean, Algae (including Ergosan 2% average, Spirulina 1.7% average), Oils, Fats and Minerals.

Additives Vitamins: Vitamin A 20,000 IU/kg, Vitamin D3 1950 IU/kg, Vitamin E 130IU/kg, Vitamin C (as Li-Ascorbic Acid Monophosphate 676 mg/kg.

Trace Elements: Copper Sulphate Pentahydrate 16mg/kg, Magnesium Oxide 47.21 mg/kg, Zinc Oxide 109.63 mg/kg, Calcium-locate Anhydrous 10.71 mg/kg.

Analytical Constituents: Protein 47%, Fat Content 10%, Crude Fibres 1.5%, Crude Ash 5.5% and ManA 16576 the latter for medical purposes.

The above is a typical ingredient make up of flake foods. However, some flake food recipes will of course vary slightly subject to legal rights and the intellectual property protection of the commercial brand in question.

HOW MUCH FLAKE FOOD DO FISH EAT

Flake foods can obviously vary in price subject to the amount you purchase. If for example you feed your tropical fish twice a day with flake food and for say 20 to 30 community aquarium fish, they will consume on average between 12 to 18 grams per week. If you are a monthly shopper, this is worth bearing in mind, and so it may be a wise decision to purchase at least a 100 gram container of flake food when you next go shopping, to your local tropical fish shop, or online store. For a flake food amount of this size will last you at least a couple of months hopefully, unless you get some new arrivals in the form of off-spring.

Today also, there is a more varied and wider range of flake foods. One I particularly used years ago, to add to certain specially prepared frozen food was "Tetra Ruby" as this food contains various additional ingredients to help enhance a fish species colours. One of the main ingredients used to help fish develop more colour is "beetroot" and sometimes this root vegetable will be found on the back of some flake food containers, where the ingredients information is provided.

Even larger species of fish still love flake foods and always eager to eat the food, species such as; Angel Fish, Blue Acara, Jack Dempsey, Convict, Ramirez, Kribensis and Firemouth Cichlids to mention a few.

In fact most fish species eat flake food, even Discus when smuggled into frozen recipes of beef heart and liver, or when the fish are particularly young and familiar with the food since birth (fry stage).

How I get fry to eat flake food is to use a spare empty flake food container and get some flake food in my hands and crush it up using my fingers, so the flake food almost goes into a powder form and keep this in the spare container. I normally start to get fry onto flake food after I have been feeding fry with live brine shrimp for several days. However, regarding live bearer species fry, you can start using this method of powdered flake food straight away, as the fry are large enough to consume the crushed flake food.

LIVE FISH FOODS

Live foods over the years have been a very popular part of the tropical fish diet. Popular live foods being Tubifex, Bloodworms and Daphnia (water fleas).

However, personally speaking I do not feed live foods to any of my fish any longer for a number of very good and sound sensible reasons. The only exception to the rule is the use of brine shrimp. With regards to this exception concerning Brine Shrimp I hatch these, rear and grow these myself in saltwater and are therefore disease free!

Now this cannot be said for other live foods and so please allow me to explain why? But also accompanied with this explanation a little history and background (facts) surrounding tropical fish and live foods, that I believe to be important regarding this case in hand.

In early days of the tropical fish keeping hobby and pastime, Tubifex and Daphnia, were especially popular live foods to feed fish, bloodworms less so, but this was down more to availability of the food.

The reason being in early days for Aquarists to feed live foods was more down to getting tropical fish to eat again. Many cichlids and tropical fish species in the 1950's, 1960's and 1970's especially, were mainly wild caught fish species for the tropical fish hobbyist.

The journeys and transportation of these fish were horrific to say the very least, as some species took several days and weeks to get to certain ports to then be able to fly fish out across the world. Many wild caught species were caught and kept in large metal 50 gallon drums when transported and the water quality was constantly deteriorating all the time both in PH, DH and temperature. Only for the water to be topped up or changed through various stages of this process and so when this livestock finally arrived in the tropical fish retailer's establishment, the poor things were already in a very poor and unhealthy state. The easiest way to get fish back to some form of health was to feed them live foods and then after several weeks with the acclimatization to the new environment the fish if not already sold will start to look slightly better in appearance and hopefully a little healthier before they embark on their next journey to the aquarists home and aquarium.

Now fortunately today, thanks to many dedicated Aquarists and Commercial Breeders around the world and the speed of air freight, most tropical fish today are tank bred and familiar with their surroundings of an aquarium, for most or all are born in them and therefore know no different.

So you can see the logic behind feeding live food to fish that are simply not eating, but there is another way to encourage fish to eat and I will cover this later in the chapter.

Live foods sadly, carry many diseases from their breeding environments and so by feeding your tropical fish live foods you are increasing the risk of disease greatly.

Tubifex for example is often found in waste pipes or drain sewage works and I am sure you will agree not a very pleasant environment, and the water is full of disease that the Tubifex are transported in. This worm species is very resilient and when feeding to large tropical fish species that may not necessarily be breaking up these worms as they chew. Sometimes these worms will eat and puncture the stomach, or intestine of the fish that has consumed the worms. Another disease known by the feeding of Tubifex is called "Hole in the head" disease and when a fish contracts such an infection, there is very often a fatal outcome for the fish.

Water Daphnia often hatches in ponds and pools, where many species of Bird Life visit, to drink, or wash. This Wild Life can carry tapeworms and many other unpleasant intestinal predator diseases including; flukes, nematodes and worms, all of which can be transported through the water, or on the Daphnia to the Aquarists aquarium.

Bloodworms are the least lethal of the three live foods mentioned, but the live food still comes from pools and ponds. Bloodworms spend most of their lives in the substrate (mud) of such venues that again house and carry many diseases from existing fish in these pools, or visiting birds and animal wild life.

In Aquarist literature over the years, there can be found many articles regarding these live foods and how to clean them? However, this is an impossible task and the idea of keeping the new live foods in fresh tap water and rinsing through the live foods is NOT full proof!

For one thing most folk are learning today, is that most viruses and diseases have cycles, take "Ebola" for example; after thirty days the virus eggs can hatch again and populate after being dormant in the contracted victims body and in this instance, the victims being in this case the tubifex, bloodworms or daphnia, that are then consumed by your highly loved tropical fish.

Lastly, another reason why I do not use live foods with the exception of microscopic Brine Shrimp for newly hatch fry is when breeding any species of fish including cichlids.

The regular eating of live foods by your fish can and does encourage parents of newly hatched fry to very often go rogue, eating their own young as a result of the frequency of eating live foods. When you have live fry wriggling in a larval state, or free swimming it can be too tempting, resulting in the parents eating the fry.

FROZEN FISH FOODS

Today the range of frozen foods has greatly widened for tropical fish and I am very pleased to see also the emergence of more specialist high protein frozen foods for Discus and other Cichlid species, these just being two examples.

Photograph above showing pre-packed frozen bloodworms available today from most tropical fish retail outlets and a picture of bloodworm in a bowl – Photographs by Alastair R Agutter

Popular off-the shelf frozen foods today are; Bloodworms, Krill, Daphnia and Lobster Eggs to mention a few.

These off the shelf frozen foods are reasonably priced these days and contribute greatly towards the health of your fish that I describe as "mind, body and soul" from having a healthy varied diet.

Bloodworms in frozen form are a particular favourite with most if not all tropical fish and a worthwhile purchase to include in your freezer.

More specialized frozen foods I like to think derived from Jack Wattley, me and others back in the early to middle of the 1980's when trying to develop high protein foods for Discus fish especially. From such humble endeavours, in those earlier years, a whole new industry exists today, where commercial breeders and tropical fish product producers and manufacturers offer a whole host of these foods for cichlids, catfish and other species.

So what is a high protein fish food and what can it do?

Well, high protein specially prepared foods is like the difference in performance between a family saloon car compared to a formula one racing car.

High protein foods are just irresistible to the fish and so healthy where you can literally see your fish growing week on week. Taking Discus that are very close to my heart after breeding them in captivity, with high protein specially prepared foods, I can get these species from fry stage to adulthood in just twelve months, as opposed to the normal growth and age to adult hood being around 24 months. Also with high protein foods the fish become very healthy and their body mass is noticeable. For with regards to Discus fed on high protein food, they are a lot larger and more heavily set in the body.

At the beginning of this chapter is a photograph of one of my high protein foods that I feed to my fish and will take you through the recipe now and accompanied with photographs. As I have promised to many folk in and out of the industry, that I would provide a new recipe of a high protein food that is irresistible to Discus, Angel Fish, Catfish and many other Cichlids and also tropical fish community members including Neon's, Cardinals, Guppies, Platies, Tetras and barbs etc.

High protein foods are specially prepared so they have all the main and essential minerals and vitamins that tropical fish require in their diet. By providing high protein food it ensures your tropical fish are at their most healthiest and therefore far more resilient in the event of contracting a disease, or seeking to bring your tropical fish into a breeding condition.

This particular recipe when fed to my Angel Fish for example will bring the pairs into breeding condition within two weeks and where they will spawn and continue to do so every fortnight, for a number weeks and months in 10 to 14 day cycles.

BEEF HEART AND SPINACH HIGH PROTEIN FISH FOOD RECIPE

When making this recipe and others, some essential tools will be required and these are; Scissors, Small Spoon, Small Glass, Wooden Spoon, Sharp Knife (small), Large Bowl (plastic or stainless steel), Small Clear Freezer Bags and an Electronic Blender or Mixer.

This recipe will make up around 20 packs of frozen high protein food for your tropical fish and can be grated from frozen and fed once a day as part of their diet.

Photographs above showing 1/. Broccoli Tops 2/. Broccoli Stems 3/. Blender Dicing Broccoli 4/. Broccoli Diced in Mixing Bowl – Photographs by Alastair R Agutter

1/. Take 1 pound of Broccoli and cut into manageable pieces using a small sharp knife and then place in the Electric Blender or Mixer, then switch on for about 5 to 6 seconds or until the Broccoli is diced into very small pieces (not liquidized). See pictures 1, 2, 3 and 4 above.

2/. Take 1 pound of Spinach and wash thoroughly in a colander under cold water and then cut the spinach into small manageable pieces, using a small sharp knife. Then place small batches of the spinach into the Electric Blender or Mixer and dice into small pieces as you did before with the Broccoli. Please see picture 5 below.

3/. Take 1 pound of Beef or Lamb Liver and cut into small pieces using a small sharp knife and remove any fat or gristle tissue from the liver. Then take small batches of the Beef or Lamb Liver and place in the Electric Blender or Mixer to dice the Liver.

Then finally place the diced Beef or Lamb Liver into mixing bowl already containing the Broccoli and Spinach. Please see pictures 6, 7 and 8 above.

Photographs above showing 5/. Spinach and Broccoli Diced in the Mixing Bowl 6/. Lamb or Beef Liver 7/. Lamb or Beef Liver Cut into small pieces 8/. Diced Beef or Lamb Liver added to the Mixing Bowl – Photographs by Alastair R Agutter

3/. Take 1 pound of Beef or Lamb Liver and cut into small pieces using a small sharp knife and remove any fat or gristle tissue from the liver.

Then take small batches of the Beef or Lamb Liver and place in the Electric Blender or Mixer to dice the Liver.

Then finally place the diced Beef or Lamb Liver into mixing bowl already containing the Broccoli and Spinach. Please see pictures 6, 7 and 8 above.

Next take the Beef Heart and start cutting into small pieces using a small sharp knife, removing all fat and gristle from the meat.

Then place the pieces of Beef Heart into the Electric Blender or Mixer for a few seconds each time or until the Beef Heart is diced and then place the diced Beef Heart into the mixing bowl with the other ingredients. Please see pictures 11 and 12.

Above showing 9/. Beef Heart 10/. Broccoli, Spinach, Beef Heart and Liver 11/. Cut Beef Heart 12/. Diced Broccoli, Spinach, Liver, Beef Heart and Peeled Prawns – Photographs by Alastair R Agutter

Next take half a pound of fresh North Atlantic Cold Peeled Prawns (not frozen) and place these in the Electric Blender, or Mixer, to dice the prawns. Then place the peeled diced prawns into the mixing bowl along with the other ingredients.

Photographs above showing 17/. Multi Vitamins dissolved in a small amount of water 18/. Sachets of Gelatine, Spoon and Small Sharp Knife – Photographs by Alastair R Agutter

Next take two Multi Vitamin Tablets (200 mg) and place these in a small glass. Then pour a small amount of water into the glass over the Multi Vitamin Tablets and stir with a small spoon, until the Multi Vitamin tablets are completely dissolved. Once the Multi Vitamins are completely dissolved in the glass, pour the contents of the glass into the mixing bowl with the other ingredients. Please see picture 17 above.

Next take a sachet of Gelatine or Gluten as it is known in the USA and empty the sachet contents into a small glass (tumbler, whiskey glass size). Then boil a kettle of water and pour a small amount of the boiling water over the Gelatine (gluten) in the glass, to around half full. Give the glass with the gelatine and water a good stir with a spoon.

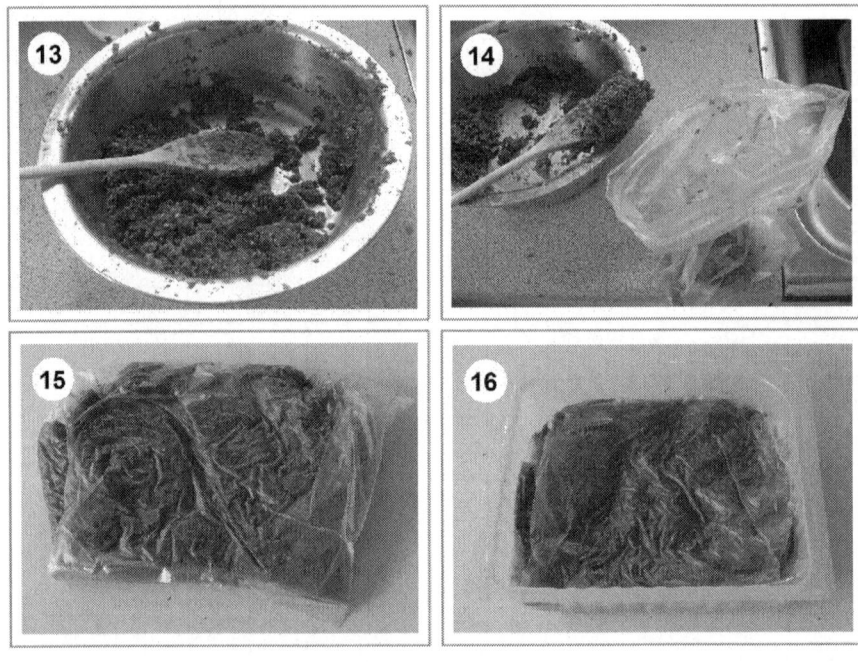

Photographs above showing 13/. Mixed ingredients Recipe in Bowl 14/. Putting Mixed Recipe into small clear freezer bags 15/. Mixed Recipe patted down into small flat blocks in clear freezer bags 16/. Flat Freezer Bag Fish Food placed in a tray – Photographs by Alastair R Agutter

Once the Gelatine sachet contents are completely dissolved in the glass, pour the contents of the glass with the gelatine into the other mixing bowl holding all other ingredients. Please see picture 18 showing Gelatine (gluten).

Next, take a wooden spoon and then thoroughly mix the contents of the bowl by hand stirring continually all the ingredients in the mixing bowl until the mix is evenly distributed.

Once the contents are mixed thoroughly, get some small clear freezer bags around 6 x 8 inches and start putting some of the fish food into the bags, using a wooden spoon. Then pat down the fish food in the freezer bags making them into thin small slabs about 6 inches long and about 4 inches wide and about ½ to 3/8 of an inch thick, about 8 to 12 mm in new money as they say. Make sure you fold the ends of the freezer bags under the fish food slabs so the fish food in the bags are sealed and closed. Next get a plastic tray or small container and place the packs of fish food on the tray, or in the plastic tray container. The containers I use are from previous purchases of meat in trays from supermarkets. I wash these trays out thoroughly and use them for this process of freezing my fish food, as they are ideal for the job and you can place around 4 to 5 thin packs (slabs) of your fish food in each tray. Please see pictures 13, 14, 15 and 16 above.

Once all the fish food has been placed in the freezer bags, patted down into slabs and placed in or on trays. Simply pop the trays of fish food into your freezer.

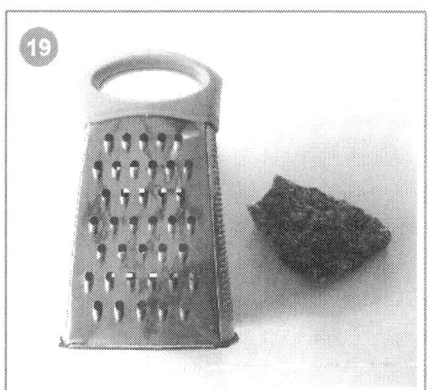 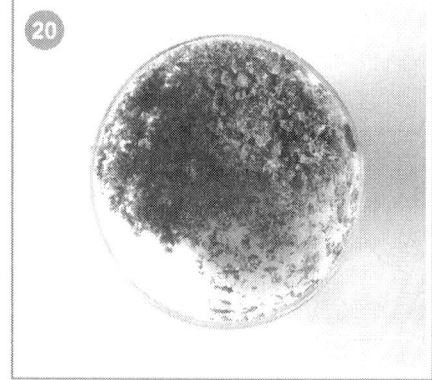

Photographs above showing 19/. Grater and a piece of fish food frozen slab to grate 20/. Grated fish food from the slab in a bowl ready to feed to your fish – Photographs by Alastair R Agutter

Once your fish food has been frozen, it is now ready to use. Simply take a slab of fish food out of the freezer and gently peel back the freezer bag away from the frozen food. Then take a normal cheese grater and use the course setting in the picture above and grate downwards your frozen fish food onto a plate, or into a bowl. Please see picture 19 and 20 above.

Your fish food is then ready to give to your fish. At first feed sparingly for the first day or so, then after that period feed as much fish food the fish can eat within a five minute period. Once your tropical fish become use to this new food, they will eat it as if the food is going out of fashion.

This fish food is so successful with my fish they even turn their noses up to the bloodworm, if I try to feed the bloodworm to my fish at the same time, when feeding this beef heart recipe. My tropical fish simply prefer this specially prepared high protein food above all else, especially cichlids and catfish.

BEEF HEART BROCCOLI AND SPINACH RECIPE

Ingredients:

1 pound of Broccoli

1 pound of Spinach

3 pound of Beef Heart

1 pound of Beef or Lamb Liver

½ pound of Peeled Prawns

2 Multi Vitamin Tablets (200 mg)

1 Sachet of Gelatine (gluten)

The above recipe is suitable for juvenile and adult fish. The following recipe is for smaller fish and the process of making and preparing the fish food is exactly the same as explained before.

BEEF HEART BROCCOLI AND SPINACH JUNIOR RECIPE

The following recipe is for smaller fish including very young cichlid fish species.

Ingredients:

1 pound of Broccoli

1 pound of Spinach

3 pound of Beef Heart

1 pound of Beef or Lamb Liver

½ pound of Herring or Cod Roe

1 Multi Vitamin Tablets (100 mg)

1 Vitamin D Tablet (80mg)

In this recipe **NO** Gelatine (gluten) is used to bind the fish food.

BEEF HEART AND SPINACH RUBY RECIPE

Ingredients:

1 pound of Broccoli

1 pound of Spinach

3 pound of Beef Heart

1 pound of Beef or Lamb Liver

½ pound of Peeled Prawns

2 cooked beetroots (peeled + chopped + diced)

2 Multi Vitamin Tablets (200 mg)

1 Vitamin D Tablet (80mg)

1 Sachet of Gelatine (gluten)

The above recipe is suitable for juvenile and adult fish with additional ingredients for bone development and colour enhancement radiance.

PELLET AND FREEZE DRIED FISH FOODS

Another range and type of tropical fish foods available on the market for today's Aquarists are pellets and freeze dried foods.

 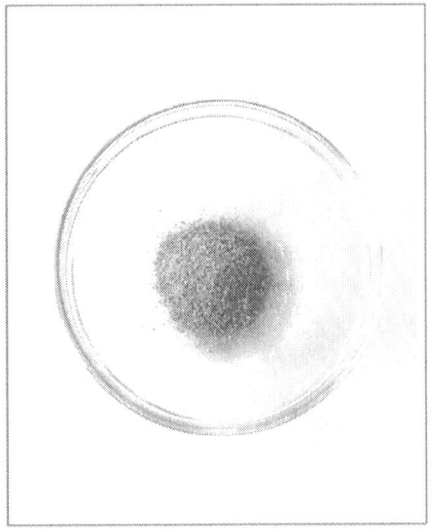

Photographs above showing Freeze Dried Daphnia in Packet Form and also the Freeze Dried Daphnia poured into a bowl for recognition purposes – Photographs by Alastair R Agutter

With regards to freeze dried foods I should say they are great for your fish, but that's not me. I love all fish and all animals and only want the best for them. So freeze dried foods cannot beat the real thing with regards to fresh frozen foods.

Freeze dried foods maybe handy in the event of an emergency from running out of fish food and where there is nothing else available.

Freeze dried food is very fibrous and I should imagine, it's like eating lumps of shredded wheat without any milk or sugar!

There is undoubtedly a wide and varied range of freeze dried foods today on the market and to encourage the eating of such a food by your tropical fish, must be based on scent and smell of the fish food in question.

This then leads us into the realms of artificial additives, and where I have never been a fan of such engineered chemicals for the food industry, be it human, pet or animal.

Many ailments and illnesses today, including very serious life threatening health problems in the form of Cancers, Alzheimer's, Multiple Cerosis, Liver, Kidney and Heart disease are caused from NOT eating healthy wholesome natural foods. Such processed foods for human, or animal consumption, I find to be very serious, commercially negligent and deeply worrying.

Photographs above showing Freeze Dried Daphnia in Packet Form and also the Freeze Dried Daphnia poured into a bowl for recognition purposes – Photographs by Alastair R Agutter

Pellets foods for tropical and cold water fish have now been around for several decades and offering today a wide and varied range.

The food is easy to administer and hassle free for aquarists and comes in many varying sizes and formula recipes for different types of fish species.

Two main forms are floating and sinking pellets. With regards to floating pellets, they can drift around on the surface of the aquarium for quite a while and can cause a protein build up around the surface walls of the aquarium if not eaten almost immediately. However, these pellets are very hard from the processing procedure and do expand in water and this could cause bloat to fish if they consume too many pellets that expand in the stomach.

Most pellets are cereal based, but they do include additives in the recipe and can cause constipation to fish if they are not being fed a balanced diet.

Sinking pellets can cause fish to root around on the bottom of the aquarium and this can be destructive to established plant life (root systems). Fish can also dig up and disturb trapped biological cultures breaking down waste material and also disturb pockets of toxins and chemicals being naturally broken down in the aquarium.

Whereas with flake and fresh frozen food, when the fish food does drop through the water it is invariably eaten before reaching the bottom (substrate) of the aquarium.

Flake and fresh frozen food is much lighter and if it does drop to the bottom of the aquarium it normally just lightly sits or suspends itself just above the substrate, where fish can very quickly and easily swim along gathering up eating the food and as a result, causing no harm to the substrate or plant life environment in the aquarium.

Finally, pellet foods can cause aquariums to become cloudy if overfed by a lazy aquarist and also resulting in a bacterial build-up in the aquarium, including the populating of infusoria and micro worms.

Recent years and today, the jury is still out on pellet foods for farmed fish!

CHAPTER FOURTEEN
Aquarium Early Days Care

I wanted to write this short chapter as a supportive part of your new or existing pastime of tropical fish keeping. This section is especially pertinent to the establishing of a new aquarium and the 28 to 30 day rule.

Photograph above showing one of the Author's Naturally Planted Aquarium's in Early Days with the inclusion of a gradual build-up of fish inhabitants – Photograph by Alastair R Agutter

The first thing to remember when keeping fellow creatures is the great burden of responsibility that falls upon our shoulders to love and care, to do the very best for our new family members.

There will be challenging moments as is the case in all walks of life and in our noble pastime of tropical fish keeping.

These moments will include sadly, the occasional loss of an inhabitant member from an illness. This can often happen more so at the beginning of an Aquarist's journey and these moments should not serve to discourage folk from keeping tropical fish, for these events happen to most if not all Aquarists at the very start.

One of the biggest processes and moments in tropical fish keeping is the establishing of an aquarium and creating a biological bacterial environment. Now a great deal of confusion is created surrounding this subject even today, and in truth there is no silver bullet, or method to bye-pass the natural process of creating a biological environment.

No chemicals or products on the market will give you instant results or perfect water conditions for tropical fish. Even with our technology today, we still have to give reverence and respect Mother Nature and where only she can create, begin and establish an inhabitable biological eco-system for marine and plant life.

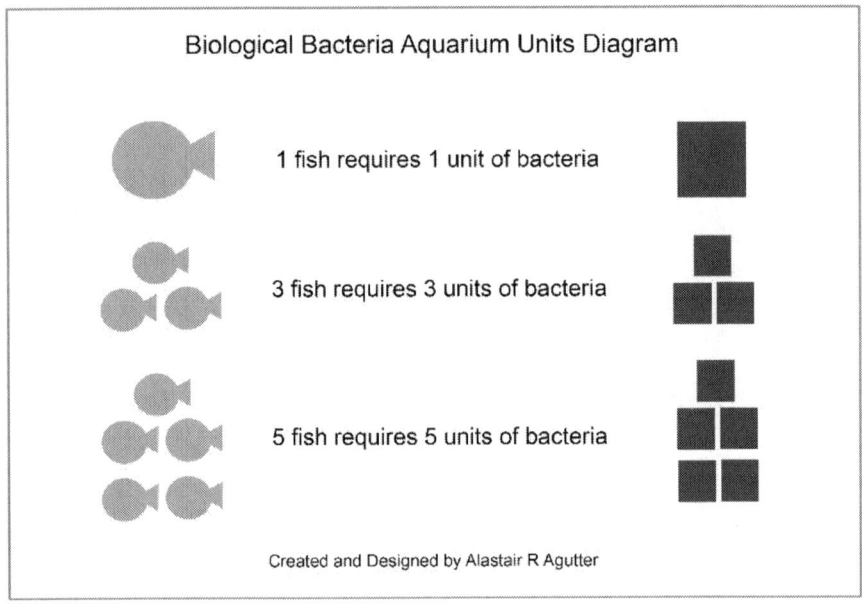

Diagram above showing fish inhabitants and biological bacterial culture in unit form to help show interdependency of both element parties – Diagram by Alastair R Agutter

Pictured above, I have created a simple diagram surrounding the biological process, for even whilst writing this book, I have read folks requests for advice and help surrounding setting up breeding and rearing tanks as a result of their tropical fish spawning, where they need to establish a new aquarium and still struggle to rationalize the process of a biological culture. This is even when very experienced commercial industry players on forums online have tried to articulate the process.

The best way to look at the process of establishing an aquarium is to look at the fish and the biological process in units. Now when you do not have an established biological culture, any fish you enter into an aquarium requires a biological culture to breakdown fish waste matter. So if we add one fish to a new aquarium, we need one unit of bacterial culture to process the fish waste and by-products. One unit of a bacterial culture created, has less impact in an aquarium, than if you were to introduce ten fish in an aquarium and where as a result, you will require ten units of a biological bacterial culture to be established.

With the presence of plants when establishing a new aquarium, they can greatly help in the process of establishing safe aquarium water conditions by filtering out toxins and waste, for plants actually have their own bacterial culture already in existence on the plants themselves.

So as for a bacterial culture being established in a filter medium for example, the plants are already doing some of the heavy lifting for the aquarist, as the aquarium becomes a naturally safe environment as we cycle through ammonia, nitrites to nitrate.

So the least pressure on any new aquarium environment the better, while this biological bacterial process is being established. So this is why in the 28 to 30 day rule when establishing an aquarium, I urge new aquarists to only buy initially a very small number of tropical fish in the 1's and 2's and to gradually build up in fish numbers overtime.

The reality is, to have a biological bacterial process in an aquarium you need a fish for the bacteria to grow and exist, to feed from the fish waste by-products. If you have the bacteria and no fish, the bacteria will die!

Feeding fish in such a new environment needs to be in small amounts and measured, ensuring no food is left, as this will help keep a control on the biological bacterial culture development and thus in turn, keeping ammonia and nitrite levels down during this process, before nitrate begins to grow and populate to counter and digest the nitrite oxides.

Carryout regular water changes as directed, this will remove and help keep down the build-up of any ammonia or nitrites.

Check fish for health issues by making sure your fish species eyes are clear, for cloudy eyes is a sign of ammonia and nitrite bacterial build-up in the aquarium water.

Keep an eye on fish inhabitant behaviour patterns, if your fish start to swim and rub against objects in the aquarium, this again is a sign of bacterial build-up in the form of ammonia and nitrite. Again this just requires regular water changes, NO chemicals.

If fish show signs of white spot or damage to the fins, this again is a sign of bacterial build up or the aquarium water temperature being too low. Check your heater thermostat by waiting to see if the neon light is coming on and working properly, indicating that your heater thermostat is functioning.

Check your thermometer to see what temperature the aquarium water is and increase the heater thermostat accordingly, if the temperature is too low. Regular water changes and the increase of water temperature will cure any fin rot or white spot.

As like all humans, when we are run down and low as a result of stress, diet or the environment, we come out in spots and this is the case with tropical fish.

Again no chemicals are required to cure an ailment such as white spot or fin rot. All chemicals in such a situation if used, just further complicates the situation even more by increasing the contamination in the water, hence the need for regular water changes only.

My First Aquarium Collectors Edition

CHAPTER FIFTEEN

Aquarium Maintenance

1/. Switch off heater thermostat as part of the maintenance process and give the heater thermostat a good clean and wipe, then switch back on the device.

Aquarium maintenance on a regular monthly basis can be an invaluable habit to adopt to ensure all your hard work is not in vain from technical failure – Photograph by Alastair R Agutter

2/. Carry out a quick check around the aquarium to make sure there are no leaks and that the Aquarium Stand is still safe and secure.

3/. Check the lighting system to make sure no part of the electrical light element system is being exposed to water, condensation or dampness.

4/. Check all plugs and electrical connections to make sure they are still safe and secure and only 3 Amp fuses used.

5/. Check the filter system to make sure there are no loose fittings in the way of pipes or airline connectors if using canister, air pump, sump or reservoir filtration systems.

6/. Check all of the Aquarium's glass and then using a small clean sponge or several pieces of kitchen roll crunched up and wipe the front glass of the aquarium internally to remove any algae build-up.

7/. Check to make sure any condensation trays are clean and free of any algae build-up and functioning properly by covering the aquarium water surface area efficiently.

CHAPTER SIXTEEN
Fish Species Safety and Health Care

In the next chapter we cover fish diseases that can occur and where the aquarist needs some answers. This chapter is more devoted to preventative cure, so your tropical fish do not become ill.

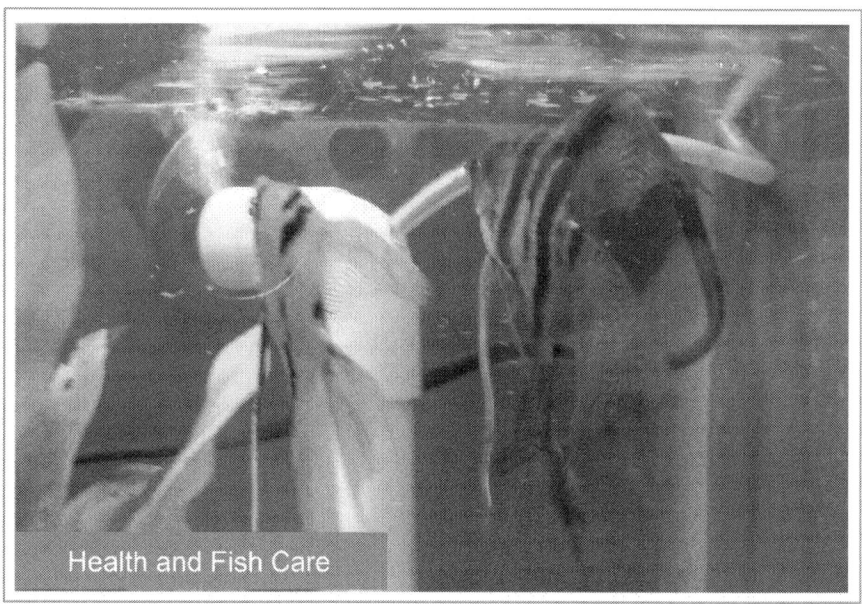

Health and Fish Care

Happy healthy tropical fish means disease free members of the family household and for your love and care they will connect with you – Photograph by Alastair R Agutter

1/. The first golden rule with regards to tropical fish and aquariums is to never tap on the glass. It's like the equivalent to someone coming up behind you and blasting you with a claxon directly in your ear. Tapping on the glass causes electromagnetic shock waves and the amplification of sound through the water that can cause permanent damage.

2/. Aquarium location is critical, make sure the aquarium is placed in the correct position so your tropical fish members of your family can see the coming and going of the family and visitors. There is nothing worse than someone creeping up on you and making you jump. This is the same for your tropical fish and stress is one of the biggest killers of tropical fish.

3/. Regular feeding and a varied diet with good quality high protein foods including flake food for most community species will see healthy thriving fish and growing to their full potential. Feeding needs to be carried out at regular times if once, twice, three or four times a day. Feeding your fish at the same time prevents fighting and the hoarding of food by other more dominant species in the aquarium that can contribute to the contamination of the water. Fish do know these times from their very own body clock mechanism and sunlight activity in a home or fish house.

4/. Regular water changes are another key preventative to ensuring healthy thriving tropical fish. Most diseases come about from fish becoming stressed as a result of a lack of routine, poor water quality leading to disease.

5/. The right food is also critical as mentioned above, no one would want to eat egg and chips every day for the rest of their lives and so fish do need a regular and varied diet, so the fish continue to be eager to eat.

6/. Correct temperatures are obviously critical regarding the health of tropical fish, so always make sure from the outset that you have the correct heater thermostat to meet the aquariums requirements for successfully heating the aquarium water in the fish tank. A table to help establish the correct heating requirements can be found in the heating chapter of the book and also the chapter containing reference tables.

7/. Correct filtration rates are very important to ensure the filtration system is biologically processing waste at a rate where the passing of the waste matter can be broken down successfully, resulting in clean quality water on exit of the filter system.

8/. Correct Lighting is essential for both plants and tropical fish to thrive. For plants, light is required to help them grow and eat by carrying out the photosynthesis process and with regards to tropical fish, for their growth and bone development. Again also having a lighting system that is scheduled that comes on at specific times and go off at set times is most desired.

CHAPTER SEVENTEEN
Fish Diseases and Cures

Sometimes when acquiring new fish for your aquarium, some species maybe infected with some common disorders such as gill flukes, worms and white spot etc. But all can be cured with tender love and care.

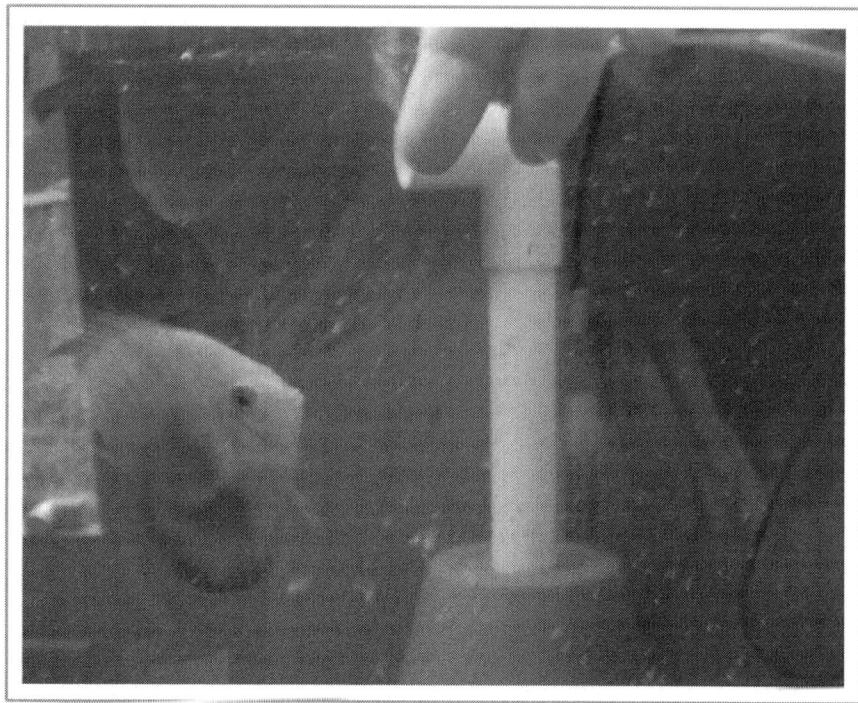

The Fish Whisperer – A Complete bond and trust between Author and Discus Fish, as the Juvenile comes up to feed from Alastair's fingers – Photograph by Alastair R Agutter

When fish are diseased for the new tropical fish keeper, this can be a very stressful period for fear of losing fish, but in such scenarios it does not have to be an alarming or worrying time. On such occasions it just requires the Aquarist to carry out a few activities to get things right!

For your peace of mind such events I have experienced throughout my fish keeping life first hand and now spanning some 5 decades (50 years) this coming year in 2017. So please do not worry, as I will provide you here in this chapter the best course of action if such an event should arise.

Most fish diseases come about as a result of stress, or water quality, and if we relate this to our own lives with regards to living in a densely polluted environment and unable to coup, it would only be a matter of time before we became ill.

As you know from reading the book so far, I try to avoid any form of chemicals, as they can cause long term lasting effects, especially when it comes to wanting species to breed in captivity and growth I might add.

Some treatments can cause more stress to fish, rather than serving as a cure, and very often most common diseases can be resolved with just a little effort as mentioned earlier by the aquarist, in relation to improving the water quality, altering the temperature and improving the diet for his or her tropical fish.

As like all our Wild Life that grace this Earth we call home, fish are fascinating creatures. Fish species like all other creatures, live each day, learning and evolving, as set down by the rules of the Divine Covenant in relation to Natural Law.

Even in my 50 years as an Aquarist I am still learning, and this process will continue for an eternity I am sure. But from my study, and one of the most popular topics in Town regarding the Science, Biology and Medical Community today being discussed is consciousness. Recent experiments with our cousins the Dolphins surrounding mirrors has proved these beloved creatures can recognize and acknowledge it is they, who is seen in the mirrors reflection. From communication by such species as just one example and the ability to collaborate, brings with it consciousness "emotion" and coupled to this at times is stress and anxiety that causes illness and disease.

When you have studied tropical fish species for so long and especially the more highly evolved and intelligent species, such as cichlids, and none more so than the Discus, it is possible to connect!

The signs of healthy fish, especially juveniles is when they are eating and then fighting, such activity confirms survival mode has passed, this meaning water conditions and the environment is fine.

Very often most cases where fish species will not eat or show signs of sickness (ill) is stress related, sometimes even losing the will to live. Now to some this may seem farfetched, but in truth as we have to become more aware of our environment from Climate Change, and the very grave impact this will have on us.

For the very first time, regarding the Human Story and Journey, we are now beginning to start scratching beyond the surface of these very important topics and subjects. I hope for the very first time in the Human Story there is a glimmer of light with the realization that our survival is only possible by learning to co-exist with all other life forms. So for us to achieve this feat of greater understanding, we must begin by finally consigning ignorance to the bin! Here below I have set out for you many, if not most of the ailments that tropical fish contract.

Today thankfully, as a result of most fish being tank bred by commercial breeders in captivity, the risk of disease has been greatly reduced in comparison to bringing in tropical fish from the wild. A good varied diet, regular routine and regular water changes will deliver disease free healthy thriving fish, but in the event of disease here follows diseases symptoms and cures.

DISEASES, SYMPTOMS AND CURES

The first thing you need to know is the following cures applied to the diseases covered below, are based on my very own first-hand experience and from my research I have endeavoured to find the safest cures and remedies.

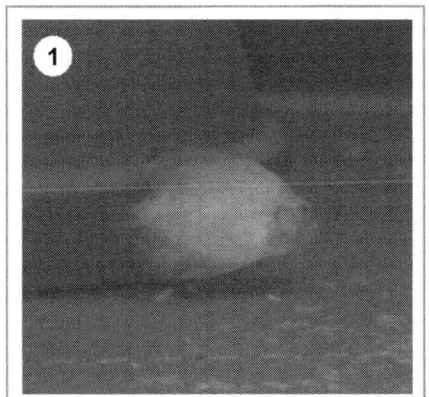 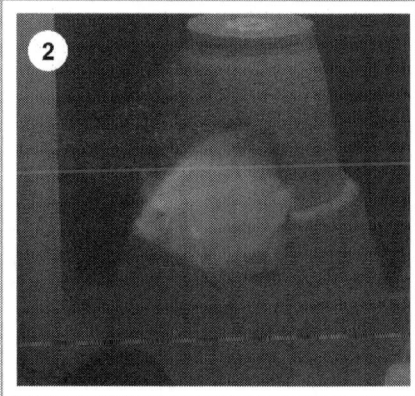

Pic 1/. Shows a Young Discus not eating from stress and Pic 2/. Shows the same Discus just two weeks later eating high protein food and putting on weight – Photographs by Alastair R Agutter

The above pictures show the same Discus, she was a small 1-1/2" fish that I found in a retail outlet with a deformed mouth, she was on her last legs and about to die see picture one. I hate seeing fish suffer like that and so I purchased the small Discus from the shop and brought her home with me. I then placed her in an aquarium with some very small ember tetra's (5) and began feeding her one of my juvenile high protein beef heart recipes that can be found in the book's food chapter and in just 24 hours at the right temperature, the right water conditions and the right food, she began to eat. Some two weeks later she had put weight on, her eyes had cleared see picture two and now she is swimming about with other fellow juvenile Discus species of the same size holding her own and happy!

I know the above photograph is not pleasant where you see a fish suffer.

But I wanted to show you how many diseases are caused by stress and the cure is not from the use of chemicals.

Today, if you are interested in the progress of this little fish. She is now with 7 other Discus friends and very bossy, in fact she is one of the very first to get to the food and will be around 3 inches in diameter in the coming few weeks and very heavily set.

TROPICAL FISH DISEASES GUIDE

Symptoms: Eye Discolouration and Cloudiness

Cause: Bacterial build-up, insufficient water changes

Treatment: Water changes immediately of natural localized tap water and warmed to the aquarium temperature. Replace as much as about 50% of the water and carry this out every other day for a week (3 to 4 times).

Symptoms: Skin reaction, patches.

Cause: The fish is fielding a barrier, Bacterial infection by Costia or Protozoan.

Treatment: Again regular water changes of localized tap water and the chlorinated content should kill the bacterial disease. 50% water changes again every other day for a week. If no improvement carry out these water changes every day for a further week.

Symptoms: Respiratory Distress Syndrome, Choking

Cause: Gill worm or flukes

Treatment: Introduce an Oxydator into the Aquarium and further air stones. Carry out regular daily water changes of 50% using localized tap water that retains small amounts of chlorine that should kill the creatures infecting the fish. Carry this out until the signs of the erratic behaviour from the fish including hitting objects when swimming or gasping for air.

Symptoms: White transparent faeces, darkening of the fish's colour.

Cause: Spiro nucleus, sometime created unknowingly by stress.

Treatment: Place the affected fish with some smaller fish that have a healthy appetite to encourage feeding again and confidence.

Symptoms: Release of transparent strings from around the head region

Cause: Hole in the head disease caused by infection transmitted by Tubifex worms and some other live foods.

Treatment: Make regular water changes and increase the temperature of the aquarium water by 5 degrees. In many instances the disease has affected the brain and little can be done. Some treatments are extreme and can kill the fish from further stress.

Symptoms: Hunger strikes

Cause: Water conditions poor, intestinal disorders

Treatment: Raise the temperature of the aquarium by 5 degrees, make daily water changes (50%) and introduce live foods such as blood worms or daphnia. The fish should be up and around in no time.

Symptoms: Long white stringy faeces

Cause: Tapeworms or Nematodes

Treatment: 50 % water changes using regular tap water every day that your fish are accustomed too. Hopefully the chlorinated water will cure the disease, or drive out the intestinal predators.

Symptoms: Skin disease or skin infections

Cause: Bacterial infection from poor quality water conditions.

Treatment: 50% water changes each day for a week using local accustomed chlorinated tap water. These water changes will remove any bacterial build-up. You can also introduce a sponge filter to further assist in the event that your existing filter is faulty or struggling to deal with these events.

Symptoms: Fish growths on skin or fins

Cause: Bacterial infections

Treatment: 50% water changes each day for a week using local acclimatized chlorinated tap water. These water changes will remove any bacterial build up.

Symptoms: Black body lying on the sides, high shimmying movements

Cause: The Plague

Treatment: Airborne viral infection. Turn all lights off and increase the temperature by 5 degrees, carry out a 50% water changes and introduce some live food like daphnia and leave the fish in peace and quiet as they are highly stressed.

Symptoms: Swelling around the Stomach Region of the Fish and Lighter in Colouration

Cause: Constipation

Treatment: Sometimes fish do suffer from constipation, this is often caused where fish have been purchased from a retail outlet and not been eating properly. Then when the fish is in the new surroundings with the right conditions, the fish can sometimes gorge food and then end up with constipation, as they have not been passing waste properly for some time. In these circumstances you can only hope that the fish will eventually begin the pass the waste build-up, sometimes the fish will jolt or look as if it is doing a dance in the water as it tries to shift the waste matter. Sometimes the fish may hit itself against an object trying to rid itself of the problem. Very often with this condition the fish will stop eating and hopefully the food waste is eventually passed.

Symptoms: Swelling of Stomach

Cause: Bloat

Treatment: Bloat is similar to constipation, but can be long lasting and fatal where fish have eaten in excess for long periods of time and damaged internal organs sometimes from fighting. There is no cure with this condition only hope that nature will take its course and he fish recovers over time.

Symptoms: Dorsal Tail and Pectoral Fin Damage

Cause: Bullying

Treatment: All fish have a pecking order amongst their own species and other aquarium inhabitants and where fighting breaks out. Some fish deliberately attack dorsal, tail and pectoral fins. This bullying behaviour can commence during and after feeding times, sometimes as a result of not enough food being fed to the fish in the community aquarium. Increase feeding to see if this helps alleviate the bickering and fighting.

Symptoms: White Spots on Body and Fins

Cause: Stress and Anxiety

Treatment: White spot is a very common disease and caused from stress and anxiety, that is brought about by too lower temperatures in most cases and water quality. Simply increase the temperature of the aquarium by around 5 degrees and carryout a 50% water change. After a few days the fish species suffering from this condition should begin to recover. Another common reason for white spot, if we are referring to just one fish in an aquarium, this condition could be down to bullying, so keep a good eye on the fish suffering and see if there is any bullying taking place from other fish.

Symptoms: Fin Deterioration (Fin Rot)

Cause: Stress and Anxiety

Treatment: Fin Rot again is often caused from stress as a result of poor water quality. Carryout a 50% water change and raise the temperature of the aquarium by around 5 degrees. This should reduce the bacterial build-up including the toxins and oxides in the water such as Ammonia, Nitrites and Nitrates. Adding chemicals to the water in any form such as Methylene Blue, only further adds more toxins to the water and creates more stress to the fish inhabitants.

My First Aquarium Collectors Edition

CHAPTER EIGHTEEN

Aquarists Reference Tables

This chapter provides you with a series of tables to help Aquarists find information and answers quickly and I hope they can be an invaluable reference point.

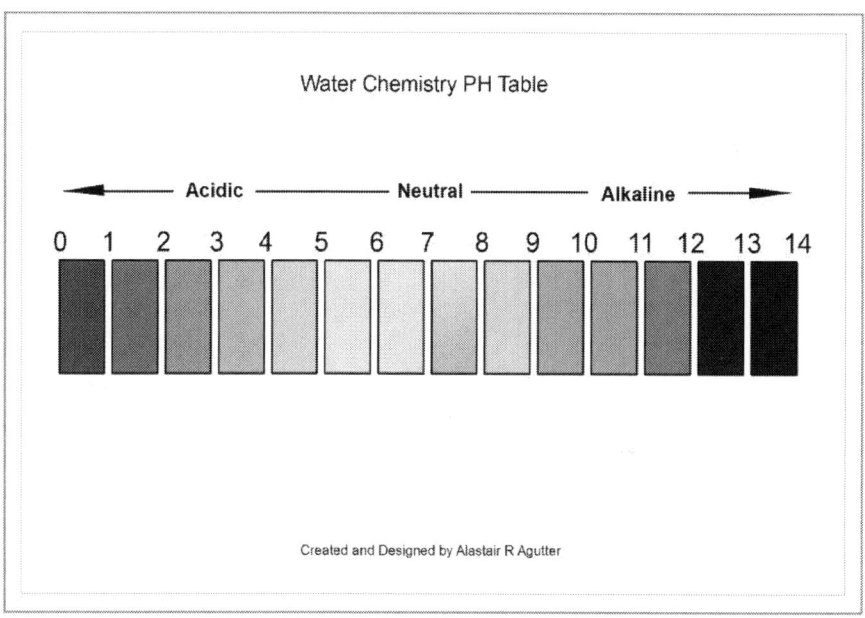

Diagram of the PH Table from 0 to 14 – Created and Designed by Alastair R Agutter

This table above shows the water hardness and softness range, so Aquarists can quickly reference PH levels regarding their own local tap and aquarium water.

The PH table also shows what I describe as the "Goldey-Locks" range of 6.0 to 8.0 PH that is an inhabitable water quality for most species of tropical fish.

Water Hardness DH Table

PPM CaCo3	DH	Conditioning
20 40 60	1.12 2.25 3.37	Soft
80 100	4.49 5.61	Moderately Soft
140 180	7.87 10.11	Ideal
220 260	12.36 14.61	Hard
300	16.85	Very Hard

Created and Designed by Alastair R Agutter

Diagram of the General Hardness Table – Created and Designed by Alastair R Agutter

This table above shows the general hardness (GH or DH) of water, so Aquarists can quickly reference DH levels regarding their own local tap and aquarium water.

The DH or GH table provides an insight to the amount of salts and minerals found in the Aquarists water, as some species can be sensitive to metals and calcium's in the water with regards to reproduction. Some species include Discus, Angel Fish, Hatchet Fish, Cardinal and Neon Tetras.

My First Aquarium Collectors Edition

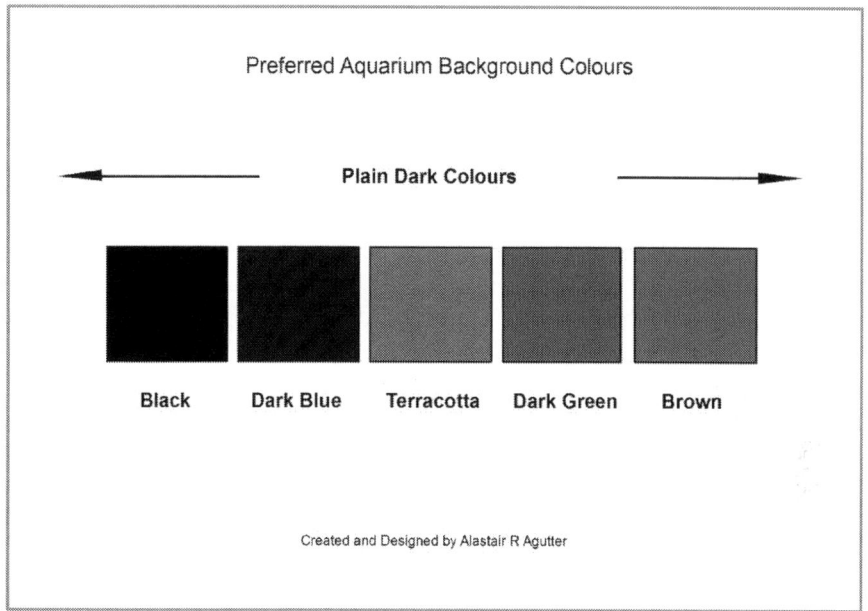

Diagram of Aquarium Backgrounds Table – Created and Designed by Alastair R Agutter

This table above shows the preferred background colours of Aquariums as this does have a significant bearing on fish species colours and desire for breeding.

Background colours are also important for fish species well-being as they can become stressed from background colours and patterns that can disorientate fish species, as they function with the use of electromagnetic energies and waves to map out their environment and can see in full colour like human beings.

Black, Terracotta and Dark Green are particularly favourable colours for fish species to bring out their colour and for breeding. But also these colours are favourable background colours for enhancing aquatic plants and ornate objects such as bogwoods.

Biological Bacteria Volume Mass Diagram

Fish Units	Temperature	BBVM's	Filter Flow Rate
5	78	40 BBVM	10 Gallons
5	84	55 BBVM	10 Gallons
10	78	80 BBVM	15 Gallons
10	84	110 BBVM	15 Gallons
15	78	120 BBVM	20 Gallons
15	84	165 BBVM	20 Gallons
20	78	160 BBVM	25 Gallons
20	84	220 BBVM	25 Gallons
Per Unit	Fahrenheit	Per Million	Gallons

Created and Designed by Alastair R Agutter

Diagram of Bacteria Volume Mass Table – Created and Designed by Alastair R Agutter

This table above shows the biological bacteria volume mass in Aquariums at certain temperature levels in relation to the number of fish species being housed and the volume of water processed as a filtration rate in gallons.

Tropical fish species in an aquarium requires the biological breakdown process of fish bye products and therefore a bacterial population culture has to exist.

Established aquariums can only be established if fish exist to allow for the populating of the bacteria that breaks down and eats the waste products of the fish and in a naturally planted aquarium, the breakdown of plant waste in the form of deteriorating leaves etc.

No chemicals can accelerate this process as it is a natural chemical phenomenon of nature populating polyatomic-ions in the form of oxides these being mainly Ammonia, Nitrite and Nitrates.

Aquarium Sizes For Number of Fish Inhabitants Table

Aquarium Size	Cubic Inches of Fish	Aquarium Size	Cubic Inches of Fish
18" x 12" x 12"	18 inches of fish	48" x 12" x 15"	60 inches of fish
24" x 12" x 15"	25 inches of fish	48" x 12" x 18"	72 inches of fish
24" x 12" x 18"	30 inches of fish	48" x 18" x 18"	108 inches of fish
24" x 24" x 24"	48 inches of fish	48" x 18" x 24"	144 inches of fish
30" x 12" x 15"	37 inches of fish	60" x 12" x 18"	75 inches of fish
30" x 12" x 18"	45 inches of fish	60" x 18" x 18"	135 inches of fish
36" x 12" x 15"	35 inches of fish	60" x 18" x 24"	180 inches of fish
36" x 12" x 18"	54 inches of fish	72" x 18" x 18"	162 inches of fish
36" x 18" x 18"	81 inches of fish	72" x 18" x 24"	216 inches of fish

Created and Designed by Alastair R Agutter

Diagram of Aquarium Sizes and Number of Fish – Created and Designed by Alastair R Agutter

This table above shows the size of aquariums and the number of fish that can be comfortably housed.

It is important to have such a reference to ensure fish inhabitant species can grow successfully when the correct numbers of fish are being housed.

When aquarists overstock aquariums there is a greater risk of disease and deformity in the fish from stunted growth.

Also, when there is a too heavy population of fish in an aquarium, there is a high risk of bacterial build-up and explosions, again causing fish to lose their appetite and exposed to disease as a result of the water conditions caused.

Aquarium Sizes and Optimal Filter Flow Rates Table

Aquarium Size	Filter Flow Rate	Aquarium Size	Filter Flow Rate
18" x 12" x 12"	11.55 Litres per hour	48" x 12" x 15"	38.50 Litres per hour
24" x 12" x 15"	19.25 Litres per hour	48" x 12" x 18"	46.20 Litres per hour
24" x 12" x 18"	23.10 Litres per hour	48" x 18" x 18"	69.30 Litres per hour
24" x 24" x 24"	61.60 Litres per hour	48" x 18" x 24"	92.40 Litres per hour
30" x 12" x 15"	24.02 Litres per hour	60" x 12" x 18"	57.75 Litres per hour
30" x 12" x 18"	28.87 Litres per hour	60" x 18" x 18"	86.62 Litres per hour
36" x 12" x 15"	28.87 Litres per hour	60" x 18" x 24"	115.50 Litres per hour
36" x 12" x 18"	34.65 Litres per hour	72" x 18" x 18"	103.95 Litres per hour
36" x 18" x 18"	51.97 Litres per hour	72" x 18" x 24"	138.60 Litres per hour

Created and Designed by Alastair R Agutter

Aquarium Sizes and Filtration Flow Rates – Created and Designed by Alastair R Agutter

Aquarium sizes and optimal filtration flow rates per hour are not often covered in any detail, but they are very important and critical if you are seeking an optimal aquarium with healthy thriving fish.

This diagram helps you to refer to popular aquarium sizes to establish the flow rate for your aquarium. Most filtration products in the form of air pumps or powerhead units today provide information of the litre output capacity and ability. With some simple calculations you can establish your needs with the help of this table.

When flow rates are too high through a filtration unit, very often waste material is passed through the biological bacterial culture housed inside the filtration system too fast, resulting in the failure to breakdown the material properly. The re-cycling of waste material in the aquarium causes a bacterial build-up in the fish tank and often reported cloudy water.

Heater Thermostats Wattage and Aquarium Sizes Table

Aquarium Size	Heater Thermostats	Aquarium Size	Heater Thermostats
18" x 12" x 12"	1 x 100 watt	48" x 12" x 15"	2 x 100 watt
24" x 12" x 15"	1 x 150 watt	48" x 12" x 18"	2 x 150 watt
24" x 12" x 18"	1 x 150 watt	48" x 18" x 18"	2 x 200 watt
24" x 24" x 24"	1 x 300 watt	48" x 18" x 24"	2 x 200 watt
30" x 12" x 15"	1 x 150 watt	60" x 12" x 18"	2 x 200 watt
30" x 12" x 18"	1 x 200 watt	60" x 18" x 18"	2 x 200 watt
36" x 12" x 15"	1 x 200 watt	60" x 18" x 24"	2 x 300 watt
36" x 12" x 18"	1 x 200 watt	72" x 18" x 18"	2 x 300 watt
36" x 18" x 18"	1 x 300 watt	72" x 18" x 24"	2 x 300 watt

Created and Designed by Alastair R Agutter

Heater Thermostat Wattage and Aquarium Sizes – Created and Designed by Alastair R Agutter

I hope this table also provides help and assists with regards to establishing the correct size of heater thermostat and wattage output for your aquarium.

All heater thermostat commercial products indicate the actual size of the device, but little is often written or covered with regards to the actual size or number of heater thermostats required for specific aquarium water volume mass in relation to gallons and litres.

These sizes of heater thermostats in the form of wattage are based on an average atmospheric temperature amongst Countries in winter and summer seasons. If you come from a region where the weather is extremely cold, well then you may need to increase this wattage as the aquarium's water battles with the external elements. If for example your weather is extreme temperature wise, well then purchase a 150 watt heater thermostat instead of a 100 watt heater thermostat.

Lighting Wattage and Aquarium Sizes Table			
Aquarium Size	Lighting Wattage	Aquarium Size	Lighting Wattage
18" x 12" x 12"	100 watts	48" x 12" x 15"	300 watts
24" x 12" x 15"	100 watts	48" x 12" x 18"	300 watts
24" x 12" x 18"	100 watts	48" x 18" x 18"	300 watts
24" x 24" x 24"	200 watts	48" x 18" x 24"	300 watts
30" x 12" x 15"	150 watts	60" x 12" x 18"	350 watts
30" x 12" x 18"	150 watts	60" x 18" x 18"	350 watts
36" x 12" x 15"	200 watts	60" x 18" x 24"	350 watts
36" x 12" x 18"	200 watts	72" x 18" x 18"	400 watts
36" x 18" x 18"	200 watts	72" x 18" x 24"	400 watts
Created and Designed by Alastair R Agutter			

Lighting Wattage and Aquarium Sizes Table – Created and Designed by Alastair R Agutter

Aquarium lighting in a naturally planted aquarium is especially important for the successful growth of your aquarium plants but also your fish regarding their growth and body bone development.

This table shows the correct aquarium wattage I have researched that works and with a lighting period of time each day being between 10 to 12 hours.

As you know fish like routine and so even the switching on and off of the aquarium lights can be achieved with the help of a plug, or wall unit timer set to 10 to 12 hours a day, starting at time A and ending at time B.

The failure to regulate the correct times and wattage of light in an aquarium will result in plant deterioration and this can be very quickly over a matter of a few days and weeks, leading to unwanted excessive numbers of toxins (pollution) building up in the aquarium.

Aquarium UK Gallons to Litres Table

Aquarium Size	UK Gallons	Litres	Aquarium Size	UK Gallons	Litres
18" x 12" x 12"	9.34	42.42	48" x 12" x 15"	31.15	141.42
24" x 12" x 15"	12.46	56.56	48" x 12" x 18"	37.38	169.70
24" x 12" x 18"	18.69	82.23	48" x 18" x 18"	56.07	254.55
24" x 24" x 24"	49.84	226.27	48" x 18" x 24"	74.76	339.41
30" x 12" x 15"	20.24	91.88	60" x 12" x 18"	46.72	212.10
30" x 12" x 18"	23.36	106.05	60" x 18" x 18"	70.08	318.16
36" x 12" x 15"	23.36	106.05	60" x 18" x 24"	93.45	424.26
36" x 12" x 18"	28.03	127.25	72" x 18" x 18"	84.10	381.81
36" x 18" x 18"	42.05	190.90	72" x 18" x 24"	112.14	509.11

Created and Designed by Alastair R Agutter

Aquarium UK Gallons to Litres Table – Created and Designed by Alastair R Agutter

Above is a conversion table of UK Imperial Gallons converted to Litres and these are accompanied with the most common aquarium sizes. No do not despair if your aquarium is not listed as the following mathematical formula will help you determine the actual size of your aquarium.

First measure the length of your aquarium, its depth and finally height. This being L x W x H then multiply these in inches to acquire the mathematical total to the equation. Example 30 x 15 x 15 = 6750, then divide into 6750 the figure of 1728 (cubic square foot in inches) and this will provide a total of 3.906 and this figure is the cubic square feet of this aquarium example. Then multiply the cubic feet of 3.90 by 6.23 (UK) gallons. This then gives you a total figure of 3.90 x 6.23 = 24.29. Then finally multiply the UK Gallons of 24.29 x 4.54 which equals 110.30 and this figure is the litres of this aquarium converted from UK Imperial Gallons.

Aquarium US Gallons to Litres Table

Aquarium Size	US Gallons	Litres	Aquarium Size	US Gallons	Litres
18" x 12" x 12"	11.22	42.10	48" x 12" x 15"	37.40	141.37
24" x 12" x 15"	14.96	56.54	48" x 12" x 18"	44.88	169.64
24" x 12" x 18"	22.44	84.82	48" x 18" x 18"	67.32	254.46
24" x 24" x 24"	62.24	235.26	48" x 18" x 24"	59.84	226.19
30" x 12" x 15"	24.31	91.89	60" x 12" x 18"	56.10	212.05
30" x 12" x 18"	28.05	106.02	60" x 18" x 18"	84.15	318.08
36" x 12" x 15"	28.05	106.02	60" x 18" x 24"	112.20	424.11
36" x 12" x 18"	33.66	127.23	72" x 18" x 18"	100.98	381.70
36" x 18" x 18"	50.49	190.85	72" x 18" x 24"	134.64	511.63

Created and Designed by Alastair R Agutter

Aquarium US Gallons to Litres Table – Created and Designed by Alastair R Agutter

Above is a conversion table of US Imperial Gallons converted to Litres and these are accompanied with the most common aquarium sizes. No do not despair if your aquarium is not listed as the following mathematical formula will help you determine the actual size of your aquarium.

First measure the length of your aquarium, its depth and finally height. This being L x W x H then multiply these in inches to acquire the mathematical total to the equation. Example 30 x 15 x 15 = 6750, then divide into 6750 the figure of 1728 (cubic square foot in inches) and this will provide a total of 3.906 and this figure is the cubic square feet of this aquarium example. Then multiply the cubic feet of 3.90 by 7.48 (US) gallons. This then gives you a total figure of 3.90 x 7.48 = 24.17. Then finally multiply the US Gallons of 24.17 x 3.78 which equals 91.36 litres and this figure is the litres of this aquarium example converted from US Imperial Gallons.

Aquarium Sizes to Cubic Square Feet Table

Aquarium Size	Cubic Square Feet	Aquarium Size	Cubic Square Feet
18" x 12" x 12"	1.5 Cu Sq ft	48" x 12" x 15"	5.0 Cu Sq ft
24" x 12" x 15"	2.5 Cu Sq ft	48" x 12" x 18"	6.0 Cu Sq ft
24" x 12" x 18"	3.0 Cu Sq ft	48" x 18" x 18"	9.0 Cu Sq ft
24" x 24" x 24"	8.0 Cu Sq ft	48" x 18" x 24"	12.0 Cu Sq ft
30" x 12" x 15"	3.25 Cu Sq ft	60" x 12" x 18"	7.5 Cu Sq ft
30" x 12" x 18"	3.75 Cu Sq ft	60" x 18" x 18"	11.25 Cu Sq ft
36" x 12" x 15"	3.75 Cu Sq ft	60" x 18" x 24"	15.00 Cu Sq ft
36" x 12" x 18"	4.50 Cu Sq ft	72" x 18" x 18"	13.50 Cu Sq ft
36" x 18" x 18"	6.75 Cu Sq ft	72" x 18" x 24"	18.0 Cu Sq ft

Created and Designed by Alastair R Agutter

Aquarium Sizes to Cubic Square Feet Table – Created and Designed by Alastair R Agutter

This table provides the Cubic Square Feet measurement of a number of aquarium sizes listed above. The Cubic Square Feet of Aquariums is obviously important in tropical fish keeping regarding a whole host of subject areas covered and where very often you may find yourself in need of the aquarium Cubic Square Foot size. Relevant areas that come to mind as a few examples are; Amount of Gallons or Litres, for Medication purposes and heating with reference to heater thermostat wattage requirements.

If your aquarium is not listed above do not despair as I will now take you through a simple mathematical formula that will allow you to establish the Cubic Square Foot capacity of any aquarium.

Simply multiply the L x W x H of the aquarium in inches and then divided the total figure by 1728.

This will then provide you with the Cubic Square Feet of the Aquarium in question.

Here is a following example for you:-

I have an aquarium that is 40 inches in length, a depth or width of 20 inches and a height of 18 inches.

So, if I multiply 40 x 20 x 18 this figure total equals = 14400. Now if I divide 14400 by 1728 it gives me a figure of 8.333 and this total figure is in fact the Cubic Square Feet of the above aquarium example.

Now if for medical or filter purposes I need to know how many gallons this represents in UK imperial gallons, I simply multiply 8.33 which is the cubic square feet of the aquarium itself by 6.23 that is the UK gallons found in one cubic square foot and so the total of UK gallons for this aquarium equals 51.91 UK Gallons.

Now if I need my gallons to be in Litres!

I simply multiply 51.91 UK Gallons by 4.54 and this will give me the number of Litres in the Aquarium and this being 235.70.

I hope in this chapter I have covered all the tables required for our pastime of tropical fish keeping and where they are together, so they are easier to find as a quick reference.

My First Aquarium Collectors Edition

CHAPTER NINETEEN

Aquarists Products and Accessories

Fish Foods: Today in tropical fish keeping, we have far more advanced and developed products available to us and ranging in price to meet every Aquarists budget and needs.

Picture above showing more user-friendly and green product tropical fish foods for today's aquarist with biodegradable containers – Photograph compiled by Alastair R Agutter

A wide and varied diet ensures your tropical fish are receiving essential vitamins, trace elements and proteins in their diet for healthy thriving inhabitants in your aquarium.

Natural fats are also important in a fish species diet to help build-up fish for reproduction.

Reproduction in a fish species life cycle can really take its toll and more so regarding some highly evolved species such as cichlids, where so often after hatching cichlids will look after their young (fry) and fail to eat themselves through these stressful periods and times when looking out for their siblings.

Feeding flake and fresh frozen foods helps create a varied diet and thus in turn always ensuring your tropical fish have a healthy appetite and always eager to eat at feeding times.

Flake and Pellet foods are what I describe as clean foods and cause the least pollution in an aquarium when feeding. However with flake and pellet foods they are what they are, processed foods dried foods, where the natural water and juices have been removed from these foods.

Fresh frozen foods can be messy, but one fresh frozen food can vary to another. It is also important to note the consumption periods by the fish of frozen foods can vary. If your fish are keen eaters and enjoy the fresh frozen foods they will eat and digest these foods before they start to become a risk to the aquarium environment regarding any increase in aquarium pollution contaminants.

Fish, like all creatures and especially us as human beings, have a preference to certain food types. Even when feeding flake foods to tropical fish, some species in a community aquarium have a particular liking towards some parts of the food and not the other. When studying your fish at feeding times with flake food you can see that Tetras for example prefer parts of the flake food and guppies or platies for example like another part of the food.

It is very clear that the ingredients and formula when making flake foods is with the aim to accommodate most community aquarium tropical fish tastes and I might add, the dieticians developing these foods have done extremely well, for I never see any flake food uneaten or remaining after about 4 to 5 minutes.

When developing fresh frozen foods just as much thought and effort needs to go into the planning as commercial food dieticians to derive at the most suitable ingredients. I make my own fresh frozen foods even for my community aquarium fish inhabitants and these recipes are different to the fresh frozen foods planned and prepared for my Discus and Angel Fish for example.

The ingredients I use for my fresh frozen fish food for my community aquarium species includes; Broccoli, Spinach, Liver, Beef Heart, Prawns, Cods Roe and Beetroot for example and the addition of multi-vitamins. Now in the Book chapter for Feeding fish, you can find my recipes of fresh frozen fish foods that are markedly different regarding ingredients used for a recipe aimed at specific cichlids and again even variations in recipes for fish species age groups and stages of growth e.g. Junior and Adult Foods.

A staple Discus diet for example will only contain beef heart, spinach and beef liver in most cases. The grating size of the food also varies accordingly to growth of fish species in question. Larger fish species food is grated on a far coarser whereas younger species food is prepared by using a smaller grating setting.

Some fresh frozen foods may not be appealing at all to some fish species and this is another reason why when introducing a new fish food to the staple diet is to only feed very small amounts initially. Mysis or Sand Eels may be popular to some larger fish species of the characin family but not at all appealing to smaller members of the characin family such as tetras.

I have never found Mysis or Sand Eels to be very popular with many members of the Cichlid family and so initially it may be worth buying a small amount of a new fish food before acquiring any larger packets or containers.

Today as mentioned there is a large range of fish foods in the form of flake, freeze dried, pellet and fresh frozen on the market today.

Aquarists have a great choice available to them and many are worth trying to hopefully achieve the best results with regards to growth and wanting to breed.

Some foods you may find are not eagerly eaten and this I have found when feeding high protein foods for the very first time to fish not accustomed to the diet. When I bring in very young Discus occasionally to help in my program and to prevent inbreeding of the same family members for genetic reasons the young are never keen on the beef heart initially, but after about two days they cannot eat enough and then you have to be careful the fish do not overeat for fear of contracting the condition known as bloat.

New fish to the community aquarium may not initially be eager to eat your fish food that the rest of the inhabitants enjoy, this is normally as a result of the existing diet, where for example the retailer or shop owner has been feeding the fish just on bloodworm for ease due to the number of aquariums he or she has to maintain. Now bloodworms is a poplar food with most fish, but not the holy grail of food as fish do need a balanced diet just like us humans and most other creatures.

Another reason why new fish from a retailer may not be keen to eat is as a result of being rundown. The moving and disruption of any fish can be stressful and contrary to the myth of fish not remembering. Fish do remember and especially more evolved species such as cichlids and especially Discus, they can be very weary and mindful of disruption for many weeks. Some of my adult Discus fish look at me sometimes as if to say "what is he doing now" when I am carrying out some maintenance, or cleaning and they will literally sit in the water at the front of the aquarium watching me for as long as it takes.

Frozen Bloodworms are well worth including in your tropical fish's diet. Bloodworms are especially a valuable food source when trying to encourage fish to eat who have been suffering from being rundown. After a couple of weeks once you have managed to get your poorly fish eating again, is to start mixing in some flake food with the bloodworms, so eventually your poorly fish in question starts to enjoy a more balanced diet.

On a final note surrounding fish food products, is to always make sure you acquire these foods from a well-known trusted brand and producer.

Obviously if you are making your own fresh fish food for freezing, you are in control of the ingredients and therefore the well-being of your fish from the outset.

The secret to feeding any food is always little and often. If your fish species have an eager appetite simply feed them more times in a day. Adult Discus for example when coming into breeding will "eat you out of house and home" to coin a phrase when it comes to food and need to be fed 4 to 5 times a day.

Products and Accessories Continued

Oxydator: This object is known as an Oxydator for delivering oxygen saturation to an aquarium invented and developed by Doctor Sochting.

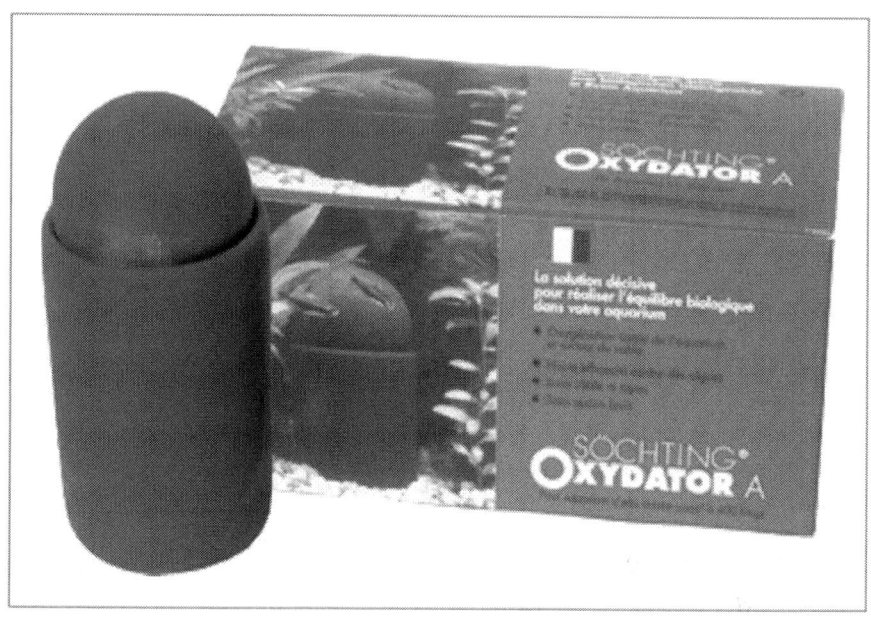

Picture above shows an Oxydator for the delivery of Oxygen Saturation to an Aquarium and especially used in breeding and keeping Discus – Photograph compiled by Alastair R Agutter

The Dr. Sochting Oxydator came to great prominence to the Aquatic World in the 1980's and was an invention that helped to provide oxygen saturation in an aquarium and for a number of very good reasons.

The Oxydator is essentially a clay based pot type container and with a large solid ball that sits on top. Another component is a clear Perspex or Plastic container that can be opened and closed. Inside the clear container is a small cylindrical element known as a catalyst.

How an Oxydator works is very smart and unique, the clear container is filed with Hydrogen Peroxide and the container is closed with the catalyst inside. Then the container in inverted (turned upside down) and placed in the Oxydators clay base tub or container and then the round solid ball is placed on top. The Oxydator is then lowered into the aquarium at a desired position and soon you can see the release of pure oxygen into the water. The reaction between the catalyst and the hydrogen peroxide releases pure oxygen into the water.

Above is a Classic picture from the 1980's with some of the Author's Wild Discus being bred in captivity and in the foreground is an Oxydator – Photograph by Ian Russell

Some species require an almost clinical condition of water quality such as Cardinals, Neon's, Hatchets, Discus and Angel fish to mention a few. So it is essential that the biological bacterial culture filtering such an aquarium system is thriving and not inhibited in any way, to ensure any waste elements and particles in the water of the aquarium are successfully broken down, providing clear water. This is greatly aided and assisted by having oxygen saturation in the water.

Above is a picture I hope you enjoy shot back in the 1980's in black and white on a 35 mm camera by Ian Russell, when I was managing to breed wild discus in captivity and in the foreground of the picture you can see an Oxydator working to provide oxygen saturation in the aquarium that was 120 gallons (500 litres approximately), housing rare Blue (Haraldi) Discus and Tefe Green (Pellegrin) Discus, where eventually from these species bred in captivity the Turquoise strains of Discus derived.

The Oxydator can also be used to serve many purposes in an aquarium. The oxydator can assist and be helpful where water conditions have a low general hardness (DH) of water, or where there are acid water conditions for example.

Oxydators are also handy in general by providing oxygen saturation that will encourage growth to both fish and plants.

Oxydators are very often used in Discus breeding tanks raising young, as there is a great intensity of fish and food in a confined area and where oxygen saturation is critical for the survival of all inhabitants these being Parents and Fry.

Oxydators are a worthwhile investment for any aquarium and a container full of hydrogen peroxide and using just one catalyst will last on average releasing pure oxygen for about a month.

Hydrogen peroxide can be purchased from your local Chemist. In Western Societies, as a result of our troubled World, it may be wise to advise your pharmacist what the purchase of hydrogen peroxide is for, as this relates to National Security issues unfortunately these days.

I have seen the Dr. Sochting Oxydator sold online via the Web, if you seek to acquire one and had problem locating them from your local shop.

Products and Accessories Continued

Polyatomic-ion Biological Reactor: For more than 40 years filtration has always been a subject that I have found fascinating and of great importance in tropical fish keeping.

Above in picture 1 shows the Polyatomic-ion Biological Reactor fully functioning delivering crystal clear water in the aquarium. Picture 2 shows the shell component parts for building a simple Polyatomic-ion Biological Reactor – Photographs by Alastair R Agutter

I knew when breeding Discus (symphysodon) in captivity that I had to crack the secrets to filtration in aquariums, to gain an edge and the best results. So I studied in great detail and depth the processes of the wild surrounding filtration, so I was able to fully understand the processes, protagonists, actors and players.

The volume exchange in the wild is ten times in most waters. Obviously areas of water that have been cut-off after flooding, or where there is more vegetative overgrown creeks, or dyke environments, where water is almost at a stagnation point, is however definitely not breaking down water at a rate of ten times an hour. So whilst I managed to invent and develop a trickle filter back in the 1980's, known as the Power Vain Filtration System to achieve such a water filtration exchange in the aquarium. I knew the story of filtration hid many more secrets.

One of our biggest failings as Scientists and Biologists is that we are all guilty so often of looking at a problem in a linear wired way of thinking and constantly referring back examining only the facts found in black and white from the past. However, Mother Nature right before our eyes in the World of Quantum Mechanics and Natural Branching shows us based on her (Mother Nature) evidence, to look at posing problems in symmetry. For example Fractal Mathematics is symmetry, Alan Turing (Father of Computers) breaking the Enigma Code and Albert Einstein surrounding the theory of general relativity looked beyond the status quo thinking laterally and multi-dimensionally.

Filtration I discovered was no different, as it has many variables and facets, in other words you can have numerous methods and rates to arrive at equal results or far different ones. For example, It is the water environment itself and the related elements in the form of minerals, fish and plant life that can determine different outcomes but all of such delivering positive results.

The mind blowingly wonderful thing about this subject and many others I might add is that Einstein's elements of time and motion, including gravity, have a significant bearing when it comes to filtration in any form.

In the chapter of filtration we discuss the different types of filtration and mediums to use. I wanted to include the Polyatomic-on Biological Reactor in the products and accessories section for one of our greatest achievements and endeavours over the decades of tropical fish keeping has been our ability to create some of our own equipment. To me the ability to make items for our hobby is all part of the pastime and goes to the very heart of hobbies and interests.

The two photographs above show the Polyatomic-ion Biological Reactor working in the aquarium successfully delivering crystal clear water and another showing the shell component parts.

Yes, the dome is a flower pot, a slightly porous but safe clay based material and with terracotta the good thing is, they retain their heat to assist the bacteria culture living inside the dome.

The PVC plastic piping I obtained from my local DIY store in the plumbing section. I have created the uplift by a piece of straight pipe, two clips by cutting a straight length of pipe and cutting across the short pipe piece so it acts as a clip and can fit over the pipe. I cut two of these, one for the base where the pipe tightly just fits just inside the flower pot and the other to fit around the neck of where the pipe fits into the flower pot like a collar.

I use a bend connection that is connected to the top of the uplift pipe and in the bend made a small hole to fit the airline tubing, so it can slide down inside the uplift pipe.

On the inside of the dome I went and found myself a plastic flower pot slightly smaller than the terracotta flower pot dome and cut around the plastic flower pot around half to three quarters of an inch from the base of the plastic flower pot. At the base of the plastic flower pot there are a series of holes, these holes work as the drawing vents for the water to flow through, similar to an undergravel filter plate. I turn the cut base of the flower pot upside down and place this inside the dome of the terracotta flower pot first.

I then cut two circular pieces of activated carbon sheet that will fit tightly into the dome of the flower pot covering the perforated plastic flower pot base housed in the terracotta flower pot dome. Next I cut two circular pieces of fine foam from a sheet that can be obtained from your local pond and koi centre. I place these fine circular pieces of foam over the activated carbon circles that were cut from the carbon material sheet. Next I cut two circles of foam from a medium foam sheet, again obtained from the Koi or Pond Centre. I insert these two foam circles now inside the dome so they cover the fine foam circles and then lastly, I cut two coarse foam circles and insert these over the medium foam circles. Now the dome should be full of foam inside.

Pic 1 shows the Polyatomic-ion Biological Reactor shell and pipe parts. Pic 2 shows activated carbon, fine, medium and coarse foam sheets to cut into circles. Pic 3 Polyatomic-ion Biological Reactor assembled – Photographs by Alastair R Agutter

Now if you have an aquarium that has a substrate you can simply gently place the Polyatomic-ion Biological Reactor in the desired location of the aquarium.

Now if you have a sterile bare bottom aquarium, all you need to do is get a small circular file and file small half circle grooves around the base of the terracotta dome at one inch intervals and these small vents or holes will be the intakes for the filter in the bare bottom aquarium.

Now the filtration flow rate for a Polyatomic-ion Biological Reactor needs to be around 60 litres per hour, for each filter. Aquariums therefore up to 30 gallons only need one filter.

Air Pumps when purchased display the flow rate and so if you buy a pump with two valves producing 120 litres per hour, you then know that you only need to use one valve on the pump for every Polyatomic-ion Biological Reactor. If you have an existing more powerful air pump, simply attach a bank of one, two, three, four or five valves to the pump's outlet and then regulate the air flow between these valves until you have 60 litres an hour as a flow rate for every Polyatomic-ion Biological Reactor.

These filters when working are absolutely brilliant for crystal clear high quality water and do not damage plant roots when used in a naturally planted aquarium.

The filing out of the hole for the pipe to fit and to cut the grooves into the base of the flower pot dome is very easy to do and only takes a few minutes. Please ensure however, that you use old clothes or overalls, as it can be a messy old job with a lot of terracotta dust ☺

Products and Accessories Continued

Foam Filters: When breeding and rearing fry, filtration is obviously very important and with regular water changes, intense food programs you need a safe working filtration solution that is also adaptable.

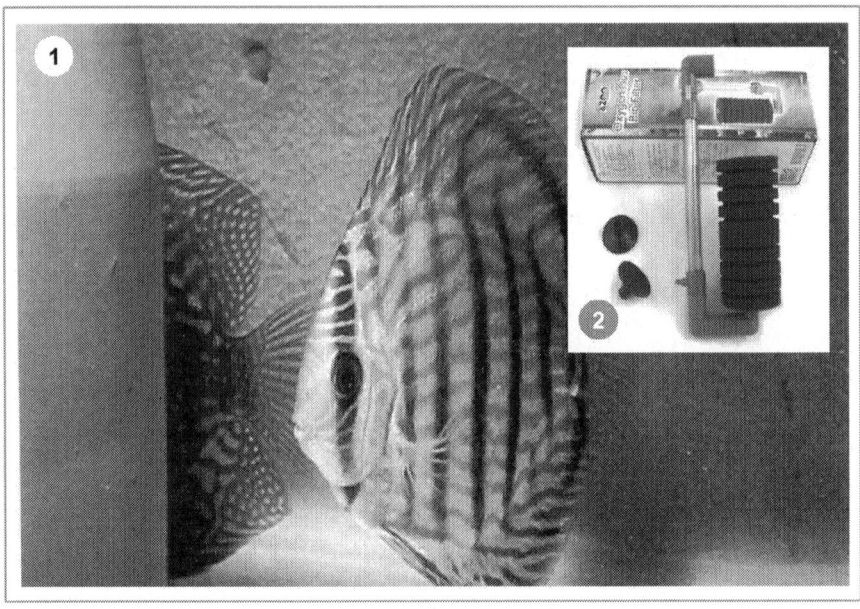

Pic 1 shows a breeding pair of the Author's Red Discus back in the 1980's. Pic 2 shows the foam filters used for breeding and rearing tanks easily available – Photographs by Ian Russell

These small foam filters are ideal for rearing fry and for small breeding fish tanks and here is why?

As soon as fish spawn, the next dilemma is the well-being of the breeding pair and the fry. My breeding and rearing fish tanks on average are 18" x 16" x 15" (15.57 UK gallons or 70.70 Litres) and house in these aquariums two foam filters in each. The reason being is that if I need to get another aquarium up and running quickly in the need for separating the fry from the parents, all I have to do is simply siphon-off half the water from one aquarium into the new fish tank and simply remove one of the established foam filters and place it in the new aquarium just set-up.

There is no need for establishing a new aquarium, as the bacteria on the foam filter that I have just moved is already active.

After this process, I then simply add another two more foam filters, one to the aquarium I have removed the filter from and a second to the new aquarium, in the event of having to repeat the process in a week or two's time, as I rear the fry and where some grow larger than others and where again a separation will be required.

The photograph above shows crystal clear water from one of my breeding aquariums back in the 1980's, using these foam filters to breed strain 5 red turquoise discus (3rd generation from wild parents).

I have read that these small filters are very popular with aquarists of community aquariums, where they add these filters to their existing fish tanks to attain clearer water.

Products and Accessories Continued

Terracotta Cones: As a tropical fish hobbyist there will come a day when your fish will want to hopefully spawn and over recent years terracotta cones have become very popular with Discus and Cichlid Aquarists.

Pic 1 shows a pair of Turquoise Red Discus with a Terracotta Cone for a Spawning Surface. Pic 2 shows the Popular Terracotta Cones on sale – Photographs by Alastair R Agutter

To my knowledge terracotta cones were first used in Germany by successful German breeders for Discus and Angel Fish in the early to mid-nineteen eighties.

Since that time they have become a very popular spawning surface for many cichlids bred in captivity.

They are easy to use and maintain, they are particular popular with the fish as they provide a slightly porous surface which allows cichlid eggs to stick more successfully and with the height of the cones, it helps to prevent eggs becoming fungus due to the raised height and level in the aquarium.

Products and Accessories Continued

Heater Thermostats: Heater Thermostats have come a long way today and available from many leading brands and varying in price.

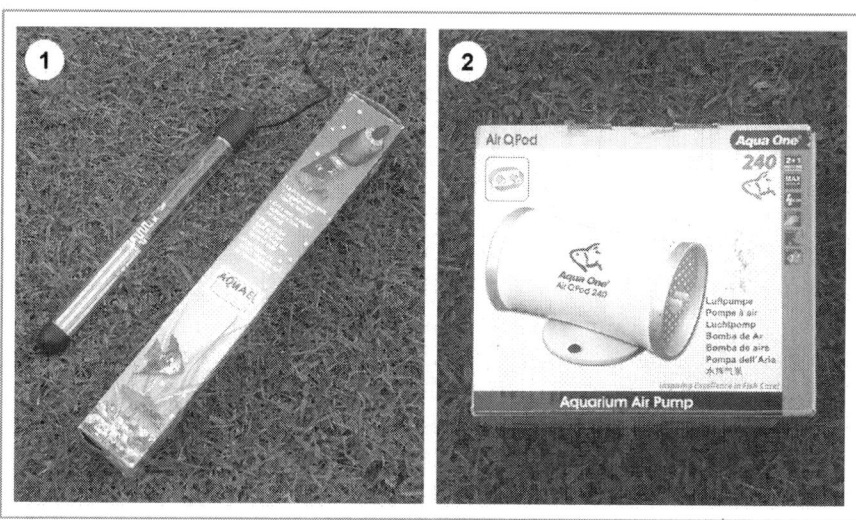

Picture 1 shows an Aquarium Heater Thermostat. Picture 2 shows a conventional Aquarium Air Pump – Photographs by Alastair R Agutter

The most popular heater thermostat sizes available normally range from 50 to 300 watt capacity and many with smarter heating elements that last longer and with easy adjustment settings on the heater thermostat device.

Obviously as tropical fish hobbyists we all need to heat our aquariums and heater thermostats are bar far the most popular. With the greater use of aquarium reservoirs or sumps being used for filtration, heater thermostats can be housed in these sections of the aquarium system thus hiding the device.

There may be the odd exception where heater thermostats are not used for example in fish houses or commercial breeding operations where another form of heating is used that actually heats the fish house or commercial premises itself.

I seem to recall Dutch breeders use an oil-fueled piped central heating system around the floor of the fish house just below the banks of the aquariums, so the heat travels up through the aquarium banks in the buildings.

Air Pumps: Today powered centrifugal pumps are more often used than air pumps for the odd aquarium in the home, as air pumps have always been renowned to be noisy. But today's air pumps are barely heard these days and if housed in a cabinet the sound will disappear altogether.

Air Pumps and Powered Pumps today are far more economical and energy user friendly.

Powerheads and Powered pumps came more to the fore in the 1980's, but it was in fact Eheim back in the 1960's that developed the first type of centrifuge motor for aquarium pumps. These are very popular devices today with aquarists and the new designs able to move large amount of water through a filtration systems.

The Air Pump however has a far longer and dignified legacy in our hobby and pastime, for it was recorded that the first ever Air Pump for an aquarium was developed in 1908 and was marked as a pivotal moment in history surrounding Aquatics. The first Air Pump was powered by water not electricity. It was not until shortly after World War One, that the first Air Pumps were recorded to be powered by electricity and in that period it was a purple patch for aquatics, as artificial lighting and heating was also developed for the aquarium using electricity.

You may well be surprised, but many traditional aquarists and commercial breeders still use air pumps today, as a preferred preference so they are able to regulate down to finite detail air flows when breeding fish species.

Products and Accessories Continued

Aquariums: Today when it comes to Aquariums in design and size we are very much spoilt for choice and a range of prices to meet every budget.

Throughout History in our pastime Engineering and Life Skills have played an important part and none more so than making our own Aquariums – Photograph by Alastair R Agutter

However there is another aspect to our pastime and hobby that has served us well over the decades and that has been Engineering and Life Skills, where many an Aquarium has been custom, or homemade.

Today unfortunately at this time glass is at a premium price due to demand in the solar panel industry. But for the best part of our hobby over the decades, the idea of making our own aquariums was always a viable option and idea. Thankfully at this time, there are still a good number of Glazier Shops in our communities and I am sure many would have some glass available for any aquarium project idea at a reasonable price.

When covering this section in the book on Aquariums it would be easy to list many great fish tank products and brands. But tropical fish keeping for me when I first started out in the hobby back in the 1960's is much more than just about products. For I think our hobby is just as importantly about people as well as our tropical fish and aquarium plants and from collective spirit and goodwill, we can see the very best in us all.

Just as gardening can get under your fingernails, Aquatics can get under your skin, and making your own aquarium is an experience and task well worth considering and undertaking if not now, perhaps in the future!

The name Aquarium was coined by the English Marine Biologist Philip Henry Gosse and built the first public aquarium in 1853 for London Zoo.

It was "The Great London Exhibition" of 1851 to 1853 that saw the hobby of tropical fish keeping really take off as fine ornamental cast iron aquariums were put on display by exhibitors.

Soon after "The Great London Exhibition" America and Germany entered the fray in Aquarium development, making aquariums from timber lined with pitch and glass fronts, angled iron aquariums made in glass with slate bottoms to heat aquariums from below.

Through the 20th Century aquarium design evolved with more robust steel welded angle frames that were enamel coated with glass panes lined by putty.

By the 1950's and 1960's, Aquarium design became works of art with ornate metal work and even bow fronted aquaria with more sophisticated enameling and anodizing or electro plating.

In the early part of the 1970's aquariums began to be constructed and made only from plate glass and using high modulus clear silicone sealants to bond the glass panes. Most common commercial sizes in those early days made with ¼ inch plate glass were; 24 x 12 x 12, 24 x 12 x 15, 36 x 12 x 15, 36 x 12 x 18, 48 x 12 x 15 and 48 x 12 x 18.

As confidence grew in this new design of all glass aquariums, larger custom designed aquariums were made using 3/8 inch plate glass and the most popular sizes were; 60 x 18 x 18, 60 x 18 x 24, 60 x 24 x 24, 72 x 18 x 18, 72 x 18 x 24 and 72 x 24 x 24.

Today even more sophisticated and larger designs of Aquariums exist made from acrylic and glass and in America, as you probably well know, even television programmes are now made and broadcast across the Discovery Channels on the subject.

The pastime of Tropical Fish Keeping I am pleased to say is growing yet again across Europe, Asia and North America. In fact, in the United States of America, tropical fish keeping is the biggest hobby after stamp collecting as reported in 1999.

If you would like to try your hand at making an aquarium, here are the following glass sizes for the aquarium in the picture at the start of this section. The silicone sealer required, can be easily obtained online and the full details of which are in the Chapter of Aquarium Sizes in the book.

Glass Sizes for a 36" x 18" x 21" Aquarium. All the glass is 6mm thick

1 @ 36" x 18" Base

2 @ 36" x 21" Sides

2 @ 21" x 17-1/2" Ends

2 @ 1-1/2" x 34" Side Ribs

2 @ 1-1/2" x 16" End Ribs

1 @ 3" x 16" Centre Rib

Products and Accessories Continued

Lighting: Today aquarium lighting comes in many styles and thankfully each day more designs are becoming more energy efficient.

One of the Author's Naturally Planted Aquariums using Energy Efficient Lighting that comes with a 10 year life product guarantee – Photograph by Alastair R Agutter

The history of lighting is very rarely ever covered in literature and is a fascinating area of the pastime for early forms of lighting for aquariums started with gas light elements often found in a home and where an aquarium was strategically placed below such a fixture. At the beginning of the 20th century (1900's) the humble light bulb began to be used for the illumination of aquariums. Eventually light bulbs began to be housed in aquarium hoods, as aquarium designs further advanced with the use of angle iron steel metals and light gauge aluminium used for aquarium hoods.

Fluorescent lighting was unleashed onto the World at "The World's Fair Exhibition in 1939" and a few years later rope lighting as it was known was soon finding its way into the World of Aquatics and still continues to be used today as white light and Grolux.

Regarding commercial aquariums today and their lighting, many or most of the fish tanks come with built in lighting systems that are either fluorescent or LED.

The lighting used for one of my naturally planted aquariums pictured above, is from green energy efficient lighting products that have a 10 year guarantee. The actual bulbs have on average a power output of between 75 to 100 watts per each bulb, but is in fact only between 15 to 20 watts in size.

Spotlights and Halogen (Mercury Vapour) Lights are an ever increasing popular choice today with many Aquarists. These light systems are normally suspended above the aquarium from wall mounts or hanging from the ceiling.

Always remember fish like routine and so the investment in a timer switch for your lighting will always be a worthwhile investment and appreciated by your fish. Remember that the lighting period needs to be between 10 to 12 hours and the actual wattage of the lighting for the size of your aquarium can be found in the reference tables chapter.

Products and Accessories Continued

UV Sterilization: In this section of products and accessories as promised in the book, I said I would cover for Aquarists valuable information surrounding UV Sterilization, Reverse Osmosis and Deionization.

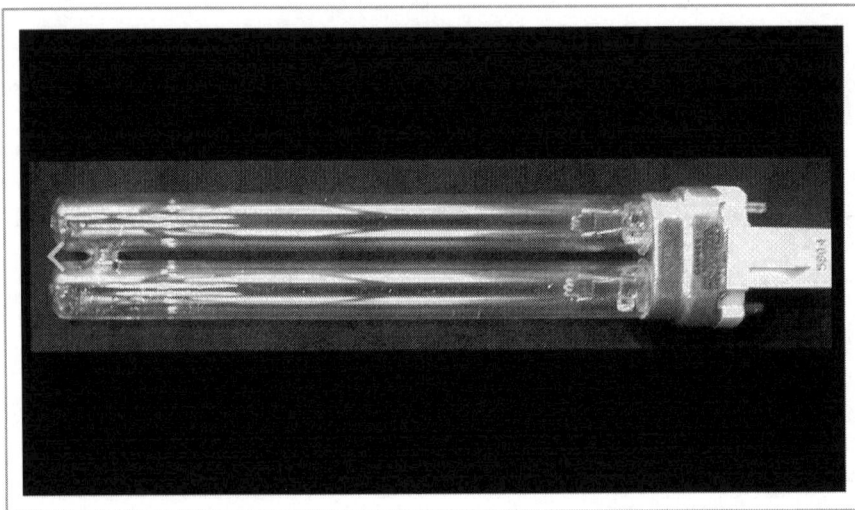

Germicidal UV Lamp in a Fluorescent Tube Unit – Photograph Courtesy of Wikipedia (Creative Commons License Permissions) and Artwork Compiled by Alastair R Agutter

I have always been a great advocate for technology and human advancement, but with a rational and balanced approach, for the more we study Natural Law in the fields of Quantum Mechanics and Natural Branching a greater appreciation is attained regarding every element we believe we know and pretend to understand.

You see we need to understand the big picture and this far extends beyond this Earth. All the time we have space and other planets that do include and house life, we need to have a constantly evolving resistant immune system to meet these changes and this can be said for all other life forms we have come to love and know who we share this small planet with.

Perhaps in a 100 or 1000 years, humankind will understand and it will be commonly known that all that we know is connected, and where this is especially relevant to seeding.

Every species on the planet from Quantum Mechanics and Natural Branching is continually advancing and this extends to microbiology and immunity.

UV Sterilization is what it is and that is a method of disinfectant of any form of microbial life forms. UV sterilization units I deem to be a lazy form of aquarium maintenance but with a contradiction. For one of the key elements in water quality is a fully functioning biological bacterial filtration system.

The presence of UV Sterilization in any form will inhibit or eliminate any bacterial activity that is critical to breaking down waste matter and oxides in the aquarium's water.

UV Sterilization can and will over time weaken the immune system of fish inhabitant species. A strong immune system in fish is the barrier to fend off and threatening bacterial infections or more prominent diseases.

If we took a very close look at our own bodies under a microscope you will find that our bodies are alive with bacterial activity and micro-organisms.

Our very own atmosphere is alive with activity and as we know is the common method of contracting colds and other viruses. Water is no different and airborne alien entities in the form of viruses do descend into the depths of our Marine World.

Scientists are today now beginning to understand where there is any form of moisture or water, micro-organisms can be carried, and this includes meteors, or asteroids, that are now being seriously considered with regards to how life was first established on Earth.

If we look closer to home with regards to Earth, every species on the planet does serve a purpose and if we equated Earth to an evolving formula one engine, we would immediately know that every component is essential for the motor to work and perform.

It is from climate change that I warned about over 25 years ago in my first tropical fish book that clearly demonstrates today how our performance engine of Earth is now starting to malfunction as components are removed in the form of animal and plant life species.

So regarding UV Sterilization, it is no friend to any form of Marine Life or environment we seek to maintain or replicate.

Reverse Osmosis: Another method of water purification I hear about is Reverse Osmosis and in truth most of these methods discussed in tropical fish magazines, or by others, I describe as Techno-geek Aquarists, is another method and technology that is dangerous to an aquarium environment and the ideas of use by such authors or columnists, indicates to me a total lack of any in-depth knowledge of our pastime.

Reverse Osmosis is a process of forcing a liquid through a filtration method, this being water through a semi-permeable membrane, a fine mesh in other words. The process is enabled by forcing the liquid through to eliminate metal trace elements, salts, minerals, calcium's and even microbial entities and bacteria.

Now to aid this process of reverse osmosis, chemicals can be used to assist this process, sounds familiar, with regards to fracking. To then deliver at the other end of the process a sterile liquid with a very low general hardness (DH or GH).

Keeping, rearing and breeding any fish species successfully is achieved by a few simple rules. 1/. An abundance of water (on tap), 2/. High Protein Healthy Foods, 3/. Correct Lighting 4/. Lastly, a Routine

If Aquarists abide by these key rules above and with a regime of regular care and maintenance, there will never be a need for additional man-made products that in truth constitute as being dangerous gimmicks.

This method can only really be of used on large scale State Region waterways where the water is so polluted nothing is able to survive. This is where Reverse Osmosis treatment plants can begin a process to purify water. But then even after that process, various metal and trace elements have to be re-introduced back into the water, to begin and start the long process of establishing natural plant and marine animal life forms once again.

Deionization: Today there are a number of processes for developing deionized water to remove minerals, anions (chlorides), copper, iron, sulphate etc. The aim of which is to lower the General Hardness (DH or GH) of Water so it becomes a purer liquid a good example being battery water.

One process is to use electrodes to remove metal trace elements and another is to again force water through a series of pipes housing ion-exchange resins that are normally microbeads to collect and trap the minerals, metals, salts etc.

The process is very long and laborious to produce small amounts of deionized water and also this process does not remove bacteria and other microbial organisms. Deionizers when not in use, such systems can in fact create a build-up of bacterial organisms from the moisture retained in these tube systems. Flushing is very often recommended but in truth how much flushing is required before you know the system is safe.

I will be honest as always and this is based on experience of using Deionizers as part of an experiment over 25 years ago when trying to breed Discus in captivity.

The deionized process could never produce enough water for me, as I had a requirement of water changes per week in excess of 450 gallons and these units on average were only capable of producing around a 120 litres (27 UK imperial gallons) at best, before cleaning and flushing, or replacing in some instances.

Deionized water is without doubt extremely useful in the medical profession and pharmaceutical industry, but not practical when it comes to keeping healthy thriving tropical fish. For one thing tropical fish need is routine and consistency. The great secret in breeding regarding water, is to get your tropical fish acclimatized to your local water, so then it is "on tap" to coin a phrase, so then you can carry out as many water changes as you wish and as often as you want.

IMPORTANT: Microbeads are soon to be banned, as they are a man-made substance pollutant now finding their way into the food chain (your tropical fish) at a dangerous level globally.

Regarding some commercial products and technology available today for the Aquarist such as; Deionizers, Reverse Osmosis and UV Sterilizers for tropical fish keeping. I think we need to sometimes step back and see things for what they truly are and in this instance, these products are nothing other than a commercial opportunity.

I am constantly reminding Students, Academia and the Public, in our Global Society, that the more we supposedly advance, the "window for error" becomes forever smaller. Very often we think we know, but then there is that old saying from time and memorial "where fools rush in."

Today from our naïve commercial world of miracle face creams and other cosmetics, all our Oceans, Estuaries, Rivers, Streams and Lakes are now under serious threat from microbeads, that are being digested by Marine Life and also polluting the water and finding their way into every part of the food table, regarding everything we eat.

Even Fowl and Farm Animals affected, as these are fed at some time intensive enriched pellet foods, containing fish meal in some form.

My First Aquarium Collectors Edition

Products and Accessories Continued

Accessories: In this last part of the products and accessories section I have written some summaries about some useful items often used or referred too for further helping the tropical fish hobbyist and dedicated aquarist.

1/. Cable Tidy Unit 2/. Polyatomic-ion Biological Reactor 3/. Condensation Tray 4/. Air Stone and Valve 5/. Heater Thermostats, Air Pump and Fish Food 6/. Powerhead 7/. Books 8/. Undergravel Filter – Photographs by Alastair R Agutter

Cable Tidy: This product is freely available and helps greatly to tidy up all those aquarium cables. The units normally allow the aquarist to connect heater thermostats, lighting and pumps.

Biological Filters: There are many types of filtration on the market today, the Polyatomic-ion Biological Reactor that I have developed is easy to make and assemble for delivering crystal clear water.

Condensation Trays: Many aquariums today come with condensation trays normally in the form of light gauge sliding glass or polycarbonate panes or panels. But conventional aquariums such as all glass, or built by you for a project, or fish house, will require condensation trays. These condensation trays can be easily obtained from your tropical fish or pet store. But what I use very often as condensation trays and as a cost saving exercise are the trays from the supermarkets that meat is sold in. These trays are ideal once washed and when the remainder of the thin plastic film is removed.

Air Stones: Are frequently used to deliver more air to an aquarium, I tend to use them especially in rearing and breeding fish tanks towards the surface of the aquarium to encourage and help fish growth.

Air Valves: Are a useful piece of equipment used between an Air Pump and filter or air stone to regulate the delivery of air to the device in question. More fashionable and better made vales are available today made form metal and with a greater regulating method.

Heater Thermostats: Always remember to ensure all heater thermostats are fitted with 3 Amp Plugs for safety reasons. Heater thermostats normally come in sizes ranging from 50 to 300 watt to heat various sizes of fish tanks.

Air Pumps: Are still very popular and more energy efficient today and a lot quieter compared to air pumps over past decades. Their purpose is to deliver air to filters and air stones etc. Again always ensure this device is fitted with a 3 Amp plug for safety reasons.

Flake Foods: Are a very popular fish food and forms part of a staple diet for most tropical fish. But always ensure you vary the diet and include high protein fresh frozen foods also to encourage healthy thriving fish and growth.

Powerheads: Are often used today on uplifts of undergravel filters (not recommended) and for biological sumps, reservoirs and trickle filters successfully.

Books: I know today the World Wide Web can offer a mass of information, but many tropical fish books carry valuable information compiled very often over many years by known competent and knowledgeable aquarists. The trouble taken to write and produce such book's, is testament to the measure of importance placed on the subject matter by the aquarists author.

Undergravel Filters: Are still used in many aquariums today, I personally do not use them, as you can create a build-up of toxins and matter in the substrate that is not broken down successfully, as a result of little, or no plat life, as undergravel filters do damage plant root systems and therefore inhibits any plant growth.

CHAPTER TWENTY

Breeding Tropical Fish Tips

Breeding Tropical fish is a subject all on its own, and with a need for countless books on specific fish species. This chapter is therefore a quick guide highlighting the main methods of reproduction.

A Breeding Pair of the Author's Angel Fish (Pterophylium Scalare) Guarding Territory just days before Spawning and accompanied by Guppies (Livebearers) and Harlequin's (Egg Scatterers) – Photograph by Alastair R Agutter

Livebearers: Are the easiest of all fish species to breed, in fact they are prolific producers of off-spring and still very much a favourite with myself and many other aquarists. In the photograph above to the right are two female Guppies heavily pregnant. Other popular livebearers include Platies, Mollies and Swordtails all of which produce off-spring on a regular basis. These fish species thrive and reproduce even when fed just flake food and at an average temperature of between 76 to 82 degrees Fahrenheit.

Very often when Livebearers seek to shed the live fry from their bodies, they tend to swim down to the bottom of the aquarium and find a secluded spot, even away from male counterparts. Once the fry are released and uncoiled, they tend to start swimming up towards the top of the aquarium and this can be a very vulnerable time in their lives. Floating plants such as Wisteria and Cabomba can very often serve to be a haven for the young fry in these early stages of growth.

After about a 7 to 10 days if there are no other predator species in the aquarium but only livebearers, the fry will start to leave the floating plants and become more active swimming around the aquarium.

Feeding young livebearers is easy and this can be done when feeding the flake food to the adults, by simply grinding a little of the flake food up between your fingers and these fine pieces of flake food will be easily consumed by the young livebearer fry. Livebearers will also eat infusoria and small microorganisms living on algae and plants throughout the aquarium. As the young fry grow even more in size, this being the case for guppies, platies, mollies and swordtails, the young fry will also eat the protein sediment that has collected on aquarium pipes and fixtures, helping to keep the aquarium clean.

If you plan to breed any of these livebearers such as; Guppies, Platies, Mollies and Swordtails, it is always advisable to have a ratio of at least 2 females to every 1 male. For the males are very vigorous breeders and sometimes I have literally seen and witnessed female guppies driven to death from constant pestering.

Aquariums for livebearers do not have to be deep at all; they can be anything from 10 to 18 plus inches high. Shallow aquariums with fine naturally coloured gravel (camouflage), planted out with Vallisneria and Cryptocoryne for example, with some floating plants such as Wisteria, are ideal conditions for breeding these livebearers.

Egg Layers: There are many species of egg layers and especially regarding members of the Cichlid Family.

Most egg layers deposit their eggs on rock substrates such as large pieces of slate, or broadleaved plants, such as Amazon Sword Plants. The photographs below clearly show the stages of spawning by one of my breeding pairs of Angel Fish on one of the wide leaves belonging to an Amazon Sword Plant and fortunately the plant in question is in good health, as these plants do go through the mill when Cichlids start frantically cleaning the leafs surface, or cleaning a rock, or slate substrate and normally for about a week. But this behaviour can go on for several weeks before a pair decides to spawn and this can be down to water, diet, or a disturbance of some kind that has changed and disrupted the regular routine in the aquarium or home.

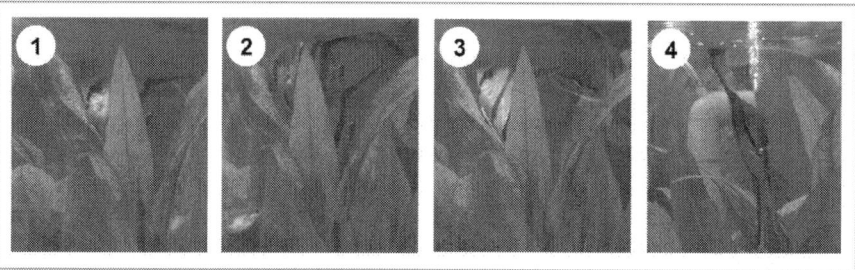

A set of pictures showing the egg laying process and sequence on an Amazon Sword Plant by one of the Author's breeding pair of Angel Fish – Photographs by Alastair R Agutter

Once the eggs are fertilized, they will normally hatch after 48 to 72 hours (cichlids) and this is dependent upon temperature and fish species.

Picture above taken 1988 of Author's Home-Made Brine Shrimp Hatcher created by using a large Pickle Jar with Airline and Air Stone attached. To the left of the picture a Pack of Brine Shrimp Eggs, to the right of the picture is a pack of Artificial Marine Salt and a Hydrometer, lastly a set of Air Line Valves to the front of the picture – Photograph by Alastair R Agutter

Young fry when free swimming will eat infusoria, algae and brine shrimp. Brine Shrimp can be easily grown and hatched in a mixed solution of aquarium saltwater in a large pickle jar. Make a small hole in the lid of the pickle jar to feed through an airline pipe, so you can then connect the airline once through the hole in the lid to an air stone to encourage the brine shrimp hatch from the movement of water after scattering the eggs in the saltwater solution.

Brine shrimp hatch easily in a warm place with a temperature ranging between 66 to 78 degrees Fahrenheit after a few days.

Brine shrimp eggs can be easily purchased along with a bag of marine salt from most tropical fish retail outlets. Feed the fry with the baby brine shrimp about three to four times a day and then after about a week, you can start feeding the fry with ground down flake food. Fry when hungry will also eat the algae in the fish tank, so never clean the glass of a breeding aquarium.

Always remember when rearing any fry to always evenly scatter the food around the rearing aquarium to make sure all the fry are getting food and so they equally grow in size. This will not be an easy task when rearing fish to keep them to an equal size, for some will start to grow stronger and larger than the others.

Eventually you will inevitably have to split the fry, especially if they are cichlids to ensure the smaller fish can catch up and not be bullied. This is where you can see the importance of sponge filters in rearing tanks and two in each aquarium. For as you split the fry, you can simply siphon off half the water into the new fish tank and transfer one of the existing sponge filters that already has an active biological culture working from the existing rearing tank.

Egg Scatterers: Tetras do exactly what is described where the female scatters her eggs around the environment and in this instance, the aquarium, closely pursued by her male counter-part.

The eggs of egg scatterers in the wild are then gently carried away by the waters currents, where the eggs will eventually settle and hopefully subject to where they lay in the habitat, be it some weed or a fine gravel substrate, the young fry will hatch and try to survive the hazardous rigors of life as they begin their journey.

Breeding egg scatterers in captivity is often achieved in shallow aquariums, these fish tanks are normally only between 9 to 12 inches in height and relatively small in size around 18 to 24 inches in length and only 12 inches deep (front to back).

Picture above showing some of the Author's Cardinal Tetras (pair) who are members of the Egg Scattering Fish Species Fraternity – Photograph by Alastair R Agutter

Again a small sponge filter is used with a gentle air flow so the water is not turbulent. The aquarium is then normally filled with horse hair often found in old fashion furniture settees. So then as the egg scatterers swim around the eggs descend slowly to the bottom of the aquarium giving the small eggs a chance to hatch without being eaten by the parents.

Feeding the parents on flake food in small regular amounts provides no reason for the parents to descend down amongst the maze of horse hair.

Never clean your breeding aquariums glass, let the algae naturally grown and form on the fish tank floor and walls, as this serves as a good food source for the young fry when they hatch after a few days, where they will then feed on infusoria and algae, plus any fine grains of flake food found that has broken down.

These breeding tanks in a commercial environment are normally between 76 to 84 degrees Fahrenheit in temperature and in the large commercial glassed roof breeding fish houses, these aquariums are normally positioned on the top of the banks of the breeding aquariums.

Mouth Brooders: This type of breeding has evolved overtime due to the very hostile environment that these Cichlid Fish Species inhabit. From the Great Lakes such as Lake Malawi, to the Great River Nile you will find Mouth Brooders, including the Egyptian Mouth Brooder, that is a prolific breeder and eaten by native inhabitants.

Picture above showing a Malawi Pseudotropheus Cichlid Mouth Brooder living in some flower pots, these species are very aggressive even when breeding – Photograph by Alastair R Agutter

The fish species very often need large aquariums if you want them to reproduce. I must confess I did breed these fish species types when they first arrived into Britain back in the early to mid-nineteen seventies.

Mouth brooders are very disruptive fish, constantly digging up and moving gravel and in some instances making great piles of seven to nine inches deep. When breeding the male makes shallow wells in the gravel to lure the female when she quickly lays the eggs, he in turn fertilizes the eggs simultaneously and then eventually the parent or parents gather up the eggs in their mouths to incubate the eggs. On frequent occasions the male will undertake this task on his own, even when the fry are hatched, the fry will stay in the mouths of the parents, as they grow and are occasionally spat out by the parent into the water so the fry can feed and swim to strengthen body muscles and learn fin control.

Mouth Brooders are not only very aggressive, but superfast swimmers, renowned for darting and splashing around, so make sure you have a decent lid or condensation tray fitted to your aquarium.

Water conditions for breeding Mouth Brooders from the Great Lakes and the Nile prefer harder more alkaline water conditions of 7.4 PH upwards and temperatures ranging from 74 to 80 degrees Fahrenheit.

One point to note, these species in higher water temperatures become more active and aggressive. Diet wise, these species will eat anything from Flake, Pellet, Bloodworms, to Beef Heart and Spinach.

Bubble Nest Builders: Gourami's are known as Labyrinth fish species and can Breath air out of water for considerable periods and this relates to the regions they inhabit in the Wild, where very often Gouramis can even be found living and breeding in Rice Paddy Fields.

Picture above showing Three Spot Gouramis in the Company of Clown Loaches at Maidenhead Aquatics – Photograph by Alastair R Agutter

Gouramis can tolerate a considerable water hardness PH range, including soft to brackish water conditions and high water temperatures ranging on average between 76 to 84 degrees Fahrenheit.

Gouramis when breeding build bubble nests on the surface of the water and use various floating plants and pieces of weed to help support the bubble nest.

Gouramis prefer very slow and tranquil water and especially at breeding times, where they also prefer shallow water conditions, even as low as six to seven inches when building their bubble nests.

Gourami fry normally hatch after about 48 to 72 hours dependent upon water temperatures and conditions. The fry will happily eat infusoria in the aquarium and algae. After several days when they become free swimming they will eat baby brine shrimp and after about 10 to 14 days eat finely ground flake food.

CHAPTER TWENTY ONE
Author's Additional Notes

When I first started out on this journey, I had intended to write a book of basics for today's folk taking up tropical fish keeping and in a format that would cover the essential aspects for new Aquarists getting started.

But as I began writing "My First Aquarium Collectors Edition" and wanted to ensure the information I provided was thorough and of encouragement. I soon found the book began to quickly expand as I endeavoured to articulate my knowledge and experience into the written word for all. At every stage writing the book I found myself saying *"this information is vital and must be included"* and so the book continued to grow in size, both physically and in stature with regards to the weight of knowledge found within the book from five decades of dedication.

Upon reflection, I am pleased to have contributed in such a way to give all Aquarists a good start and to expand the topic by writing this book, where I hope such information found will be enlightening for all tropical fish hobbyists.

I am confident there will be valuable nuggets of information for all aquarists in some shape or form to draw from found in the book and the recorded material is based on factual first-hand experience and proven methods.

Sincere Best Wishes,

Alastair R Agutter

Author

My First Aquarium Collectors Edition

Mr Agutter's Famous Discus Book
"A Best Seller for Over 25 Years!"

"The Author is one of a select few in the world to breed Wild Discus successfully in captivity"

Available through all good book stores world-wide!

Manufactured by Amazon.ca
Bolton, ON